IFIP Advances in Information and Communication Technology 503

Editor-in-Chief

Kai Rannenberg, Goethe University Frankfurt, Germany

IFIP – The International Federation for Information Processing

IFIP was founded in 1960 under the auspices of UNESCO, following the first World Computer Congress held in Paris the previous year. A federation for societies working in information processing, IFIP's aim is two-fold: to support information processing in the countries of its members and to encourage technology transfer to developing nations. As its mission statement clearly states:

> IFIP is the global non-profit federation of societies of ICT professionals that aims at achieving a worldwide professional and socially responsible development and application of information and communication technologies.

IFIP is a non-profit-making organization, run almost solely by 2500 volunteers. It operates through a number of technical committees and working groups, which organize events and publications. IFIP's events range from large international open conferences to working conferences and local seminars.

The flagship event is the IFIP World Computer Congress, at which both invited and contributed papers are presented. Contributed papers are rigorously refereed and the rejection rate is high.

As with the Congress, participation in the open conferences is open to all and papers may be invited or submitted. Again, submitted papers are stringently refereed.

The working conferences are structured differently. They are usually run by a working group and attendance is generally smaller and occasionally by invitation only. Their purpose is to create an atmosphere conducive to innovation and development. Refereeing is also rigorous and papers are subjected to extensive group discussion.

Publications arising from IFIP events vary. The papers presented at the IFIP World Computer Congress and at open conferences are published as conference proceedings, while the results of the working conferences are often published as collections of selected and edited papers.

IFIP distinguishes three types of institutional membership: Country Representative Members, Members at Large, and Associate Members. The type of organization that can apply for membership is a wide variety and includes national or international societies of individual computer scientists/ICT professionals, associations or federations of such societies, government institutions/government related organizations, national or international research institutes or consortia, universities, academies of sciences, companies, national or international associations or federations of companies.

More information about this series at http://www.springer.com/series/6102

Matt Bishop · Lynn Futcher
Natalia Miloslavskaya
Marianthi Theocharidou (Eds.)

Information Security Education for a Global Digital Society

10th IFIP WG 11.8 World Conference, WISE 10
Rome, Italy, May 29–31, 2017
Proceedings

 Springer

Editors
Matt Bishop🆔
University of California, Davis
Davis, CA
USA

Lynn Futcher
Nelson Mandela Metropolitan University
Port Elizabeth
South Africa

Natalia Miloslavskaya🆔
National Research Nuclear University
MEPhI
Moscow
Russia

Marianthi Theocharidou🆔
European Commission
Joint Research Centre
Ispra
Italy

ISSN 1868-4238   ISSN 1868-422X (electronic)
IFIP Advances in Information and Communication Technology
ISBN 978-3-319-58552-9   ISBN 978-3-319-58553-6 (eBook)
DOI 10.1007/978-3-319-58553-6

Library of Congress Control Number: 2017939724

Printed on acid-free paper

This Springer imprint is published by Springer Nature
The registered company is Springer International Publishing AG
The registered company address is: Gewerbestrasse 11, 6330 Cham, Switzerland

Preface

This volume contains the papers presented at the 10th World Conference on Information Security Education (WISE10) held during May 29–31, 2017 in Rome, in conjunction with the 32nd International Conference on ICT Systems Security and Privacy Protection (IFIP SEC 2017). WISE10 was organized by the IFIP Working Group 11.8, which is an international group of people from academia, government, and private organizations who volunteer their time and effort to increase knowledge in the very broad field of information security through education. WG11.8 has worked to increase information assurance education and awareness for almost two decades. This year, WG11.8 organized the 10th conference of a successful series, which is an important milestone for the working group. The theme for this year's WISE conference was "Information Security Education for a Global Digital Society."

This year's conference received 32 submissions from around the world. Each submission was reviewed by at least three Program Committee members. The committee decided to accept 14 full papers and one workshop proposal. The acceptance rate for the papers is thus 45%.

This conference took place thanks to the support and commitment of many individuals. First, we would like to thank all TC-11 members for continually giving us the opportunity to serve the working group and organize the WISE conferences. Our sincere appreciation also goes to the members of the Program Committee, to the external reviewers, and to the authors who trusted us with their intellectual work. We would like to thank our colleague Diana Burley for proposing and co-organizing the workshop on "Workshop on the Joint Task Force Cybersecurity Curricular Guidelines." We are grateful for the local organizers and hosts, especially the WISE10 Logistics Chair, Erik Moore. Finally, we would like to thank the IFIP SEC 2017 General Chairs, Sara Foresti and Luigi V. Mancini, for enabling this continuous collaboration with the IFIP SEC conference series.

As for the preparation of this volume, we sincerely thank Erika Siebert-Cole and our publisher Springer for their assistance. Moreover, we acknowledge the EasyChair conference management system, which was used both for managing the conference and creating this volume.

March 2017

Matt Bishop
Lynn Futcher
Natalia Miloslavskaya
Marianthi Theocharidou

Organization

Program Committee

Matt Bishop	University of California at Davis, USA
Reinhardt Botha	Nelson Mandela Metropolitan University, South Africa
William Caelli	IISEC Pty Ltd, Australia
Melissa Dark	Purdue University, USA
Lynette Drevin	North-West University, South Africa
Steve Furnell	Plymouth University, UK
Lynn Futcher	Nelson Mandela Metropolitan University, South Africa
Ram Herkanaidu	Plymouth University, UK
Erland Jonsson	Chalmers University of Technology, Sweden
Audun Josang	University of Oslo, Norway
Suresh Kalathur	Boston University, USA
Christos Kalloniatis	University of the Aegean, Greece
Vasilis Katos	Bournemouth University, UK
Sokratis Katsikas	Center for Cyber and Information Security, NTNU, Norway
Elmarie Kritzinger	University of South Africa, South Africa
Hennie Kruger	North-West University, South Africa
Costas Lambrinoudakis	University of Piraeus, Greece
Javier Lopez	University of Malaga, Spain
Leonardo Martucci	Karlstad University, Sweden
Vashek Matyas	Masaryk University, Czech Republic
Natalia Miloslavskaya	National Research Nuclear University MEPhI (Moscow Engineering Physics Institute), Russia
Erik Moore	Regis University, USA
Kara Nance	Virginia Polytechnic Institute and State University, USA
Jacques Ophoff	University of Cape Town, South Africa
Günther Pernul	Universität Regensburg, Germany
Carlos Rieder	isec ag, Switzerland
Jill Slay	University of New South Wales, Australia
Rumen Stainov	Fulda University of Applied Science, Germany
Tye Stallard	University of California, USA
Marianthi Theocharidou	European Commission, Joint Research Centre
Kerry-Lynn Thomson	Nelson Mandela Metropolitan University, South Africa
Alexander Tolstoy	National Research Nuclear University MEPhI (Moscow Engineering Physics Institute), Russia
Sven Uebelacker	Hamburg University of Technology and University of Cambridge, Germany/UK
Ismini Vasileiou	Plymouth University, UK

Rossouw Von Solms   Nelson Mandela Metropolitan University, South Africa
Edgar Weippl   SBA Research, Austria
Louise Yngstrom   Stockholms universitet och KTH i Kista, Sweden

Additional Reviewers

Ali, Raian
Hassan, Sabri
Nisioti, Antonia
Richthammer, Christian
Rostami, Shahin
Stallard, Tye

Workshop on the Joint Task Force Cybersecurity Curricular Guidelines (Workshop Proposal)

Matt Bishop[1], Diana Burley[2], and Lynn Futcher[3]

[1] University of California at Davis, Davis, USA
mabishop@ucdavis.edu
[2] The George Washington University, Washington, D.C., USA
dburley@gwu.edu
[3] Nelson Mandela Metropolitan University, Port Elizabeth, South Africa
Lynn.Futcher@nmmu.ac.za

Abstract. The goal of the Joint Task Force on Cybersecurity Education is to develop comprehensive curricular guidance in cybersecurity that will support future program development and associated educational efforts. This workshop is to present the current draft of the proposed guidelines and obtain feedback that can be incorporated into the next version.

In 2016, the professional computing societies ACM, IEEE-CS, AIS SIGSEC, and IFIP WG 11.8 assembled a Joint Task Force on Cybersecurity Education.[1] The goal of this working group is to develop cybersecurity curricular guidelines for programs that emphasize different areas of specialization. The intent is that these guidelines can drive curricula, with each curriculum being tailored for the specific discipline and goals while ensuring that professionals (or prospective professionals) obtain the knowledge and skills they need.

The model consists of four parts: knowledge areas, cross-cutting concepts that span, or underlie, the knowledge areas; disciplinary lenses that provide the views of the knowledge areas and cross-cutting concepts based upon the discipline; and application areas, which help define the coverage for each knowledge areas.

The Joint Task Force is seeking community feedback to improve the current draft curricular guidelines. Two workshops have been held; the third, and the first international one, is this workshop. As other nations and communities have differing needs and educational environments, comments from those communities will be invaluable in making the guidelines as useful to all as possible.

Thus, this workshop will explore the current guidelines, their goals, the organization, and how the guidelines might be used. We will invite the audience to provide insights, identify problems their institutions might have in using the guidelines, and propose changes and additions that will improve the guidelines.

---

[1] http://www.csec2017.org.

Acknowledgements. We gratefully acknowledge the work of the Joint Task Force on Cybersecurity Education in developing these guidelines, and the valuable contributions of participants in our 15 community engagement efforts. This workshop is based upon work supported by the National Science Foundation under Grant No. DGE-1623104, the National Security Agency's CNAP Curriculum Development effort (RFI-2017-00022), the Education Board of the ACM, and Intel Corporation. Any opinions, findings, and conclusions or recommendations expressed in this material are those of the author(s) and do not necessarily reflect the views of the National Science Foundation, the National Security Agency, the ACM Education Board, or Intel Corporation.

Contents

Training Information Security Professionals

Information Security Education

Cybersecurity Curricular Guidelines

Matt Bishop[1]([✉]) [iD], Diana Burley[2], Scott Buck[3], Joseph J. Ekstrom[4],
Lynn Futcher[5], David Gibson[6], Elizabeth K. Hawthorne[7], Siddharth Kaza[8],
Yair Levy[9], Herbert Mattord[10], and Allen Parrish[11]

[1] University of California at Davis, Davis, CA, USA
mabishop@ucdavis.edu
[2] The George Washington University, Washington, DC, USA
dburley@gwu.edu
[3] Intel Corp., Hillsboro, OR, USA
scott.buck@intel.com
[4] Brigham Young University, Provo, UT, USA
jekstrom@byu.edu
[5] Nelson Mandela Metropolitan University, Port Elizabeth, South Africa
Lynn.Futcher@nmmu.ac.za
[6] United States Air Force Academy, Colorado Springs, CO, USA
david.gibson@usafa.edu
[7] Union County College, Cranford, NJ, USA
hawthorne@ucc.edu
[8] Towson University, Towson, MD, USA
skaza@towson.edu
[9] Nova Southeastern University, Fort Lauderdale, FL, USA
levyy@nova.edu
[10] Kennesaw State University, Kennesaw, GA, USA
hmattord@kennesaw.edu
[11] United States Naval Academy, Annapolis, MD, USA
aparrish@usna.edu

Abstract. The goal of the Joint Task Force on Cybersecurity Education is to develop comprehensive undergraduate curricular guidance in cybersecurity that will support future program development and associated educational efforts. This effort is a collaboration among the ACM, the IEEE Computer Society, the AIS Special Interest Group on Security and Privacy (SIGSEC), the IFIP WG 11.8, and the Cyber Education Project. In January 2017, the Joint Task Force released a draft of those guidelines. This paper describes the framework underlying the guidelines, examines one set of topics, and then places this work in the context of an exemplary curriculum on cybersecurity education.

Keywords: Cybersecurity education · Curricular guidance · CSEC2017

© IFIP International Federation for Information Processing 2017
Published by Springer International Publishing AG 2017. All Rights Reserved
M. Bishop et al. (Eds.): WISE 10, IFIP AICT 503, pp. 3–13, 2017.
DOI: 10.1007/978-3-319-58553-6_1

1   Introduction

Recent accelerated growth in the number and variety of computing security education academic, training, and certification programs has led to an increased interest in what a cybersecurity professional[1] should know and what skills they should have. Agreement has been uncommon; disagreement is the norm. There is no agreed-upon body of knowledge that such a professional should know, no agreement on a specific set of practices that a cybersecurity professional should have experience with, and no agreement on the competency levels of the desired skills.

This lack of commonality arises from the nature of cybersecurity. It encompasses many disciplines, and is used in many roles. As a result, the knowledge and skills that a cybersecurity professional will use varies depending upon the job description. The knowledge and skills of one who makes policy differs considerably from one who architects defenses for a given installation. Certainly, both need to know something of what the other does; but the depth of knowledge and set of skills will vary considerably. Underlying all knowledge and skills of cybersecurity professionals, though, is a core body of knowledge that all should know and experiences they should have, regardless of role.

With this in mind, the ACM, IEEE-CS, AIS SIGSEC, and IFIP WG 11.8 assembled a Joint Task Force on Cybersecurity Education.[2] The goal of this working group is to develop cybersecurity curricular guidelines for undergraduate programs that emphasize different areas of specialization. For example, the guidelines will provide a basis for a training institute's certification program, a university's degree program in cybersecurity, and for a business school's MBA program. The certification program would emphasize practice, the university's program both theory and critical thinking, and the business school would emphasize policymaking to support a company's business mission.

This approach avoids the conflicts that arise when one tries to prescribe a common body of knowledge that defines a "cybersecurity professional". More important is the considerable flexibility of this approach. One program might emphasize the role people play in cybersecurity, and so incorporate literature, sociology, psychology, and language classes into its program. Another might simply focus on how to design and implement a security-based network architecture, for example that protects medical records housed at a hospital. Both can draw from the guidelines. Both will emphasize aspects of the guidelines that provide their professionals (or prospective professionals) with the knowledge and skills they need. Both can decide to discount specific areas, but will be aware that they are doing so—and knowing what one does not know is a hallmark of a well-educated, knowledgeable, skilled person.

The goal of this paper is to present the framework and basis for the guidelines in their current form, and examples of the guidelines themselves and how they

---

[1] We use this term to mean anyone working in an occupation requiring her to protect data, cyberinfrastructure, or computing resources.

[2] http://www.csec2017.org.

might be used. The draft of these guidelines is called the CSEC2017, and is available for comment [2]. The final version is still under development.

2 Background

"Cybersecurity" is a widely used term that speaks to the security of systems and data but has many different definitions. Examples include "[p]revention of damage to, protection of, and restoration of computers, electronic communications systems, electronic communications services, wire communication, and electronic communication, including information contained therein, to ensure its availability, integrity, authentication, confidentiality, and nonrepudiation" [9]; "defensive methods used to detect and thwart would-be intruders" [13]; and "the organization and collection of resources, processes, and structures used to protect cyberspace and cyberspace-enabled systems from occurrences that misalign *de jure* from *de facto* property rights" [7]. Agresti [3] notes that four forces (rebranding, organizational imperative, cyberspace domain, and national defense priority) shape the definitions. Thus, any guidance aimed at cybersecurity must begin by defining that term.

To make clear the scope of the guidance, the Joint Task Force defined "cybersecurity" as:

> A computing-based discipline involving technology, people, information, and processes to enable assured operations. It involves the creation, operation, analysis, and testing of secure computer systems. It is an interdisciplinary course of study, including aspects of law, policy, human factors, ethics, and risk management in the context of adversaries.[3]

Cybersecurity first arose as a technical issue when multiprocessing systems were developed; then, the question was how to keep processes from interfering with one another. Time-sharing raised issues of users interfering with one another, and theory and controls were developed to understand the problem and prevent or hinder compromise [6,12,15,17]. As a discipline, cybersecurity first appeared in a 1970 report from a group chaired by Willis Ware [16]. The U.S. Air Force subsequently chartered a Computer Security Technology Planning Study [4], led by James P. Anderson; that 1972 study defined many basic concepts such as the Trojan horse. The theory of cybersecurity was developed [5,8,10,11,14]. As networking grew, the need for cybersecurity increased, and the Internet and the World Wide Web stretched the reach of attackers so much that even non-technical users were put at risk. Attackers became more ingenious, and defenses improved, and the attackers then improved. This cyber arms race continues to this day.

As the discipline of cybersecurity has grown, so have educational programs, professional training programs, and certification programs. Each emphasizes

---

[3] The CSEC2017 draft has the last words, "in the context of adversaries" at the end of the first sentence of the defintion [2, p. 10]. That is a misprint.

aspects of cybersecurity in their own way. Cybersecurity jobs span the gamut from homes to small offices to governments to international corporations. The wide variety of jobs, and hence professionals, in this field has made defining an educational body of knowledge difficult, because each type of job requires different knowledge and skills. Thus, cybersecurity education programs should be based on core cybersecurity knowledge and skills. They should have a computing-based foundation, teach concepts that are applicable to a broad range of cybersecurity expertise, and emphasize ethical responsibilities and obligations. Finally, many programs will tailor their curriculum so their graduates can go into specialities that are in demand at the time.

The goal of the CSEC2017 guidelines is to provide a basis for developing such programs. It begins with a model that unifies these concepts and views them through different specialities, as well as the application of the knowledge, skills, and concepts.

3   Model

The model consists of four parts:

1. Knowledge areas, the basic organizing structure and core ideas;
2. Cross-cutting concepts, which span the knowledge areas;
3. Disciplinary lens, which provides views of the model based upon specific disciplines; and
4. Application areas, which help define the level of coverage for each knowledge areas.

In this section, we discuss each of these parts in detail.

3.1   Knowledge Areas

The six *knowledge areas* define the subject matter of cybersecurity. They form a body of knowledge for practitioners, researchers, teachers, and others. They are composed of *knowledge units*, which describe the sets of topics and what students should know about each. Each unit also describes learning outcomes.

The knowledge areas meet three criteria:

1. The area is important for multiple disciplines;
2. The area provides a tool for understanding or exploring cybersecurity ideas; and
3. The material in the area can be learned in varying levels of detail and understanding over time.

The areas, and a brief description of what each encompasses, follows.

- **Data Security.** This knowledge area focuses on the protection of stationary and moving data. It requires an understanding of both algorithms and analysis, and deals with both the theory and application of these. Example units in this area are confidentiality, integrity, and cryptography.

- **Software Security.** This focuses on the design, development, implementation, deployment, maintenance, and operation of software that meets security requirements, both explicit (security) and implicit (robustness). It includes all types of assurance in software, reverse engineering, and analyzing and handling malware, as well as what is often termed "secure software".
- **System Security.** This area speaks to the composition of components that make up a "system" such as a computer or the infrastructure supporting networks. Aspects of this area dealing with software focus on its integration and use as a component of a system rather than the security of the software (although that may affect how the software is handled). The supply chain, digital forensics, devices (hardware), authentication, access control, and cyberphysical systems fall into this area.
- **Human Security.** Protecting people's data in the context of organizations (i.e., as employees) or personal life, and their privacy, is a critical task of cybersecurity that this area covers. It also includes security-related behaviors such as how people react to social engineering attacks, social engineering itself, and identity management.
- **Organizational Security.** The organizational security knowledge area deals with security in the context of organizations. The type, size, and function of the organizations are not constrained. An important element of this area is risk—what it is and how it can be mitigated in the context of the organization. Examples of other knowledge units are disaster recovery, business continuity, compliance, and security evaluations.
- **Societal Security.** The ubiquitousness of computers, networks, and devices that computers control makes cybersecurity a necessity in society. This knowledge area deals with those facets of cybersecurity that impact society as a whole. Example knowledge units are ethics, cyber law and crime, professional codes of conduct, intellectual property, and cultural constraints and controls on cybersecurity processes, procedures, and technologies.

There is some overlap among these areas, in the sense that a knowledge unit often can be put into more than one. A good example is the design of a library that reads and processes packets from a network. This can go in the software security knowledge area, because it is a question of assurance: how does the library ensure that the packets are protected and handled as required? It can also go into the system security area, as the library interface is used in the composition of components (that is, network to system). The above organization minimizes this overlap, and when it occurs suggests that the same knowledge unit would have two different views, each view based upon the knowledge area.

3.2   Cross-Cutting Concepts

These concepts provide a framework for making connections among the knowledge areas. They unify underlying ideas, and so help students understand the material in the areas regardless of the discipline the student encounters them in. The model defines the following cross-cutting concepts:

- **Confidentiality (C)** is a property defined by rules that control the spread of information. Such a set of rules may define who can and cannot access data or resources, for example.
- **Integrity (I)** is a property that describes the accuracy and trustworthiness of information. A key component of this property is assurance, which defines the evidence provided to convince the audience that the objects meet some desired level of accuracy or trustworthiness.
- **Availability (A)** is a property defined by rules describing when and in what manner data or resources can be accessed. Note that mere accessibility of an entity is not enough to make that entity available. If, for example, a network connection to a server does not meet the required quality of service (the property defining availability in this context), the entity may be accessible but not available.
- **Risk (R)** describes the exposure of the entity to threats. It is a product of the probability of the threat being realized and the damage incurred should the threat be realized.
- **Adversarial Thinking (AT)** is a manner of thinking in which one determines how threats can be realized. It requires understanding what threats will compromise the entity under consideration, and how to realize them.

As an example of why these are cross-cutting, consider "confidentiality." It is a key component of data, system, and organizational security. In the guise of privacy, it is a component of human security. Through the combination of all these, it speaks to societal security. So the precise meaning of the term depends on the context in which it is used, as does its application. But the underlying concept of confidentiality, that of restricting access to something based on a set of requirements and a (possibly unstated) policy, cuts across these knowledge areas.

Each of these areas is broken down into units, and the units into topics. For example, the System Security knowledge area is broken down into units that include availability and secure system design, which in turn have the topics system availability, measures of availability, and attacks on availability; and security design principles, security architectures, trusted computing base, and security modes of operations, respectively.

3.3   Disciplinary Lens

While the knowledge areas are common to all of cybersecurity, the depth and approach that students and practitioners are expected to know varies depending on how they will use the knowledge. For example, a programmer needs to know something about the policies that control the data her program will use, as data in medical records must be handled very differently than data in a store's inventory. Similarly, a policymaker needs to know that software cannot distinguish between the "good guys and gals" and the "bad guys and gals", so backdoors in software and systems to aid law enforcement can be used by others, illicitly. The programmer need not know how policy is made; the policymaker need not understand how backdoors can be implanted or exploited. Both need to understand enough of the other's world to see the consequences of their actions.

For curricular purposes, we use the disciplines as defined by the ACM [1]:

- **Computer Science (CS)** is the discipline of developing software, developing ways to use computers to solve problems, and indeed developing new ways to use computers. It includes theory and applications, and is a broad subject.
- **Computer Engineering (CE)** focuses on the design and implementation of computing devices. This requires understanding how the devices will be used, what software they must run, and in what environment they will be used.
- **Information Systems (IS)** deals with use of information processing technology in enterprises such as businesses, with an emphasis on the use of information that can be obtained from the use of the systems. It examines how to integrate that technology into the processes by which the enterprise attempts to meet its goals.
- **Information Technology (IT)**, like information systems, focuses on information technology but with an emphasis on "technology." This encompasses what type of technology is appropriate for the needs of the organization, how the technology is to be deployed and maintained, and how to support both the technology and the users of that technology.
- **Software Engineering (SE)** is the discipline of defining, developing, implementing, testing, and maintaining software systems.
- **Mixed Disciplinary (MD)** programs contain elements chosen from the disciplines above.

3.4 Summary

A program can view the knowledge areas and cross-cutting concepts through the appropriate disciplinary lens to determine which concepts it should consider

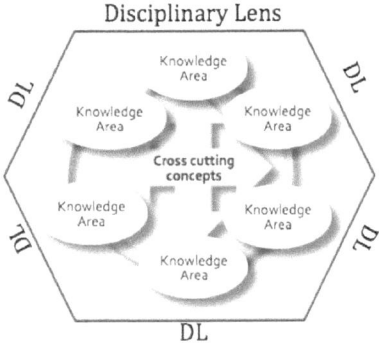

Fig. 1. The relationships of the elements making up the thought model.

core, and which need to be touched only lightly upon. Figure 1 summarizes how these elements are put together.

4   Professional Practice

The CSEC2017 model for cybersecurity curricular guidelines are linked to professional practice through seven application areas. Workforce frameworks can then codify bodies of knowledge for their target audience by going from the application areas back to the model, and extracting both the core knowledge and cross-cutting concepts they deem appropriate, and view them through the disciplinary lenses appropriate for their audience.

The application areas are simply organizing frameworks to allow the definition of competency levels needed for each area. The content of the areas overlaps, as is expected; each area provides guidance for the depth of coverage needed for each idea.

The application areas are organized along the lines of the system and software life cycle as well as supporting areas. They are:

- **Public policy** is affected by several groups. Legislators and regulators make laws affecting the development, deployment, and use of computing. In the U.S., judges pass upon the constitutionality (legality) of the laws and of their application to specific cases and circumstances. Corporate managers (CEOs and members of the Board of Directors or similar entity) will also interact with public policy, either advising those who set it or ensuring that their computing technology and procedures comply with those policies. They must understand how these laws, regulations, and requirements will affect the use of the systems, how people interact with the systems, and most especially the risks that those rules reduce or increase. This suggests they know basics of the design of systems, so they understand what computing technology can—and, more critically, cannot—do, and be able to work out the budgetary and human costs of the rules.
- **Procurement** requires understanding how the systems will fit into, and advance, the work of the organization. This may involve changing aspects of the organization's procedures to enable the systems to be useful. Risk management and business continuity issues come into play in this application area, as does an understanding of how people in the organization, and other stakeholders, will interact with the systems being procured. So this application area requires a knowledge of those areas, in addition to understanding concepts of assurance, infrastructure, and organizational, human, and social dynamics.
- **Management**, which refers to people, systems, and data in an organization, is guided by policies, both internal and public. Understanding compliance, business continuity, and recovery from attacks and other types of disasters is a part of management. Managers decide who has access to data and resources, what type of access, and how they may use that access; thus, they must understand identity and authorization management. As they will oversee, and be

responsible for, the effect of changes made to the system, understanding how both assurance and testing speak to the goals of the organization and of the mission of that particular system. They must also have a basic understanding of incident handling and recovery in order to deal with attacks.

- **IT security operations** are to keep the system secure, "secure" being defined by a set of requirements. This requires that operations personnel know how to translate those requirements into configurations, procedures, and their implementation. For example, the security infrastructure must ensure that identity management systems are installed, initialized, configured, and used properly. Validating that the requirements are properly implemented requires testing the infrastructure, systems, and procedures, and analyzing the results of those tests. In addition, the operators must be able to maintain the systems under both normal conditions and under abnormal conditions, such as during an attack.

- **Software development** begins with requirements for the software to meet. These requirements come from laws, regulations, policies, business plans, and societal and organizational constraints. So developers interpret these requirements in their design and implementation. The development must ensure the software is robust ("secure programming"), which means they must know how to determine which exceptions to handle and understand how to do so. The environment, users, and installers all must be taken into account when the software and interfaces are designed. Testing enables the developers to gather assurance evidence to verify the software system meets its requirements, and convince other stakeholders this is so.

- **Research** requires all researchers to know the basics of access control and availability, confidentiality, integrity, risk, and adversarial thinking. Cryptography is commonly used to supply the last two areas, so its basics are important to know. Beyond that, the specific area in which the research is being conducted defines what the researcher needs to know. For example, a researcher in cryptography should understand how it is used in practice in order to understand how the application affects the parameters of the cryptosystems; it is probably unnecessary to understand the proof of the HRU theorem and the associated results. But someone studying formal models of access controls would need to know the proof of the HRU theorem, and not the details of cryptography.

- **Enterprise architecture** is in some sense a capstone of the application areas, as it draws on all the other areas. Policy drives the architecture; the design of the architecture drives procurement, management, and operations. The architecture also affects the goals of the software, because the architecture includes the systems and infrastructure needed to keep the enterprise running smoothly. Enterprise architects must understand the policy, procurement, management and operations application areas, as well as elements from the area of software development.

5   Conclusion

CSEC2017 presents the basis for curricula. An institution desiring to have a specialization, major, or other course of study in cybersecurity may use this to design and implement their program. No single program will be able to cover all knowledge areas and cross-cutting concepts in full depth; instead, they should cover these broadly, and select specific aspects of those areas to explore in more depth. The selection will be based on the goals of the program, and the needs of the students attending the program and of the workforce that they expect, or will be expected to, join.

The inclusion of human, organizational, and societal knowledge areas emphasizes that cybersecurity is not a strictly technical discipline. The humanities and social sciences play a key role in cybersecurity. The connection with social sciences is clear, as those deal with society and organizations. The connection with humanities is equally important, because art, literature, languages, and other such subjects teach about the human condition and about people— and ultimately the goal of cybersecurity is to enable people to protect people, through the medium of guarding data and resources. Hence, including these two humanistically-oriented subjects in a cybersecurity program increases the likelihood that cybersecurity will protect the right people, data, or resources, in the right way, and at the right times.

Cybersecurity as a discipline is still maturing. Community input is important, and the Joint Task Force encourages comments, suggestions, and improvements. The 2016 International Security Education Workshop, held in June 2016 in Philadelphia, PA, USA provided one such avenue; a subsequent global stakeholder survey in late 2016 provided more input. The CSEC2017 web site, http://www.csec2017.org, provides a mechanism to submit comments. In this way, the curriculum guidance will meet the needs of the cybersecurity teaching, research, and practice workforces.

Acknowledgements. We gratefully acknowledge the valuable contributions of participants in our 15 community engagement efforts.

This material is based upon work supported by the National Science Foundation under Grant No. DGE-1623104, the National Security Agency's CNAP Curriculum Development effort (RFI-2017-00022), the Education Board of the ACM, and Intel Corporation. Any opinions, findings, and conclusions or recommendations expressed in this material are those of the author(s) and do not necessarily reflect the views of the National Science Foundation, the National Security Agency, the ACM Education Board, or Intel Corporation.

References

1. Computing curricula 2005: the overview report. Technical report, ACM, New York (2005). http://www.acm.org/education/education/curric_vols/CC2005-March06Final.pdf

2. Cybersecurity curricula 2017: curriculum guidelines for undergraduate degree programs in cybersecurity. Technical report Draft version 0.5, ACM Joint Task Force on Cybersecurity Education (2017). http://www.csec2017.org/csec2017-v-0-5
3. Agresti, W.W.: The four forces shaping cybersecurity. IEEE Comput. **43**(2), 101–104 (2010)
4. Anderson, J.: Computer security technology planning study. Technical report ESD-TR-73-51, ESD/AFSC, Hanscom AFB, Bedford, MA, October 1972
5. Bell, D.E., LaPadula, L.J.: Secure computer system: Unified exposition and multics interpretation. Technical report MTR-2997 Rev. 1, The MITRE Corporation, Bedford, MA, USA, March 1976
6. Conway, R.W., Maxwell, W.L., Morgan, H.L.: On the implementation of security measures in information systems. Commun. ACM **15**(4), 211–220 (1972)
7. Craigen, D., Diakun-Thibault, N., Purse, R.: Defining cybersecurity. Technol. Innov. Manage. Rev. **4**(10), 13–21 (2014). https://timreview.ca/article/835
8. Denning, D.: A lattice model of secure information flow. Commun. ACM **19**(5), 236–243 (1976)
9. Dukes, C.W.: Committee on national security systems (CNSS) glossary. Technical report CNSSI No. 4009, Committee on National Security Systems, National Security Agency, Ft. George G. Meade, MD, USA. https://cryptosmith.files.wordpress.com/2015/08/glossary-2015-cnss.pdf
10. Graham, G.S., Denning, P.J.: Protection: principles and practice. In: AFIPS Conference Proceedings: 1971 Fall Joint Computer Conference, vol. 39, pp. 417–429. ACM, New York, November 1971
11. Harrison, M., Ruzzo, W., Ullman, J.: Protection in operating systems. Commun. ACM **19**(8), 461–471 (1976)
12. Hoffman, L.J.: The formulary model for flexible privacy and access controls. In: AFIPS Conference Proceedings: 1972 Spring Joint Computer Conference, vol. 40, pp. 587–601. ACM, New York, May 1972
13. Kemmerer, R.A.: Cybersecurity. In: Proceedings of the 25th International Conference on Software Engineering, pp. 1–11 (2003)
14. Lampson, B.W.: Protection. ACM SIGOPS Operating Syst. Rev. **8**(1), 18–24 (1974)
15. Saltzer, J.: Protection and the control of information sharing in multics. Commun. ACM **17**(7), 388–402 (1974)
16. Ware, W.: Security controls for computer systems: report of Defense Science Board Task Force on computer security. Technical report R609–1, Rand Corporation, Santa Monica, CA, February 1970
17. Weissman, C.: Security controls in the ADEPT-50 time-sharing system. In: Proceedings of the 1969 Fall Joint Computer Conference, pp. 119–133. ACM, New York, November 1969

Designing Degree Programmes for Bachelors and Masters in Information Security

Natalia Miloslavskaya[(✉)] and Alexander Tolstoy

The National Research Nuclear University
MEPhI (Moscow Engineering Physics Institute),
31 Kashirskoye shosse, Moscow, Russia
{NGMiloslavskaya, AITolstoj}@mephi.ru

Abstract. The effectiveness of ensuring information security (IS) largely depends on the IS specialist's professional level. It is important to design the relevant degree programmes (DPs) for their training within the framework of academic education. This process involves the definition of initial data and the implementation of a certain number of interrelated stages. The peculiarities of national educational systems as well as inadequate coordination of educational activities at the international level are the main reasons for the lack of uniform requirements for the DPs' formation. A DP's design procedure, based on the experience of the international organizations engaged in the accreditation of individual DPs, is considered. The paper defines the typical DP's structure and the basic stages of its design for the example of the Bachelor's and Master's in IS DPs.

Keywords: Information security · Information security professionals · Professional standards · Competency · Degree programme · Bachelors · Masters · Design

1 Introduction

The effectiveness of ensuring information security (IS) largely depends on the professional level of specialists in the field. It is important to design the relevant degree programmes (DPs) for their training. A DP refers to a set of educational and methodical documents, which set forth the basic provisions relating to the implementation of the educational process of training professionals of a certain level.

Each educational institution develops its own DPs based on its experience, others' experiences, and various regulations adopted at the national or international level. The peculiarities of the educational systems of different countries as well as an inadequate coordination of educational activities at the international level are the main reasons for the lack of uniform requirements for the DPs' formation.

In this paper, a DP's design procedure, based on the experience of the international organizations engaged in the DP's accreditation, is considered. As a successful example of such activities, we examine the experience of the Agency for Accreditation of the DPs in the field of engineering, informatics, natural sciences and mathematics (ASIIN, www.asiin-ev.de). The Agency proposes and implements quality control at the

Published by Springer International Publishing AG 2017. All Rights Reserved
M. Bishop et al. (Eds.): WISE 10, IFIP AICT 503, pp. 14–26, 2017.
DOI: 10.1007/978-3-319-58553-6_2

international level for the DPs. The core of the DP's accreditation criteria, regardless of the country in which an applicant (educational institution) operates, consists of the following:

- The orientation of the learning outcomes;
- The feasibility of the DP;
- The quality features associated with the professional community and labor market;
- The applicant's potential, including its quality management maturity;
- The accounting of the requirements of the European Association for Quality Assurance in Higher Education (ENQA) (set out in the "European Standards and Guidelines") and the European Quality Assurance Register (EQAR).

Thus, the paper proposes a generalized (typical) description of a DP's structure, based on the formulation of its key implementation goals, objectives and intended learning outcomes with their features, the development of its curriculum and the description of requirements for the education quality control and the resource support of the DP's implementation. The effectiveness of the proposed approach is confirmed by the NRNU MEPhI's experience in designing the DPs for Bachelors and Masters in IS.

2   Typical Degree Programme Structure

The shared experience of educational institutions, which successfully passed the procedure of their DPs' accreditation in the organizations like ASIIN (presented at http://www.asiin-ev.de), allow us to describe a typical DP's structure (Fig. 1).

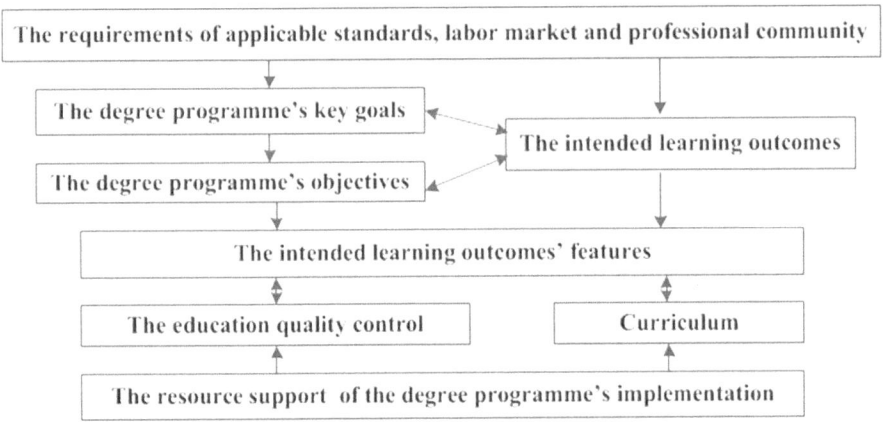

Fig. 1. Typical DP's structure

The educational and methodical documents relating to any DP should clearly describe all these structural elements. The DP's key goals and objectives, as well as the intended learning outcomes formulation should be guided by the requirements set forth by the applicable standards, labor market and professional community (consumers of the educational institutions' graduates, etc.). [To simplify the presentation of our findings and in condition of limited paper size, the requirements resulting from general public interest, IS science itself, etc. are not discussed]. The intended learning outcomes should be described by the relevant features. The DP's curriculum content should be focused on the solution of problems formulated to achieve the key goals and intended learning outcomes. The education quality control should be ensured at all stages of the curriculum implementation. The resources supporting the DP should provide the necessary quality of curriculum implementation. Thus, all the components of a typical DP's structure are interrelated. These relations are causal, allowing the high-quality DP implementation to achieve the key goals of education. In this case, any DP can be regarded as a description of the professional training system with a certain level of operational quality. The optimization of the education quality is associated with an efficiency of management of this system.

3 Procedure of a Degree Programme's Design

The DP's structure description and its elements' interrelations determine its design procedure, consisting of the following consequent steps:

1. Analysis of the requirements of the applicable standards, labor market, and professional community.
2. Selection of the DP type (for Bachelors/Masters).
3. Definition of the DP's key goals and objectives.
4. Formulation of the DP's intended learning outcomes.
5. Definition of the intended learning outcomes' features.
6. Development of the DP's curriculum.
7. Selection of resource support for the DP's implementation.
8. Selection of the education quality control measures.

For the quality of the educational process, it is important to embed the DP's design processes into the processes implemented by a professional training system in a particular field. Any educational institution is interested in improving the overall efficiency of these processes. Hence, the using the continuous process improvement model (called the Deming-Shewhart model or the PDCA cycle) is reasonable [1, 2]. The PDCA cycle is closely connected with quality management [3] where the process control and optimization are especially important. This model assumes a cyclic repetition of four steps. Plan (P): the establishment of objectives and the processes necessary to achieve them, the planning of activities for achieving the objectives and satisfying the customers, and the necessary resource allocation and distribution. Do (D): the planned activities' implementation. Check (C): the collection of information and control of the process implementation results based on the key performance indicators, the identification and analysis of deviations, and their causes. Impact, management, updating (A): the adoption of measures to address the causes of the deviation, and the changes in the planning and allocation of resources.

The application of the first PDCA cycle to the educational process is the first process implementation: P: the DP's design; D: the implementation of the DP's curriculum; C: the educational process's quality control in order to determine the level of the tasks solution set out above and the objectives' achievement degree, detection of abnormalities and their reasons' analysis; and A: the DP's adjustment, which involves the elaboration of measures to change the design process content.

The subsequent PDCA cycles correspond to the continuous improvement of the educational process. In this case, it is important to choose the intervals between the full cycles and to define the control procedures.

Taking into account the educational process's inertia (study duration) and its phasing (semesters, academic years) two options for its improvement are recommended. The *tactical improvement* is associated with the correction of the curriculum and resource support. This adjustment should occur after the educational year based on the DP's quality self-assessment. The *strategic improvement* is associated with the correction of all DP's components. This adjustment should occur after the completion of a full cycle of training on the programme (e.g. four years for a Bachelor's DP and two years for a Master's DP) based on the self-assessment and external audit of the DP's implementation quality. It is possible to associate the quality control with the processes of the DP accreditation.

We also consider an example of the design procedure for any Bachelor's and Master's DP in the field of IS that takes into account all the specific peculiarities and requirements (national and international) for education in this field. The general (non-technical) education requirements (e.g. in humanities, social sciences, etc.) are out of scope of this paper.

3.1 The Requirements of Applicable Standards, Labor Market and Professional Community

The requirements of a separate segment of the labor market and professional community for the qualification of professionals who are capable of fulfilling the kinds of professional activity can be found in various national or international regulations. The documents developed in the USA, Australia, the Russian Federation, the European Community and the International Organization for Standardization (ISO) are the most interesting in the IS field.

The National Cyber Security Division of the U.S. Department of Homeland Security (DHS/NCSD) published the "Information Technology Security Essential Body of Knowledge: A Competency and Functional Framework for IT Security Workforce Development" [4]. NIST prepared the more specialized National Initiative for Cybersecurity Education (NICE) [5]. The Australian Government Information Management Office developed "Cyber Security Capability Framework & Mapping of IS Manual Roles" [6]. The European Commission approved the e-Competence Framework version 3.0 (e-CF 3.0) [7]. ISO has drafts of new standards. ISO/IEC 27021 covers "… [c]ompetence requirements for information security management systems professionals." Three parts of ISO/IEC 19896 describe knowledge, skills, general and effectiveness requirements for ISO/IEC 19790 testers and ISO/IEC 15408 evaluators.

The state-level requirements' formulation features in the documents of the USA, Australia, the European Community and ISO were analyzed in detail in [8].

In our research, we used the requirements of the generalized Russian labor market in the field of IS, combining government, industry and academia. The Russian Federation has developed a set of IS professional standards [9]. At the beginning of 2017 this includes the following professional standards: "Specialist in automation of information and analytical activity in the sphere of security"; "Specialist in security of computer systems and networks"; "Specialist in IS of automated systems (ASs)"; "Specialist in IS in telecommunication systems and networks" and "Specialist in technical information protection". The "Specialist in IS of ASs" professional standard has been approved at the state level. The remaining standards have a project status.

All these standards have a common methodology for forming the requirements. Each professional standard formulates the name of the professional activity; the key goal of the type of professional activity; the generalized job functions included in the type of professional activity; the specific job functions related to a certain generalized function, etc. In our research, we take all this information from the standard as initial data for the DPs and hence we do not show how key goals, learning outcomes and requirements are derived from one another.

Each job function relates to a specific professional qualification level (PQL). The graduates of the educational institutions on the Bachelor's DPs can fit on their qualification to the 6th level (PQL = 6); the graduates on Master's DPs, to the 7th level (PQL = 7). For each job description, the job activities that a professional with a specific PQL can perform are described and the necessary knowledge and abilities that he/she must possess are identified.

As an example, the main provisions of the "Specialist in IS of ASs" professional standard are considered.

The name of professional activity: IS ensuring for ASs.

The key goal of the type of professional activity: IS ensuring for ASs, which operate under the threats in the information sphere and describe the information and technological resources to be protected.

The generalized job functions, corresponding PQLs, work functions, positions held and the required levels of education: are presented for the Bachelor's and Master's DPs in Table 1 (where HPE means Higher Professional Education). Russia uses a three-tier HPE system: Bachelor (4 years), Master (2 years after Bachelor) or Specialist (5–6 years), Post-graduate school (3–4 years after Master or Specialist)). Bachelor graduates with or without work experience can perform a generalized job function B (PQL = 6), occupying one of the positions listed in Table 1. Master or Specialist graduates without work experience can perform a generalized function D (PQL = 7), occupying one of the positions listed in Table 1.

An example of job activities that can perform a professional, referred to a specific PQL, and the necessary knowledge and abilities that he/she should possess: Table 2 shows the "Administration of IPSs for ASs" job function (the generalized job function B; at the same time, he/she should complete a Bachelor's DP and have no work experience) and for the "Development of the design decisions for the AS's information protection" job function (the generalized job function D; at the same time, he/she should complete a Master's DP and have no work experience).

Table 1. The generalized job functions, corresponding PQLs, positions held and required levels of education from the "Specialist in IS of ASs" professional standard

Generalized job functions		Work functions	Position held	Required level of education
Code	Name	Name		
B (PQL = 6)	Ensuring IS for ASs during their operation	Diagnosis of information protection systems (IPSs) for ASs Administration of IPSs for ASs IS management for ASs Providing IPSs functioning in emergency situations Monitoring of information protection in ASs Audit of information protection in ASs	Information Protection Engineer Information Protection Specialist Software Engineer for Technical Information Protection Software Engineer	HPE, Bachelor
D (PQL = 7)	Design of IPSs for ASs	Testing of IPSs for ASs Design decision development for the AS's information protection Development of the maintenance documentation for IPS for ASs Development of software and hardware IPSs for ASs	Leading IPSs' Development Engineer Leading Information Protection Specialist IPS's Development Project Head IPS's Department Head	HPE, Master, Specialist

Our analysis of the "Specialist in IS of ASs" professional standard and its comparison with the results of similar analysis of the regulations of the USA, Australia, European Community and ISO standards' drafts [7] leads us to conclude that all these documents have their own peculiarities, reflecting the experience and specifics of the respective countries, and some terminological inconsistency.

However, they have common features: they contain the qualification requirements for IS professionals related to a separate type of work they can perform at a certain position. This information is extremely important for the educational institutions, which are developing and implementing the educational programmes for training IS professionals of a certain level. It allows them to define the key goals and objectives of training and to formulate the requirements for the intended learning outcomes.

Table 2. An example of job activities and the necessary knowledge and abilities from the "Specialist in IS of ASs" professional standard

	Basic education – Bachelor's DP	Basic education – a Master's DP
Job activities	Installing AS's software updates Protecting information, taking into account the requirements of the efficient AS's functioning Managing AS's users authorities Informing users about AS's operation rules, accounting the IS requirements Conducting training of personnel to work with AS's IPS, including the workshops with staff on models or in a test area Changing of operational documentation and organizational and administrative documents for AS's IPS	Developing the IS threats' models of and the intruders' models for ASs Developing the models of ASs and ASs' protection subsystems Developing the regulation drafts, regulating the information protection activities Developing the proposals on improvement of AS's IS management system
Necessary knowledge	The formation principles for IS policy for ASs Hardware and software IPSs for ASs The key cryptographic methods, algorithms and protocols, used to protect information in ASs The methods of protection effectiveness control for information leakage via technical channels The criteria for evaluating the effectiveness and reliability of ASs' software protection The technical tools for monitoring the information protection measures' effectiveness The organization principles and structure of AS's software protection system The content and procedure of the personnel activities on operating the protected ASs and AS's IPSs The main information protection measures for ASs	The guidelines and methodological documents of the authorized executive bodies on information protection The regulations and national standards for licensing in the sphere of protection of state secrets and information protection tools' certification The principles of construction and functioning, examples of implementations of modern local and global computer networks and their components The information protection features in the automated technological processes' control systems The evaluation criteria for ASs' software protection effectiveness and reliability The organization principles and structure of AS's software protection system The main characteristics of IPTs against leakage via technical channels The formation principles for AS's IS policy

(*continued*)

Table 2. (*continued*)

	Basic education – Bachelor's DP	Basic education – a Master's DP
Necessary abilities - To	Create, delete and modify AS users' accounts Write an IS policy for AS's software components Install and configure operating systems, database management systems, computer networks and software systems to meet the IS requirements Use the cryptographic information protection methods and tools in ASs Register the events associated with information protection in ASs Analyze the events associated with information protection in ASs	Apply the existing regulatory framework in the field of IS Apply the regulations on countering technical intelligence Classify the protected information by types of secrets and confidentiality degrees Define the types of access subjects/objects to be protected Identify the access control methods, types and differentiation rules for the access objects to be implemented in ASs Select the information protection measures to be implemented in AS's IPTs Identify the kinds and types of IPTs, ensuring the implementation of technical information protection measures Determine the structure of AS's IPTs according to the requirements of the regulations in the field of IS for ASs

3.2 Definition of the DP's Key Goals and Objectives

Defining the DP's key goals and objectives must take into account the key goals and objectives set by the standards mentioned above, and the labor market's requirements. In our case, the DP's key goal can meet the needs of professionals who can do the types of professional activity in a particular segment of the labor market. An example of such a segment is the area of IS that requires professionals of a certain level (e.g. Bachelors or Masters). The types of their professional activities may include, but are not limited to: operation of IPTs or protected information processing systems; design of IPTs or protected information processing systems; management of systems ensuring IS or protected information processing systems; research in the field of IS; and pedagogical activities in the field of IS.

As an example, the definition of the Bachelor's and Master's DP's key goals and objectives for the "Specialist in IS of ASs" professional standard of the Russian Federation is considered.

The overall key goal of the Bachelor's and Master's DP: the training of professionals in the field of IS of ASs, which operate under the threats in the information sphere and protect information and technological resources.

The particular key goal of the Bachelor's DP: the training of professionals in the field of IS for ASs during their operation (as defined in Table 1, based on a generalized job function B).

The objectives of the Bachelor's DP: the training of professionals for the job functions which are defined in Table 1 (column 3, based on the job functions related to a generalized job function B).

The particular key goal of the Master's DP: the training of professionals in developing IPTs for ASs (as defined in Table 1, based on a generalized job function D).

The objectives of the Master's DP: the training of professionals for the job functions defined in Table 1 (column 3, based on the job functions related to a generalized job function D).

The definition of the DP's key goals and objectives directly influences the intended learning outcomes.

3.3 Formulation of the Learning Outcomes

When determining the requirements for the DP's implementation results, the DP's key goals and objectives should be taken into account, as well as the requirements of the labor market and professional community. These requirements can be found in various regulations of the national or international level.

The modern approach to their definition is based on the establishment of professional competencies of a professional's ability to solve given problems and to perform specific work within his/her sphere of activity [10]. As an example, the definition of the intended learning outcomes for the implementation of the Bachelor's and Master's DPs based on the requirements of the "Specialist in IS of ASs" professional standard of the Russian Federation. The professional competencies in this case can be formulated for each job function (Table 1) based on the determination of the job activities relating to this job function (Table 2).

The intended learning outcomes for the Bachelor's DP: the professional competencies that a Bachelor should have to perform for the "Administration of IPSs for ASs" job function (a generalized job function B). The Bachelor must be able to demonstrate (according to the job activities defined in Table 2) the ability to install AS's software updates; secure information, taking into account the requirements of the efficient functioning of the AS; manage the AS's user rights; inform the users about the rules of AS operation, taking into account the IS requirements; train personnel to work with the AS's IPS, including workshops with staff on models or in a test area; and change the operational, organizational, and administrative documents for the AS's IPS.

The intended learning outcomes for the Master's DP: the professional competencies, that a Master should have to perform for the "Development of the design decisions for AS's information protection" job function (a generalized job function D). The Master must be able to demonstrate (according to the job activities, which are defined in Table 2) the ability to develop the IS threats' and intruders' models for the ASs; the models of the ASs and the ASs' protection subsystems; the regulation drafts regulating the information protection activities; and proposals for improveing the AS's IS management system.

If a DP trains professionals to perform multiple job functions, then a set of professional competencies should be formulated for each job function.

The DP may also include general professional competencies, the formation of which is necessary as a basis for the subsequent formation of the professional competencies. This is especially true for the Bachelor's DPs.

3.4   Definition of the Intended Learning Outcomes' Features

Characterization of the intended learning outcomes is traditionally associated with a specific competency by combining observable and measurable knowledge (K), skills (S), and abilities (A) [10]. Knowledge is the cognizance of facts, truths and principles gained from formal training and/or experience. A skill is a developed proficiency or dexterity in mental operations or physical processes that is often acquired through specialized training; using these skills results in successful performance. Ability is the power or aptitude to perform physical or mental activities that are often affiliated with a particular profession.

In accordance with the recommendations of the "The European Qualifications Framework for Lifelong Learning" (EQF) [11], the definition of the learning outcomes' features in the form of requirements to the level of K, S and A depends on the DP's level: EQF level 5 for Bachelors and EQF level 7 for Masters in IS. When defining their features, the "Specialist in IS of ASs" professional standard for Bachelors and Masters (Table 2) were used. The EQF's recommendations were also considered.

The features of Bachelor's and Master's DP intended learning outcomes: The K, S and A are shown in Table 2, where job activities are equal to S.

All these data should be taken into account in the design of appropriate DPs' curricula.

3.5   Development of the DP's Curriculum

The curriculum contains a list of training activities for the entire period of study. These activities include classes (C) and students' independent work (IW). As a rule, these activities are implemented within the framework of different curriculum elements: academic disciplines, internships, implementation, and protection of a Final Qualifying Work (FQW). The workload for each element is assessed in conventional units (CUs) or credits (Cs) correlated with the training hours (THs). For example, 1 credit is equal to 36 THs in Russia. The workload is distributed by semesters and study weeks. Each semester covers 18 weeks. Each curriculum element has its own knowledge progress testing (KPT): Exam (E) or Test (T).

The curriculum implementation workload for the Bachelor's DPs is more oftenusually valued at 240 credits. It corresponds to 8640 THs and 4 years (8 semesters) of study.

The curriculum implementation workload for the Master's DPs is usually valued at 120 credits. It corresponds to 4320 THs and 2 years (4 semesters) of study.

Table 3. A curriculum structure's sample for a Master's DP

Curriculum elements	KPT	Workload				Distribution by years, Hours per week (C/IW)			
						1st year		2nd year	
		Credits, CUs	Training hours			1st sem	2nd sem	3rd sem	4th sem
			Total	C	IW				
Discipline 1	T	2	72	36	36	2/2			
Discipline 2	T	…	…	…	…	…	…	…	…
Discipline N	E	5	144	72	72		4/4		
Internship	3 Es	30	360	0	360	0/6	0/7	0/7	
FQW	E	30	360	0	360				0/20
Total		120	4320						

An example curriculum structure for a Master's DP is shown in Table 3. It is necessary to identify a list of disciplines, as well as KPT forms, workload (in credits and THs) and the distribution of THs by study weeks for each curriculum element.

A programme for each curriculum element, the implementation of which is focused on the formation of specific competencies and intended learning outcomes, should be designed. A certain professional competence is formed by several disciplines [10]. In that case, all the curriculum elements should be combined into the separate training modules. For example, a Bachelor's DP curriculum can be designed based on four modules: General Educational, General Professional, Professional, Internship & FQW's Protection. The General Educational Module combines elements of the discipline; mastering it will create a basis for the students' mastering of disciplines to be included in the General Professional Module. It, in turn, combines elements of the discipline; mastering it will create a basis for the students' mastering of disciplines from the Professional Module. A Master's DP curriculum can be designed similarly based on three modules: General Professional, Professional, Internship & FQW.

The given structure separates the requirements for the intended learning outcomes for each module and expands the range of competencies that should have been formed at the end of the educational process. Another positive effect of modular curriculum structure is the ability to support the mobility of students in passing their training, when the students can study the individual modules in different educational institutions (this is typical of the dual-diploma DPs).

The ASIIN's recommendations [12] can be used to describe a training module.

3.6 Selection of Resource Support for the DP's Implementation

To implement any DP, the following resources are required: human resources, laboratories, educational and methodical resources, and financial resources. The faculty (their quantity and quality) forms the human resources. The required number of instructors depends on the workload and the number of students enrolled. The faculty's quality depends on the instructors' experience and professionalism (their educational titles, academic degrees, publication activity, etc.). Laboratory support is determined by the number and level of equipment of educational and scientific laboratories. Educational and methodological support is determined by the educational institution's library capacity, accessibility to different information sources, availability of textbooks and training manuals, design of a separate DP's implementation, etc. Financial support for the DP's implementation is based on the funds received from the students (paid training), from various organizations and funds (targeted training), and from the state (budget training).

The resource requirements for the provision of the educational process in the Russian Federation are formulated in the educational standards, and are developed and approved at the state level for each training direction (including that of IS).

3.7   Selection of the Education Quality Control Measures

Any educational institution implementing a DP for Bachelors/Masters should be a guarantor of the education quality based on continuous multilevel education in order to best meet the learning outcomes of all stakeholders. For that purpose, a Quality Management System should exist with the appropriate control measures in place. Their formation and development are based on global trends focused on the concept of Total Quality Management, the requirements of ISO 9001:2015 [3], the guidelines for Quality Assurance Agencies in Higher Education, etc.

4   Conclusion

The above design procedure has been tested at the Institute of Cyber Intelligence Systems of the National Research Nuclear University MEPhI in the development and implementation of the following DPs in IS: *for Bachelors*: "Automated Systems Security"; *for Masters*: "Cryptographic Methods for Cybersecurity", "Information Security of Crucial Objects" and "Information Security and Intelligence Analysis for Financial Monitoring". All these DPs have been successfully accredited in Russia, proving the consistency of our approach. In addition, these DPs are currently passing the international accreditation by ASIIN. Using our approach, we prepared the DPs' self-assessment report as an initial data for this procedure. During this self-assessment, we found a few ASIIN requirements were not met (for example, in dividing DPs in training modules, the distribution of disciplines within the modules for the Bachelors' DP). We corrected the curricula to satisfy those requirements. One lesson we learned is that we needed to pay more attention to consumer's demand for graduates of our DPs and their expectations of graduates' knowledge, skills and abilities.

Currently, the third generation of students is being trained with a total enrollment of 105 students (15 Bachelors + 90 Masters). After every graduation year we reviewed and adjusted the curriculum of each DP due to the changes in the requirements and educational content.

Acknowledgement. This work was supported by Competitiveness Growth Program of the Federal Autonomous Educational Institution of Higher Education National Research Nuclear University MEPhI (Moscow Engineering Physics Institute).

References

1. Shewhart, W.A.: Statistical Method from the Viewpoint of Quality Control. Department of Agriculture. Dover, vol. 1939, p. 45 (1986)
2. Deming, W.E.: The New Economics, p. 135. MIT Press, Cambridge (1993)
3. ISO 9001:2015 Quality Management Systems – Requirements
4. State Government Information Security Workforce Development Model. A Best Practice Model and Framework, Final Version 1.0 (U.S.), June 2010
5. The U.S. National Cybersecurity Workforce Framework. https://www.dhs.gov/national-cybersecurity-workforce-framework, Accessed 18 Jan 2017
6. The Cyber Security Capability Framework & Mapping of ISM Roles. Final Report. Australian Government Information Management Office, June 2010
7. The European e-Competence Framework 3.0. A common European Framework for ICT Professionals in all industry sectors. CWA 16234:2014 Part 1. CEN
8. Miloslavskaya, N., Tolstoy, A.: State-level views on professional competencies in the field of IoT and cloud information security. In: Proceedings of the 2016 4th International Conference on Future Internet of Things and Cloud Workshops, The 3rd International Symposium on Intercloud and IoT (ICI 2016). Vienna (Austria), August 2016, pp. 83–90 (2016)
9. The professional standards draft (Specialists in the field of IS). (in Russian), http://infosystems.ru/library/proekt_professionalnogo_standarta.html, Accessed 18 Jan 2017
10. Miloslavskaya, N., Tolstoy, A.: Professional competencies level assessment for training of masters in information security. In: Bishop, M., Miloslavskaya, N., Theocharidou, M. (eds.) WISE 2015. IFIP AICT, vol. 453, pp. 135–145. Springer, Cham (2015). doi:10.1007/978-3-319-18500-2_12
11. The European Qualifications Framework for Lifelong Learning. http://ec.europa.eu/dgs/education_culture, Accessed 18 Jan 2017
12. Criteria for the Accreditation of Degree Programmes (ASIIN). http://www.asiin-ev.de/media/kriterien/0.3_Criteria_for_the_Accrediation_of_Degree_Programmes_2015-12-10.pdf, Accessed 18 Jan 2017

Assessing the Effectiveness of the Cisco Networking Academy Program in Developing Countries

Odwa Yekela[✉], Kerry-Lynn Thomson[✉], and Johan van Niekerk[✉]

Nelson Mandela Metropolitan University, Port Elizabeth, South Africa
{s212314653,kerry-lynn.thomson,johan.vanniekerk}@nmmu.ac.za

Abstract. Ensuring students are equipped with the necessary skillsets for the workplace has become a priority for Higher Education Institutions (HEIs). This is especially true in the ever changing field of network security. Competency frameworks can contribute towards the creation of relevant curricula. Various approaches to delivering such education exist. Blended learning, one of the most popular approaches, has shown promising results yet there are still many factors that plague the successful adoption and implementation of e-learning programs at HEIs. This paper investigates how the Cisco Networking Academy Program (CNAP) has integrated blended learning effectively to prepare graduates for network security positions while adhering to global competency standard needs.

Keywords: Blended learning · Cybersecurity · Competency · CNAP · Higher education

1 Introduction

Information Communication Technology (ICT) has assumed a critical role in facilitating social-economic development in many countries. According to ENISA [1], ICT solutions such as communication networks and information systems are necessary for economic and social development and are fast becoming universal utilities, much like water and electricity. Due to the strong reliance on information, the protection of information resources has become of critical importance to many organizations, both in developed and developing countries. Already more than 50 nations have published their official stance on cybersecurity [2]. Cybersecurity related fields such as information security and communication network have been placed as a leading priority by ICT managers [3]. More and more graduates are seeking for employment in cybersecurity related jobs, yet there is still a lack of an adequate cybersecurity workforce. Not only is there a shortfall of a skilled cybersecurity workforce which is a critical vulnerability for companies and nations, but there is also little consistency in terms of how cybersecurity work is defined or described.

This absence of a common language to describe and understand cybersecurity work hinders the establishment of a consistent baseline of capabilities, the identification of skills gaps and the assurance of a steady pipeline of future talent. Hence many

M. Bishop et al. (Eds.): WISE 10, IFIP AICT 503, pp. 27–38, 2017.
DOI: 10.1007/978-3-319-58553-6_3

organizations and countries have adopted competency frameworks as an industry wide approach to describing competencies in cybersecurity [4]. These competencies are based on industry standards and can be learned and assessed through competency-centered learning programs. One of the most widely accepted and administered competency-centered learning program at HEI is the Cisco Networking Academy Program (CNAP) [5]. The CNAP encompasses communication networks as a whole, as it seeks to prepare graduates for competency intense job positions and for industry certifications [6]. The program also consists of a dedicated network security course. The network security course program is industry recognized and is currently being implemented at many HEI. Even with the wide spread popularity of e-learning platforms such as blended learning at universities, there are many challenges that still plague the large scale integration of these competency-centered learning programs at HEI. This is more apparent in countries where there is little to no ICT infrastructure for education. Most e-learning initiatives in developing countries have not been successful [7–9], this is largely due to fact that developing countries are mimicking the e-learning trends of developed countries with the expectations of reaping the same benefits enjoyed by HEI in developed countries [7, 9].

Furthermore, cybersecurity needs and expectation for developing countries are different from cybersecurity needs in developed countries [10]. Even with these obstacles the CNAP program has been able to effectively integrate Blended learning to prepare graduates from all around the world for cybersecurity related positions while adhering to global industry competency needs. The Objective of this paper is to evaluate the effectiveness of CNAP as a network security curriculum in HEIs, by evaluating it against cybersecurity competency framework and well-known blended learning best practices.

2   Competency in Cybersecurity

It is generally accepted that to be regarded as proficient at a profession; one has to have significant knowledge and skill in a particular domain or discipline, have been accepted by the community, either through certification or general recognition as one who is qualified to practice in that discipline, operates with authority and responsibility, and be of service to the community [11]. But does this abstract view of professionalism apply to cybersecurity? The individuals who are at the forefront of protecting information resources are known as cybersecurity professionals. However, little is known about the work practices of these professionals. In reality, the cybersecurity industry is much more complex [12]. Note that job titles vary considerably across organizations, and there is a lack of functional job descriptions of cybersecurity related professions, such as network security professionals. Furthermore, studies have shown that even ICT professions that do not have the word "security" in their job titles also spend a considerable amount of time performing security-related activities on a daily basis [13].

To address the lack of a common description for cybersecurity work, competency frameworks are used by organizations to account for cybersecurity competencies. Competency frameworks consist of a classification of the attributes required to be competent at a profession. In general competency is an individual's ability to draw on the knowledge, skill and attitude (KSA), necessary for performing activities to a specified standard. This standard is referred to as competency standard [14]. Competency standards can be described as an industry-determined specification of performance which sets out the KSA required to operate effectively in a job role [15].

HEIs are the primary source of initial education and training for cybersecurity professionals [47]. Such institutions play a role in shaping the public perceptions of a profession through provisioning of educational programs that prepare students for a chosen profession. In reality there is a short supply of ICT skills and it cannot keep pace with the growing demand [3]. While much promotion for ICT related degrees use career outcome to market potential students, for many of these degrees there's little evidence whether these outcomes are truly embedded into the curriculum [16]. With growing pressure from industry, HEIs are required to perform a series of actions that can improve the current situation. This suggests that ICT courses should focus on building the skills and competencies that lead students to successful employment, rather than just traditional university objectives, which are aimed at teaching students the general skills of problem solving and how to find and transform knowledge to useful information. Oliver [17] further states that curricula are now favoring competency and performance, "Curricula are starting to emphasize capabilities and to be concerned more with how the information will be used than with what the information is". Competency frameworks and competency standards are now being mapped to HEI curriculum, but narrowing the gap between industry and HEI requires more than a tick-the-box approach, embedding professional skills and competencies into the curriculum should be done as part of a holistic educational design. Thus the new challenge faced by HEIs is articulating and developing employability skills that are still sustainable, pedagogically sound, and of high quality.

3   Cisco Networking Academy Program (CNAP)

The Cisco Networking Academy Program (CNAP) is a global competency-centered, on-line educational program, delivered through a Blended Learning approach. The program seeks to educate and train students, so they can design, troubleshoot and secure communication networks [5]. The CNAP program's curriculum is industry competence-centered and is congruent with industry certifications [18]. Cisco Systems first officially launched the CNAP program in 1997, when they observed that many HEIs lack adequate network competencies. They began partnering with institutions from all around the world, to date more than 16 500 Institutions from over 165 countries have enrolled in Networking Academy courses since its initial start [6, 19] CNAP is able to leverage public-private partnerships, along with government and HEIs to help students from vastly different social and economic backgrounds to develop competencies needed to align with global industry standards. As Cisco System's largest Corporate Social Responsibility (CSR) education program, CNAP aids in achieving the goal of delivering practical and relevant learning experiences. The CNAP has seen an increase in the participation of developing countries, which have been consistently higher than their more developed counter parts [19]. CNAP constitutes the core curricula for communication network [5, 43], this includes network security. In South Africa over 60 HEIs use CNAP as part of their curriculum [46].

Cisco Systems has established partnerships in many developing regions of the world, to deliver sustainable and effective capacity-building programs. In 2000, the Least Developed Countries initiative (LDCi) which established over 58 learning institutions in 20 developing countries, in this particular endeavor Cisco donated CNAP curricula, e-learning infrastructure, and hands-on lab equipment [20, 21]. Although the LDCi concluded in 2006, Cisco and its affiliated partners continue to support Institutions that were established within the ITU Centers of Excellence Initiative worldwide. Research from surveys indicates that CNAP has a strong and positive impact within participating communities, especially in developing countries. Most of the students that participated in the surveys found jobs in network related positions after completing the program. More than one in ten students who were surveyed also started their own businesses [22]. "Through this partnership, we have been able to touch more than 1 million students in 51 countries in addition, more than 10 000 students have graduated from the program in Africa" – Alfie Hamid, Regional Corporate Affairs Manager at Cisco Systems [20].

4   Blended Learning at HEI

Elliott [23] argues that the fundamental learning environment has changed, this is largely due to the introduction of technology, and therefore classical pedagogies need to also evolve to reflect this reality. The emergence of ubiquitous computing renders this reality necessary for HEIs. The way information is accessed has dramatically changed due to the increase use of the Internet, which has emerged as the most important tool for e-learning. E-learning covers a spectrum of activities from supported learning to blended learning and to learning that is delivered entirely online.

"Learning environments are becoming more blended in nature as students make choices about whether to attend all traditional face-to-face sessions or to adopt a mix of asynchronous and synchronous activities" [24] Blended learning is a teaching model that comprises of various teaching methods brought together by technology to meet specific objectives. Blended learning is delivered through a combination of personalized online learning, with face-to-face traditional instructor-led onsite support and hands-on application. Through the use of blended learning, students are given control over certain attributes of learning such as time, place, path and pace [25]; for example, a student might attend classes in a real-world classroom setting, and then supplement the lesson plan by completing online multimedia coursework. As such, the student would only have to physically attend class once a week and would be free to go at their own pace [26].

The use of blended learning has increased in HEI, it is likely to be more widely used in the tertiary and school sectors. In many cases, E-learning component in Blended learning programs is delivered through a virtual learning environment. This virtual environment is constructed for online learning [23]. The new pedagogical challenge is not a lack of information, but rather too much. Students must now learn how to conceptualize and criticize information available on the internet. One of the major benefits of this form of learning is that online learning is accessible from anywhere at any time. It is argued that traditional classroom learning should be better off spent on discussing rather than delivering content [23]. Research shows that students who interact with online learning perform better than students with no such involvement. Furthermore, surveys indicate that students consider online learning beneficial to their studies.

For many developing countries, education is a key factor in remediating poverty and encouraging economic growth [27–29]. E-learning is seen as a cornerstone for new delivery methods for education. However, implementing e-learning programs faces a lot of obstacles and challenges in developing countries. According to Khan [30], developing countries are a long way behind developed countries in e-service implementation, and the gap is widening over time. This especially applies to e-learning. Institutions in developing countries are mimicking the trends of e-learning with the expectations of reaping the same benefits enjoyed by institutions in developed countries. Anderson [29] describes several factors that prohibit the successful implementation of e-learning programs in developing countries, these include:

Classical views on Education: for e-learning to be fully appreciated, it is essential that classical views on pedagogy be rethought. Classical passive-information-transfer approaches used by HEIs are restrictive when compared to the more interactive student-centered application of e-learning [31]. The problem is that technology in HEIs is seen as just an educational tool, separate from pedagogy. Essentially ICT is a medium for the 'message' (pedagogy), and thus its inter-connectedness should not be seen as isolated [23].

Attitude on IT and e-learning: It is commonly believed that attitudes come from socio-economic views, student's and teacher's views on whether e-learning is 'as good' as traditional face-to-face pedagogies; pose a challenge for e-learning if not addressed openly [32–34]. Therefore, the attitude and behaviors that are reflected in a society should permit positively on e-learning development.

Teaching and Learning Activities: This challenge directly refers to the numerous learning activities that may be taken up in a learning environment, activities that are interactive and allow students to collaborate or have a hands-on practical element affect positively on student performance the most [35, 36]. In this regard, e-learning is viewed as limited when it comes to assessing student performance.

Support and Guidance for Students: Support provided by the institution and the teacher is important for the success of the e-learning programs. Students in developing countries usually are not technologically confident, they are neither used to the e-learning culture or distance centered learning, this coupled with the cultural views on e-learning in turn makes them expect the same kind of immediate feedback experienced in traditional face-to-face classrooms teaching [37]. Psycharis [38] elaborates by stating that when new e-learning technologies are adopted, usually little attention is given to student support.

Computer Anxiety: According to Tucker, Pigou and Zaugg [39], students with restricted experience on computers are four times more likely to withdraw from the e-learning initiatives, than students who are used to working with them. Many students in developing countries have little to no exposer to ICT solutions, and thus have low levels of confidence and comfort with ICT solutions [40].

Flexibility: One of the major benefits of e-learning is its flexibility, in that it can be used anywhere, anytime and by anyone [23], but this benefit is twofold as it brings out concerns with how much flexibility should be given to the students, such as if student should be allowed to learn at their own pace, when would be the most ideal time to take examination and if students should be allowed choose the medium of content delivery [29] students in developing countries may not have the means to be at school all the time or to have access to ICT solutions, some students may be taking several other subjects at the institution which makes flexibility an issue.

Accessibility: The use of the internet for e-learning makes accessibility an enabling or disabling factor. Access is not just restricted to physical infrastructure, it also refers to the accessibility to the content itself, factors such as bandwidth and reliability of internet connection also affects user ability to fully access content, this factor is critical in a student-centered learning environment such as e-learning.

Localization of Content: Content provided in e-learning programs must reflect local culture, language and religious beliefs or the content may not be well received by the audience. Much research shows that localization is of benefit for the students and language is often a good predictor of outcome [41, 42]. For many developing countries English many not be the predominate language used.

5   Implementation of CNAP at HEI

The CNAP plays an important role in helping educate the next generation of network and cybersecurity professionals. The program is essentially collaboration between Cisco Systems and affiliated Institutions. HEIs choose to partner with Cisco Systems for their technical orientated courses. Since the CNAP is a blended learning approach, it usually runs congruently with HEI coursework. Cisco Systems provides the CNAP on-line curricula and on-line assessment free to HEIs. The HEI in turn are required to send instructors to instructor training, monitor student outcomes, and include hands-on activities (hands-on equipment may be donated by Cisco Systems to institutions) in the classroom [43]. In addition, Cisco Systems also provides a network simulator for students to practice on and for teachers to assess student competence [44].

CNAP content is developed according to a set of learning objectives. Educators have long used learning objectives based on Bloom's Taxonomy. Bloom's Taxonomy is useful for developing learning objectives and ensuring learning outcomes reflect the learning objective. The CNAP learning objectives map well with industry competency frameworks to ensure that student who go through the program develop the necessary competencies required in the field. The most prominent competency framework in cybersecurity is the National Cybersecurity Workforce Framework [4]. The National Cybersecurity Workforce Framework establishes a common taxonomy that can be used to reference cybersecurity related skills. These skills overlap significantly with the CNAP Network Security learning objectives. The CNAP Learning objectives are reflective of the expected competency in the aligned competency as listed by the NCWF. The curriculum thus provides an adequate introduction to the core security concepts and skills needed for the installation, troubleshooting, and monitoring of network devices to maintain the integrity, confidentiality, and availability of data and devices.

Bloom's Taxonomy also provides a convenient way of describing the degree in which educators can expect students to understand in order to demonstrate particular skills. Therefore, it is strategic for teachers to use Bloom's Taxonomy to determine the level of expertise required of students, as this determines which classroom assessment techniques are most appropriate for the course. Bloom's Taxonomy consists of six levels of the cognitive domain, these levels consist of a collective of statement that outlines the learning objectives of an educational program. Usually a learning objective statement will be used to create a set of learning activities. Learning activities are described as activities designed to help students meet the learning objectives. Verbs can be correlated with specific learning activities at specific levels of the cognitive domain to describe the type of learning objectives needed. Van Niekerk and Thomson [5] illustrate how activities currently in the CNAP curricula can be expressed using Bloom's Taxonomy, as depicted in Table 1. The CNAP learning model's cognitive complexity can be expressed not just theoretically, but also from a practical hands-on frame of reference. Student competency is further assessed through practical hands-on exercises, projects and examinations. These practical endeavors assess students' performance at higher levels of degrees in the cognitive domain. During practical exercises students may be required to analyze a network's requirements, and then decide which network protocols are applicable for that specific scenario.

Table 1. Comparing CNAP learning activities to Bloom's Taxonomy

Level	Verb	Sample activities
Create	design	Design a converged information network to meet the needs of Company A?
Evaluate	critique	Critique these two converged information network designs. Which would be best for Company A?
Analyze	analyze	Analyze the given design for a converged information network and determine whether it meets Company A's requirements?
Apply	execute	Implement a converged information network
Understand	discuss	How does a converged information network differ from the traditional approach of separate networks?
Remember	define	What is the definition of a converged information network?

Other examples of the application of higher levels of the cognitive domain during practical assessment include students evaluating and then implementing specific access-control statements to suit security requirements given. Practical exercises are based on real-life scenarios and thus translate well into job related competency requirements.

There are many different things to consider when designing and delivering an e-learning program, for an e-learning initiative to be effective it must be of good quality. The Food Agriculture Organisation (FAO) e-learning methodology describes a list of attributes that signify good quality in an e-learning program [45]. As one of the world's largest and most innovative e-learning programs, CNAP captures many of these attributes associated with quality e-learning.

Student-Centered Content: CNAP learning objectives are based on industry standards and t map well with competency frameworks such as the National Cybersecurity Workforce Framework. Furthermore, CNAP content is based on real-world application, students' part-take in practical exercise and self-assessment quizzes that highlight scenarios that simulate real problems faced by professions in the field.

Granularity: CNAP content is segment into chapters and section for easy assimilation. Each chapter consist of summary and some form of interactive formative assessment to help student assess their progress systematically, chapter exams are taken by students, normally at their own pace, although working within certain limits set by the study calendar.

Engaging Content the CNAP on-line platform uses a wide range of multimedia instructional instruments, this includes interactive video clips, hand-on simulator exercises, discussion boards, multimedia chat, text questions, performance-based reviews, alerts, notifications, blogs, and more. The on-line learning platform can help also enhance instruction and customize courses by embedding content from social media channels. In addition, many tools and guidelines are provided to teachers via the CNAP online management system.

Interactivity: Due to the blended nature of CNAP, student benefit from the self-paced online material and the traditional classroom environment. In addition, career support is also provided to students via the CNAP on-line platform, such as Career Path assistance, Job hunting resources and motivational success stories from graduates.

Personalization: Students are provided with a number of tools to customize their learning experience to meet their self-paced needs, this includes dashboards where they can oversee and schedule events such as quizzes and chapter exams. Teachers are able to keep track of each student's performance through an on-line gradebook.

6   Discussion

The is a need to incorporate competency-centered programs in cybersecurity related courses by HEIs, these learning programs need to be measurable against a well-defined industry competency framework and delivered through sound pedagogical means. Through CNAP, Cisco Systems together with HEIs has been able to effectively deliver and implement an e-learning program that is measurable and pedagogically sound, while ensuring that the program is robust enough to also be provided in developing countries. As such, these following factors serve to validate this argument.

- **Meeting competency:** CNAP learning objectives are measurable against the National Cybersecurity Workforce Framework.
- **Sound Pedagogy:** CNAP learning activities adheres to the Bloom taxonomy model's view on strategic student assessment.
- **Effective delivery:** CNAP e-learning aspects consist of many characteristics of a quality e-learning program as defined by FAO e-learning methodology.
- **Anticipating challenges:** Cisco Systems has made efforts in identifying and addressing factors that may prohibit the successful adoption and delivery of CNAP.

CNAP has seen much success in many HEIs, since its initial conception over a million students have participated in the program with over 5% being from Africa [43]. Statistic indicate a steady and progressive completion rate in developing countries, although less than in developed countries. The study also concluded that there was a strong correlation between a country's successful CNAP student participation and its networking skills readiness [6]. Interestingly in another independent study it was indicated that instructor quality and use of technology tools, where the strong factors in determining the successful adoption and implementation of CNAP [43]. Therefore, successfully addressing instructor quality and use of technology tools could directly or indirectly contribute a country's networking skills readiness. Since developed countries have shown a stronger CNAP student participation then developing countries, in could be conceived that these institutions may have stronger instructors and/or technology tools, research into how they have accomplished this could help developed countries improve their own CNAP.

7   Conclusion

CNAP has in many ways been able to effectively adopt and implement e-learning platforms in HEIs to help these institutions produce competent graduates. Competencies gained through CNAP are able to be leveraged in order to find job placement. As such, the CNAP complements efforts of addressing the skills shortage crisis, in fact CNAP involvement could be considered an indicator of a country's network skills capacity or its propensity to invest in technology education.

References

1. ENISA., A step-by-step approach on how to set up a CSIRT (Technical report). ENISA (2006). http://www.enisa.europa.eu/activities/cert/support/guide
2. Klimburg, A.: National cyber security framework manual. NATO CCD COE Publications (2012). https://ccdcoe.org/publications/books/NationalCyberSecurityFrameworkManual.pdf
3. Schofield, A.: JCSE ICT Skills Survey. Joburg Centre for Software Engineering (JCSE), pp. 1–35 (2014). http://www.jcse.org.za/sites/default/files/[filename]_2.pdf

4. National Institute of Science and Technology. The National Cybersecurity Workforce Framework (2013). http://csrc.nist.gov/nice/framework/national_cybersecurity_workforce_framework_03_20\n13_version1_0_for_printing.pdf
5. Niekerk, J.F., Thomson, K.-L.: Evaluating the Cisco Networking Academy Program's Instructional Model against Bloom's Taxonomy for the purpose of information security education for organizational end-users. In: Reynolds, N., Turcsányi-Szabó, M. (eds.) KCKS 2010. IFIP AICT, vol. 324, pp. 412–423. Springer, Heidelberg (2010). doi: 10.1007/978-3-642-15378-5_40
6. Stockford, S., Wright, D.: Impact of Cisco Networking Academy Participation on the Growth of Networked Readiness for Developing Nations (2016)
7. Khan, G.F., Moon, J., Rhee, C., Rho, J.J.: E-government skills identification and development: toward a staged-based user-centric approach for developing countries. Asia Pacific J. Inf. Syst. **20**(1) (2010)
8. Borstorff, P.C., Keith, L.S.: Student perceptions and opinions towards e-Learning in the college environment. Acad. Educ. Leadersh. J. **11**(2) (2007). ISSN 1095-6328
9. Sharma, R.C.: Barriers in using technology for education in developing countries. In: Information Technology: Research and Education, Proceedings, ITRE 2003, 11-13 Aug 2003 pp. 512- 516 (2003)
10. Tagert, A.C.: Cybersecurity Challenges in Developing Nations. Doctoral thesis, Princeton University (2010). cmu.edu/cgi/viewcontent.cgi?article=1021&context=dissertations
11. Rochester, J.: Becoming a Professional. IEEE Antennas Propag. Mag. **43**(6), 151–153 (2000)
12. D'Amico, A., Whitley, K.: Real work of computer network defense analysts. In: Goodall, J.R., Conti, G., Ma, K.-L. (eds.) Proceedings of VizSEC 2007, pp. 19–37. Springer, Heidelberg (2008)
13. Adnan, M., et al.: Investigating the work practices of network security professionals. Inf. Comput. Secur. **23**(3), 347–367 (2015)
14. Wahba, M.: Competence Standards for Technical and Vocational Education and Training TVET (2012). http://cva-acfp.org/article/competence-standards-for-technical-and-vocational-education-and-training-tvet/
15. National Volunteer Skills Centre, A Guide to Writing Competency Based Training Materials. Training (2003)
16. Rudzajs, P., et al.: Towards narrowing a conceptual gap between IT Industry and University. Sci. J. Riga Techn. Univ. Comput. Sci. **41**(1), 9–16 (2010)
17. Oliver, R.: creating meaningful contexts for learning in web-based settings. In: Proceedings of Open Learning. Brisbane: Learning Network, Queensland (2000)
18. Al-rawi, A.: Integrating IT Certifications in Networking Courses: Cisco CCNA versus CompTIA Network (2006). https://peer.asee.org/integrating-it-certifications-in-networking-courses-cisco-ccna-versus-comptia-network.pdf, Accessed 30 Apr 2016
19. Cisco Systems, Cisco Networking Academy (2010). http://www.cisco.com/c/en_in/training-events/networking-academy-program.html, Accessed 5 Jan 2017
20. Rwanda News Agency, Cisco contributing to skills in developing countries - ITU Rwanda: Doing Malnutrition au Rwanda FAO au Rwanda. Rwanda News Agency (2010). http://rnanews.com/subscribe/12065-cisco-contributing-to-skills-in-developing-countries-itu, Accessed 10 Jan 2017
21. Cisco Systems, Using ICT to Build Capacity in Developing Nations (2008). http://www.cisco.com/c/dam/en_us/about/citizenship/docs/CapacityBuildingProgramsJun08.pdf, Accessed 5 Jan 2017

22. Dubie, B.D.: Cisco training offers jobs in developing countries Study shows Networking Academy Program in 6 African nations helped two-thirds find jobs. NetworkWorld (2007). http://www.networkworld.com/article/2292731/infrastructure-management/cisco-training-offers-jobs-in-developing-countries.html
23. Elliott, B.: E-pedagogy & e-assessment. Scottish Qualifications Agency
24. Crisp, G.: Teacher's Handbook on e-Assessment (2011). www.transformingassessment.com
25. Bailey, J., Ellis, S., Schneider, C., Vander Ark, K.: Blended Learning Implementation Guide, Version 1.0 (2013). www.digitallearningnow.com/site/uploads/2013/09/BLIG-3.0-FINAL.pdf
26. Adesemowo, A.K., Gerber, M., E-skilling on fundamental ICT networking concepts – Overcoming the resource constraints at a South African university. In: Proceedings of the e-Skills for Knowledge Production and Innovation Conference 2014, Cape Town, South Africa, pp. 1–16 (2014). http://proceedings.e-skillsconference.org/2014/e-skills001-016Adesemowo796.pdf
27. United Nations Development Programme. Role of UNDP in information and communication technology for development, New York (2001). web.undp.org/execbrd/pdf/DP2001CRP8.PDF
28. UNESCO, United Nations Decade of Education for Sustainable Development (2005). unesdoc.unesco.org/images/0013/001399/139937e.pdf
29. Anderson, A., Seven Major Challenges for E-Learning in Developing Countries Case Study eBIT, Sri Lanka Annika, pp. 1–14. (2016)
30. Khan, B.H.: People, process and product continuum in e-learning: the e-learning P3 model. Educ. Technol. 44(5), 33–40 (2004)
31. Dede, C.: A seismic shift in epistemology. EDUCAUSE Rev. 43(3), 80–81 (2008)
32. Gammill, T., Newman, M.: Factors associated with faculty use of web-based instruction in higher education. J. Agric. Educ. 46(4) (2005)
33. Rajesh, M.: A study of the problems associated with ICT adaptability in Developing Countries in the context of Distance Education. Turk. Online J. Distance Educ. 4(2) (2003)
34. Usun, S.: Factors affecting the application of Information and Communication Technologies (ICT) in Distance Education. Turk. Online J. Distance Educ. 5(1) (2004)
35. Jiang, M., Ting, E.: A study of factors influencing students' perceived learning in a web-based course environment. Int. J. Educ. Telecommun. 6(4), 317–338 (2000)
36. Mason, R., Weller, M.: Factors affecting students' satisfaction on a web course. Aust. J. Educ. Technol. 16(2), 173–200 (2000)
37. Sekakubo, G., Suleman, H., Marsden, G.: Issues of adoption: have E-learning management systems fulfilled their potential in developing countries? In: SAICSIT (2011)
38. Psycharis, S.: Presumptions and actions affecting an e-learning adoption by the educational system implementation using virtual private networks. Eur. J. Open Distance E-Learning 8(2), 1–10 (2003)
39. Tucker, S., Pigou, A., Zaugg, D.: E-learning - Making it happened now. The ACM Library Update (2002). http://dl.acm.org/citation.cfm?id=588726&jmp=abstract&dl=portal&dl=ACM, Accessed 9 Jan 2017
40. Minton, C.M.: Is your organization ready for E-learning? Commun. Project Mag. 3(1) (2000). http://www.comproj.com/Minton.htm, Accessed 6 Jan 2017
41. Eastmond, D.: Realizing the promise of distance education in low technology countries. Educ. Tech. Res. Dev. 48(2), 100–111 (2000)
42. Pagram, P., Pagram, J.: Issues in E-learning: a Thai case study. Electron. J. Inf. Syst. Developing Countries 26(6), 1–8 (2006)
43. Kudyachete, G.: An Assessment of Factors That Impact On the Performance of Cisco Academies: The South African Situation (2012)

44. Cisco Systems, Cisco Packet Tracer. Cisco Networking Academy, pp. 1–3. Cisco Networking Academy, 2014. CCNA Security At-a-Glance (2010). http://el.el.obs.utcluj.ro/cisco/pdf/CCNAsecurity_AAG.pdf, Accessed 5 Jan 2017
45. FAO, E-learning methodologies a guide for designing and developing e-learning courses, Rome, Italy (2011)
46. Cisco Systems, Cisco Networking academy - South Africa. http://www.cisco.com/c/en_za/about/csr-programs/networking.html, Accessed 5 Mar 2017
47. Intel Security. Hacking the Skills Shortage, Santa Clara (2016). https://www.mcafee.com/ca/resources/reports/rp-hacking-skills-shortage.pdf

Pathways in Cybersecurity: Translating Theory into Practice

Susanne Wetzel[(✉)]

Department of Computer Science,
Stevens Institute of Technology,
Castle Point on Hudson, Hoboken, NJ 07030, USA
`swetzel@stevens.edu`

Abstract. In this paper, we report on a pilot project which was geared to explore the possibility of enabling a pathway in Cybersecurity education between community colleges and four-year institutions where students enter the four-year institution with Junior status after graduating from the community college with a suitable Associate in Science degree. The pilot was carried out in the context of the Cybercorps[®]: Scholarship for Service program, also focusing on exploring whether it is possible to support students pursuing such a pathway through the Cybercorps[®]: Scholarship for Service program and successfully placing them in the government to complete their internship and post-graduation service requirements. The pilot included two students from a community college pursuing an Associate in Science degree in Computer Science/Engineering and then transferring to the Bachelor of Science in Cybersecurity degree program at a nearby four-year institution. This paper reviews the various components of the pilot project, discusses challenges and opportunities, and provides some suggestions for future directions from the perspective of the four-year institution.

1 Introduction

There is a reported shortage of professionals in Cybersecurity—not just in the United States (e.g., [6]) but around the world (e.g., [9,11]). The challenge in addressing this problem is to not only identify a short-term solution for educating and (re-)training professionals to enter the field of Cybersecurity but instead establish sustainable options that will lead to a steady-state pipeline for workforce development in Cybersecurity. In the United States, one possible approach that is met with increasing interest is that of recognizing the role of community colleges and thus the establishing and fostering of pathways in Cybersecurity between community colleges and four-year institutions (e.g., [4,12,16]). The feasibility of such pathways from a curricular perspective has been studied in theory (e.g., [18]). Furthermore, a number of national centers have been established in recent years to foster Cybersecurity education on the community college level,

Published by Springer International Publishing AG 2017. All Rights Reserved
M. Bishop et al. (Eds.): WISE 10, IFIP AICT 503, pp. 39–48, 2017.
DOI: 10.1007/978-3-319-58553-6_4

to build partnerships, and to develop curricular guidelines and standards (e.g., [3,5,8,10,14]). While great progress has been made already, there is considerable room and need for improvement and growth—in particular with regards to implementation in practice.

It is in this greater context that the paper at hand reports on a pilot project which was geared to explore the feasibility of a tightly time-constrained pathway in Cybersecurity between a community college and a four-year institution. The goal of the project was not just to establish the feasibility of students transferring from a community college into a four-year institution to pursue and complete a cybersecurity-focused degree program. Rather, the pilot was to explore whether it is possible for students to transfer to a four-year institution with Junior status, complete the cybersecurity-focused degree program within two years of joining the four-year institution, and secure employment in the government upon graduation. The results of the pilot project have provided interesting insights which are expected to further inform and shape the implementation of recent legislation [13] which calls for the inclusion of community colleges in the Cybercorps®: Scholarship for Service (SFS) program [7]. In particular, following the pilot project, the four-year institution is currently engaging in a collaboration with additional local community colleges in supporting two community college students under the new program criteria of the SFS program [7].

Outline: The remainder of the paper is organized as follows: In Sect. 2 we detail the various program components based on the three stages of the pilot program: final year of study at the community college; summer bridge program; and the two years of study at the four-year institution. This is followed by a discussion of encountered challenges and lessons learned (Sect. 3) from the perspective of the four-year institution. The paper closes with some general recommendations (Sect. 4) and some remarks on possible next steps (Sect. 5).

2   Program Components

In the following, we describe in detail how the pilot program was implemented at both the community college and the four-year institution. In particular, we detail the components that were put in place to support the students with the goal to maximize the chance for success—meaning students graduating from the four-year institution within two years of joining with a GPA ≥ 3.0 and securing employment in the government.

From an institutional perspective, the pilot project spanned across four years—from the time that the first student was selected and admitted into the program until the second student graduated from the four-year institution with a Bachelor of Science (B.S.) in Cybersecurity degree and was placed in the government to fulfill the post-graduation requirements of the SFS program [7,15]. From a student's perspective, the involvement lasted for a total of five years: during the first year, each student completed his/her Associate in Science (A.S.) degree in Computer Science/Engineering at the community college. During the following two years, the student pursued the undergraduate degree program in

Cybersecurity at the four-year institution—graduating with a B.S. degree within two academic years of joining. Subsequently, each student was required to secure placement in the government to complete the two-year post-graduation scholarship requirement.

2.1   At the Community College

Faculty from both the community college and the four-year institution worked closely in identifying suitable candidates and eventually selecting the two students to participate in the pilot project. Specifically, the community college faculty reviewed student transcripts and progress after the students' first year at the community college. The focus was on students pursuing computing and math-centric degree programs. The main criteria included a high GPA, student progress w.r.t. completed courses that could not just be transferred to a four-year institution but would count towards obtaining Junior standing in the B.S. in Cybersecurity program at the four-year institution, and the likelihood of completing the A.S. degree by the end of the second year at the community college with a high GPA. The students meeting the criteria were encouraged to consider the opportunity and submit an application. As part of the application, students were asked to prepare a statement describing their interest in pursuing a career in cybersecurity and government service. The latter was due to the fact that the students were expected to receive funding through the four-year institution's SFS program. Subsequently, candidates were interviewed by faculty from the community college and the four-year institution. One student each was selected for two consecutive years to pursue the opportunity and receive the scholarship.

Faculty Support at the Community College and the Four-Year Institution. From the very beginning, the students were supported by faculty at the community college and the four-year institution. Following the selection as participants in the pilot project and scholar, faculty from both institutions worked closely in tailoring the course of study for each student such that the students would meet all program requirements to complete the A.S. degree at the community college as well as ensuring that a maximum number of courses would transfer to the four-year institution to count towards obtaining Junior status in the B.S. in Cybersecurity program.

The students met with the faculty at the community college frequently in order to guarantee progress and allow for possible problems to be identified and remedied early. Similarly, the students and the community college faculty were in touch with the faculty from the four-year institution on a regular basis—also visiting the campus of the four-year institutions on multiple occasions throughout the academic year.

All faculty supported the students in the application process as transfer student to the four-year institution—reviewing application materials, providing letters of recommendation, and preparing the students for the in-person interviews. Given their academic standing (including grades, progress, and honor society membership), the students did not face any major challenges in obtained admission to the four-year institution.

Student Mentor. As soon as the students were selected to participate in the pilot program, they were assigned a student mentor at the four-year institution. On purpose, we selected a student as mentor who had also come to the four-year institution as transfer student and as such had first-hand experience that could be shared with the community college students. The mentor was charged to be in touch with the community college students on a regular basis, invite them to campus, and be generally available to answer questions and address concerns. Starting with the second year, the first community college student participating in the pilot project was also able to support the mentor activities for the second student in the pilot project.

Financial Support. Many community college students hold at least part-time employment in order to support themselves or their families. As such, it was crucially important for the pilot program to provide the students with substantial financial support—especially also during their final year at the community college in order to allow them to fully focus on their studies. The pilot program was funded through a supplement to the SFS program at the four-year institution. The financial support to the students included tuition, books, and some stipend. In return, the students were required to quit the jobs they held previously.

2.2 Transferring to the Four-Year Institution

The selection of courses transferring to the four-year institution was somewhat different for each one of the two students participating in the pilot project. This was due to the fact that the students had chosen slightly different paths for their A.S. in Computer Science/Engineering degree at the community college [2], including the selection of courses to fulfill math, science, and general education requirements (see Appendix for details). Both students had eighteen courses that transferred to the B.S. in Cybersecurity program at the four-year institution [1]. Generally speaking, Junior status at the four-year institution means that a student has completed twenty major courses in the first two years and needs to complete another twenty major courses during the Junior/Senior years in order to graduate with a B.S. in Cybersecurity degree.

Consequently, both students had a gap of two courses to Junior status. Furthermore, while both students had completed the typical CS 1 and 2 sequence [17] at the community college, at the four-year institution all students in the B.S. in Cybersecurity degree program must also complete an Algorithms course during their second year of studies which builds on the Freshmen CS 1 and 2 sequence and is a prerequisite for many Junior and Senior-level courses in the major.

Given the gap in the number of courses as well as the material (i.e., the Algorithms course), the pilot program included a summer bridge program which the two students had to complete during the summer in between graduating from the community college and joining the four-year institution for the Fall semester of following academic year.

Summer Bridge Program. For each of the students, the summer bridge program included two courses. The courses the students had to take were determined based on the courses they could transfer from their A.S. degree and what was most needed in order to bring them to Junior status. Both students completed the Algorithms course as part of the summer bridge program.

Aside from the academic merits, the summer bridge program also served another important means namely that of providing the students with more opportunity to get to know the four-year institution and starting to settle in before they had to "hit the ground running" at the beginning of the Fall semester. While both students had already visited the four-year institution multiple times during the previous academic year, the summer bridge program allowed them to further explore the campus—no longer just as visitor but as students, yet in a more quiet setting in the summer taking some classes but not a full course load like during a regular semester.

2.3 At the Four-Year Institution

In the Fall semester following the summer bridge program, both transfer students started to pursue their studies at the four-year institution with Junior status. Eventually, both transfer students graduated from the four-year institution within two years of first joining the institution for the summer bridge program. In between their Junior and Senior years, both students completed an internship as part of fulfilling their scholarship requirements. Furthermore, both students secured final placement in the government upon graduation. While one student secured the placement starting immediately after graduation, one student started the government employment within a few months of graduation.

Faculty Support at the Four-Year Institution. The faculty at the four-year institution were involved in the supervision of the transfer students from the very beginning of the selection process. Their role grew in importance once the students joined the four-year institution as part of the summer bridge program. The faculty at the four-year institution served as academic advisor for the students, being responsible for the tailoring of the students' course of study, and providing help and guidance as necessary. In particular, the faculty was also responsible for recruiting the student mentor and tutors and overseeing the respective activities. The faculty met with the students on a regular basis.

Student Mentor and Tutors. While at the four-year institution, the students continued to work with the student mentor who had already provided guidance to them during their final year at the community college. In addition, the second student was able to greatly draw on the experience and knowledge of the first student in the pilot project. Furthermore, the students were assigned tutors for the various classes they had to complete during their Junior and Senior years at the four-year institution. Initially, the first student was offered the opportunity to work with a tutor as soon as the student felt that it would be beneficial to get some help. This approach was changed during the second year. Specifically, a tutor was then recruited from the onset for classes that tend to be challenging for students—especially classes that are heavy on theory and math. The experience with the first student showed that if the decision is left to the student to seek help from a tutor, then there is a high risk that this help is requested too late and catching up proves difficult—if not impossible. Instead, working with a tutor from the beginning preemptively addresses the problem and has generally resulted in the students obtaining better grades in the challenging courses.

Financial Support. Upon joining the four-year institution, both students were awarded a scholarship through the four-year institution's SFS program. Through this program, both students had their tuition covered and received other benefits such as a stipend, books, etc. as per the scholarship guidelines [7]. In addition, the pilot project included funding for the student mentor and the tutors.

3   Challenges, Successes, and Lessons Learned

Generally speaking, a transition from a community college to a four-year institution is challenging for the students. Courses at a four-year institution tend to be more rigorous and fast paced than at a community college. Furthermore, while Freshmen typically have some time to ease into college life at the beginning of their college experience, transfer students have to "hit the ground running" from the very first day as they enter the four-year institution at a point where the other students are already well-settled into the college life and routine.

Also, oftentimes transfer students are at the top of their class at the community college, mastering any and all program requirements with ease (i.e., "being a big fish in a small pond"). In transferring to a four-year institution, they are then suddenly faced with a lot of uncertainty and competition (i.e., "being a new fish in a new large pond"). This change in perspective is challenging for the transfer students to cope with. The student mentor, tutors, and faculty play a crucial role during the transition in providing the necessary support to the transfer students.

Moreover, transfer students typically face a more challenging course sequence for their Junior and Senior years than their peers. This is due to the fact that the courses that transfer to the four-year institution generally cover (almost) all science and general education requirements—which for students at the four-year institution are spread across their curriculum in order to balance their course of study. Instead, transfer students tend to leave little to no such means for balance but their course of study rather includes only computing and security-focused courses. Consequently, we have seen the transfer students' GPAs drop by as much as half a grade point. It is crucially important that the course of study for a transfer student is well-designed and that the transfer student is provided with suitable mentor and tutor support so that the challenging course sequence can be mastered as best as possible. In looking towards job placement in the government to fulfill the SFS program requirements, we noticed a direct correlation between the GPA and how challenging it was for the students to secure such placement—the higher the GPA was, the easier it was and a GPA below 3.0 seems to literally make placement in the government impossible.

The transfer students must feel at home on campus by the time they are expected to successfully carry a full course load at the four-year institution. As such it is necessary to have the transfer students visit the campus frequently before joining and make good use of the summer bridge program to have the students familiarize themselves as much as possible with the campus, resources, and social activities.

4   Recommendations

Support Infrastructure: In order to allow the transfer students to succeed, it is necessary to build a comprehensive support structure including faculty, student mentors, and tutors. In order to remove the burden or need to ask for help and potentially risk procrastination, it is better to simply impose measures such as mentor and tutor support, as well as regular meetings with the faculty.

Campus Environment: Similarly, it is important for the transfer students to be involved in on campus activities such as students organizations and clubs. Ideally, transfer students will have the opportunity to get to know future classmates already during visits to campus or as part of the summer bridge program. While upper classmen oftentimes opt for off-campus housing, it has proven beneficial to require for transfer students to stay on campus for at least one year as it will make fitting in, finding friends, and exploring extra-curricular activities on campus easier.

Selectivity: The challenge with achieving a graduating GPA ≥ 3.0 at the four-year institution can be addressed preemptively by adjusting the selection criteria, e.g., by requiring the transfer students to achieve a graduating GPA >3.5 at the community college. Obviously, this directly impacts the size of the candidate pool.

Areas of Study: Depending on the characteristics of the Cybersecurity curriculum at the four-year institution, not just computing-focused studies at the community college should be considered. For example, for a four-year Cybersecurity degree program with core components in math and theory it might be better to recruit students pursuing an A.S. degree in Mathematics as these students typically have to complete extensive calculus requirements and do calculus-based sciences. Oftentimes, it proves less challenging for students to acquire computing skills based on a sound foundation in Mathematics than the other way around.

Transfer of Courses and Summer Bridge Program: While [18] provides some general guidance for identifying courses that can possibly be transferred from a community college to a four-year institution in the context of establishing pathways in Cybersecurity, in practice the courses of the respective degree programs must be evaluated in greater detail. Courses at the community college which generally lend themselves more easily for transfer to the four-year institution are science courses (such as Physics, Chemistry, or Biology), calculus courses, or courses to meet general education requirements (e.g., Sociology, Psychology, English Composition, History). For a computing-focused A.S. degree, courses which typically transfer include the CS 1 and 2 sequence [17], a Computer Organization/Assembly course, or a Systems Analysis course. For a math-focused A.S. degree, courses which may transfer include Discrete Mathematics or Probability and Statistics. In most cases, courses which are taught at an introductory level at the community college but are part of the curriculum in Junior or Senior years at the four-year institution (i.e., are taught at an advanced level) generally do not count for transfer credit. Typical examples include introductory vs. advanced courses in Operating Systems, Architecture, and Database Management Systems.

Based on the outcome of the transfer credit evaluation, the summer bridge program must be tailored on a per student basis to provide an effective means for remediation of individual deficiencies before the transfer student can take on a full course load at the four-year institution.

5   Conclusions and Next Steps

The pilot project showed that it is possible for transfer students to complete a B.S. in Cybersecurity degree within two years of joining a four-year institution if a suitable and tailored support structure is in place. However, it is not a-priori clear how such pathways can be easily scaled to accommodate a larger number of transfer students. Even if baselines for the transfer of standard courses (or transfer agreements) are established with a number of community colleges, there still is the need for individualized support and oversight of the transfer students in order to ensure timely graduation with good GPAs. This is due to the fact that there are always some deviations in the students' transfer credits (and thus their respective course of study) as well as the different strengths and interests that students exhibit.

In order to increase the candidate pool and ease the burden on the students, faculty, student mentors, and tutors alike, we suggest the exploring of a so-called *super-sophomore* model where transfer students join the four-year institution during the second half of their Sophomore year with the goal to complete their B.S. in Cybersecurity degree within three years of joining the four-year institution (i.e., pursuing undergraduate studies for a total of four and a half years instead of just four year). In order to complete the A.S. degree, the students would then transfer credits back to their community college. Such an earlier transfer to the four-year institution will allow the students to spread some of the science and general education requirements throughout their studies. Similarly, a three-year timeframe to graduation from the four-year institution will result in some easing of the students' course of study—which is also expected to positively impact the students' GPA. Alternatively, a high-achieving transfer student may be able to use the extra time to obtain a graduate certificate and as such earn some advanced qualification that is expected to be of advantage when entering the workforce. Furthermore, the super-sophomore approach may also simplify the funding, e.g., through the SFS program of the four-year institution. In receiving one year of funding while at the community college with an additional two years of funding at the four-year institution, transfer students take on a considerable financial liability in case issues arise with the transfer to the four-year institution. With the earlier transfer as part of the super-sophomore model, the three years of funding would be exclusively received at the four-year institution only after transfer admission was already successfully obtained.

Acknowledgments. The author would like to thank Elizabeth Hawthorne and Cynthia Roemer from Union County College for their collaboration in this pilot project.

This material is based upon work supported by the National Science Foundation under Grant No. DUE 0830846. Any opinions, findings, and conclusions or recommendations expressed in this material are those of the author and do not necessarily reflect the views of the National Science Foundation.

Appendix

List of sample courses which transferred from the A.S. in Computer Science/Engineering program at the community college [2] to the B.S. in Cybersecurity program at the four-year institution [1]:

Community college		Four-year institution	
UCC		Stevens	
MAT 171	Unified Calculus I	MA 121	Differential Calculus
MAT 172	Unified Calculus II	MA 122/123	Integral Calc., Series, Vectors,
MAT 271	Unified Calculus III	MA 124	Calc. for Functions of Two Variables
MAT 267	Discrete Mathematics	CS 135	Discrete Structures
PHY 111	Mechanics	PEP 111	Mechanics
PHYL 111	Mechanics Lab	PEP 221	Physics Lab I
PHY 201	Electricity and Magnetism	PEP 112	Electricity and Magnetism
CSC 101	Computer Algorithms	CS 115	Introduction to CS
CSC 102	Data Structures	CS 284	Data Structures
CIS 210	Principles of Info. Security	CS 306	Introduction to IT Security
CSC 222	Comp. Org., Arch. and Assembly	CS 383	Comp. Org. and Assembly
ECO 201	Principles of Economics	BT 243	Macroeconomics
ENG 111/112	English Composition	CAL 103	Writing and Communication
SOC 101	Principles of Sociology	HSS 141	Introduction to Sociology

References

1. Academic Catalog Stevens Institute of Technology–B.S. in Cybersecurity. https://www.stevens.edu/academics/academic-catalog
2. Academic Catalog Union County College–A.S. in Computer Science/Engineering. http://onlinecatalog.ucc.edu/preview_program.php?catoid=2&poid=381&returnto=128
3. Centers of Academic Excellence in Cyber Defense 2-Year Education. https://www.iad.gov/NIETP/reports/cae_designated_institutions.cfm
4. Community colleges are new gateways to hot cybersecurity jobs. https://www.edsurge.com/news/2016-04-28-community-colleges-are-new-gateways-to-hot-cybersecurity-jobs
5. CSSIA National Center For Systems Security and Information Assurance Innovation in Cyber Security Education. http://www.cssia.org/
6. Cyber-security skills shortage leaves companies vulnerable. http://www.informationweek.com/strategic-cio/security-and-risk-strategy/cyber-security-skills-shortage-leaves-companies-vulnerable/
7. CyberCorps® Scholarship for Service (SFS) Defending America's Cyberspace, Program Solicitation National Science Foundation NSF 15-584. https://www.nsf.gov/pubs/2015/nsf15584/nsf15584.htm
8. Cyberwatch West. http://www.cyberwatchwest.org/
9. Global study reveals businesses and countries vulnerable due to shortage of cybersecurity talent. https://newsroom.intel.com/news-releases/global-study-reveals-businesses-countries-vulnerable-due-shortage-cybersecurity-talent/
10. National Cyberwatch Center. https://www.nationalcyberwatch.org/
11. One million cybersecurity job openings in 2016. http://www.forbes.com/sites/stevemorgan/2016/01/02/one-million-cybersecurity-job-openings-in-2016/
12. Protecting information-the role of community colleges in cybersecurity education. https://www.nationalcyberwatch.org/ncw-content/uploads/2016/03/Workshop_Rpt-Role_of_CCs_in_Cyber_Ed-2002.pdf
13. Public Law 113–274 - cybersecurity enhancement act of 2014. https://www.gpo.gov/fdsys/pkg/PLAW-113publ274/content-detail.html
14. The C5 project-catalyzing computing and cybersecurity in community colleges. http://www.c5colleges.org/
15. U.S. Office of Personnel Management—CyberCorps® Scholarship for Service. http://www.sfs.opm.gov
16. Virginia's 21st century career pathway cybersecurity. http://www.doe.virginia.gov/administrators/superintendents_memos/2016/040-16a.pdf
17. Joint Task Force on Computing Curricula Association for Computing Machinery (ACM) & IEEE Computer Society: Computer Science Curricula 2013: Curriculum Guidelines for Undergraduate Degree Programs in Computer Science. ACM, New York (2013)
18. Pérez, L.C., Cooper, S., Hawthorne, E.K., Wetzel, S., Brynielsson, J., Gökce, A.G., Impagliazzo, J., Khmelevsky, Y., Klee, K., Leary, M., Philips, A., Pohlmann, N., Taylor, B., Upadhyaya, S.: Information assurance education in two- and four-year institutions. In: Proceedings of the 16th Annual Conference Reports on Innovation and Technology in Computer Science Education - Working Group Reports, pp. 39–53, NY, USA. ACM, New York (2011)

Teaching Information Security

Evaluating Secure Programming Knowledge

Matt Bishop[1]([✉]) [ID], Jun Dai[2], Melissa Dark[3], Ida Ngambeki[3], Phillip Nico[4],
and Minghua Zhu[1]

[1] University of California at Davis, Davis, CA, USA
{mabishop,mhzhu}@ucdavis.edu
[2] California State University at Sacramento, Sacramento, CA, USA
jun.dai@csus.edu
[3] Purdue University, West Lafayette, IN, USA
{dark,ingambek}@purdue.edu
[4] California Polytechnic State University, San Luis Obispo, CA, USA
pnico@calpoly.edu

Abstract. Secure programming is a widely used term for programming robustly. Applying the principles and methodologies of this style of programming would significantly improve the quality of software in use today. Teaching students how to program robustly, or securely, is a first step towards this goal. This paper presents a concept map for secure programming and then some questions used to evaluate students' knowledge of this subject. These questions have been given both before and after a term of programming, computer security, and other classes that cover this subject. In this paper, we discuss how the questions reveal the students' understanding of material in the concept map, and what erroneous ideas the questions reveal.

1 Introduction

In the United States, there has been considerable concern about the problem of poor software. One of the effects has been to examine how to teach students to program robustly.[1] There are two approaches commonly considered. The first, adding this material to classes, would require existing material to be dropped, and the instructors to understand and apply this style of programming to all class work. But in an algorithms class, for example, the students are assumed to know how to program, so the teachers and graders focus on whether the programs correctly implement the algorithms and meet the assignment requirements. Thus,

---

[1] In this paper, we use the terms "secure" and "robust" synonymously. In practice, they are slightly different. "Secure" programming refers to a program that meets specific security requirements. "Robust" programming refers to programs that do not crash, and handle bad inputs in a reasonable way ("reasonable" being defined in the context of use). Nevertheless, people refer to "secure programming" when they mean "secure and robust programming", and we adopt this use.

Published by Springer International Publishing AG 2017. All Rights Reserved
M. Bishop et al. (Eds.): WISE 10, IFIP AICT 503, pp. 51–62, 2017.
DOI: 10.1007/978-3-319-58553-6_5

whether the students write their programs securely is not considered, and — like any other aspect of practice — their skill atrophies (or is never acquired). The second, creating a separate class that covers the principles and practice of robust programming, adds a new class to an already crowded curriculum. The class would need to be required to ensure students learned the material. But the students would need to practice it after the class, and this would require the co-operation of other instructors, resulting in problems similar to those identified earlier.

A third approach is to provide support for students through a mechanism other than a class [3]. Writing clinics in law schools and English programs do this. The clinics provide assistance on the mechanics of good writing: grammar, organization, and expression. They do not determine if the content is correct or meets the requirements of the assignment. With this clinic, the teachers can focus on the content, and leave the mechanics to others. Similarly, a "secure programming clinic" would assist students by showing them how to improve the robustness and security of their programs without determining if they satisfied the requirements of the assignment. Teaching robust programming techniques in the context of assignments where robustness is not the focus, motivates the students because they will see that programming robustly produces better overall results. For example, making a habit of checking library and system calls for error return values speeds development and produces more correct programs because programming mistakes are likely to be discovered quickly and remedied. While analysis tools can provide much of this information, the clinic focuses on student understanding. In addition to improving the students' programming, the knowledge obtained from the clinic enables the students to analyze the results produced by the tools, specifically to distinguish false positives from true positives.

A key part of starting such a clinic is to understand how students think about robust programming and to assess whether the clinic is having the desired effect on their understanding of secure programming. To do this we have designed an assessment consisting of a pre-test and a post-test administered to the students at the beginning and end of the term during which they use the clinic. These questions are the start of a concept inventory. In order to develop these questions, we started by developing a concept map of secure programming to make sure we were assessing a reasonable body of knowledge. We then developed questions based on the concepts represented in the map. This paper presents the concept map of secure programming and discusses several questions designed to test students' knowledge and misconceptions of secure programming based on the concept map. We explain how the questions relate to the concept map, and how well a set of 162 students performed when asked the questions.

2   Concept Inventories

Concept inventories are assessments designed to identify students' misconceptions; the questions, administration, scoring procedures, and interpretations are consistent and in adherence with a predetermined standard/protocol. They are not intended to be used to "grade" student learning, and therefore do not replace examinations, homework, discussions, and other methods used to measure student learning. Instead, the intent of concept inventories is diagnostic. Concept inventories are designed to measure core concepts of a topic and the extent to which students have achieved expert level thinking in a domain. The scores are used to tell us how many students do and do not understand a concept, and which conceptual picture they hold instead.

Concept inventories are useful for helping diagnose particular levels of students' conceptual understanding. Research on addressing misconceptions in science suggests that a new concept cannot be learned until the student is forced to confront the paradoxes, inconsistencies, and limitations of the mental model that already exists in the student's mind [7]. Students persist in erroneous beliefs, not intentionally, but because their erroneous beliefs seem plausible, useful, and accurate [11]. Concept inventories aim to identify these erroneous beliefs, so that once they are manifest, they can be addressed and corrected. The results from concept inventories are primarily intended to improve pedagogy, though the results can be used to help instructors make comparisons of teaching over time.

This method for assessing students' conceptual understanding was first developed 50 years ago, in the field of physics education to measure students' understanding of Newtonian forces [1,9]. This initial concept inventory, the Force Concept Inventory, is still widely used today in physics and engineering. Since then several studies have validated the effectiveness of concept inventories for distinguishing between students who have understood concepts and students who merely memorized them [6]. Concept inventories have also been validated as effective in the evaluation of teaching methods [8,10,14]. Today concept inventories also exist in astronomy, chemistry, engineering design graphics, biology, thermodynamics, heat transfer, statics, statistics, electro-magnetism, circuit theory, genetics, nursing, and many other disciplines.

The concept inventory is based on the group of learning theories classified as conceptual change theories. Concepts are an abstract mental representation of a particular phenomenon. Conceptual learning therefore is the process of identifying and correctly categorizing concepts such that they can later be used to make predictions or decisions [4,12]. Correct categorization involves making links to prior knowledge and so may require adjustment or correction of prior knowledge. Ausubel's assimilation theory contrasts rote learning (temporary acquisition of disorganized or poorly understood isolated or arbitrarily related concepts) with meaningful learning (long-term acquisition of organized, interrelated concepts into existing cognitive structures) [2]. In this theory, meaningful learning requires the connection of new knowledge to pre-existing understanding. This theory has been supported by subsequent research into student learning [4]. Another theoretical basis for concept inventories comes from the National Research Council publication, *Knowing What Students Know: The Science and Design of Educational Assessment* [13]. This study lays out an "assessment triangle" as the basis for assessment instruments. This triangle has three elements: cognition, a theory that describes how students learn in a particular content domain; observation, tasks that allow students to demonstrate their knowledge; and interpretation, a coherent method to make inferences about student knowledge based on observations from the assessment [13,14]. Therefore, the assessment instrument must be designed to align the beliefs about how students learn in the content domain with the assessment tasks and interpretation of those tasks. Based on these theories, the development of the concept inventory begins with a clear understanding of the content domain, in this case secure programming, and an understanding of how students learn in this domain.

3   Concept Map and Inventory

Figure 1 shows the concept map developed for this project. Figure 2 describes each element of the concept map. This concept map depicts epistemologically important sets of concrete and abstract objects in secure programming. This concept map was developed using the input of subject matter experts. Development of the concept map is described in full in a related paper [5]. To date, this project has developed and tested 26 questions, based on the concept map, aimed at diagnosing students' conceptual misunderstandings in secure programming. The questions have been tested through the implementation of the Secure Programming Clinic at University of California Davis, California Polytechnic State University San Luis Obispo, and California State University Sacramento. Roughly half of the questions have been used and revised three times now, and half have been used and revised twice. The team continues to add additional questions with the goal of eventually covering all concepts depicted in the concept map. Examples of the questions and explanations of how distractors are used to target misconceptions are presented below.

4   Example Questions

The goal of the questions presented in this section is to determine how well the students understand the concepts underlying secure programming. The questions therefore have to have carefully designed distractors to ensure that the students who answer the questions correctly do so based on understanding the concept and not based on simply eliminating obviously wrong answers. The questions presented here were selected from a larger set of 27 questions. Each question has several distractors, the rationale for each is discussed, and the effectiveness of the distractors are shown as percentages of the 162 students who completed the assessment.

4.1   Handling User Input

This question deals with the important concept "If you have no reason to trust it, don't trust it. Take greater care with any input you have not generated." The goal of this question is to see if students know how to handle such input.

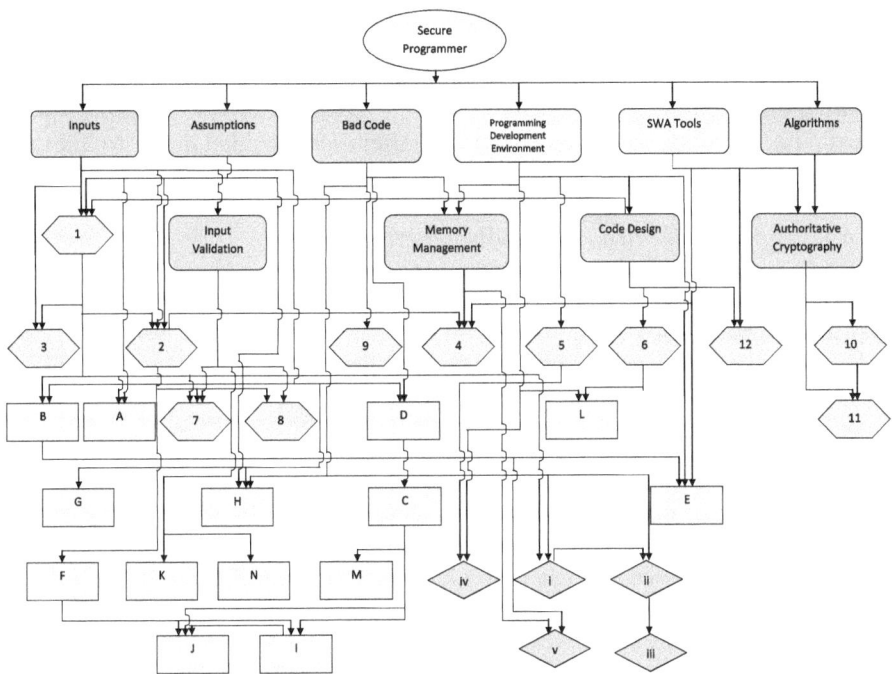

Fig. 1. The concept map. Figure 2 provides the captions for the content.

Very Important ⬡

1. Assume whatever can go wrong will
2. Assume any input is going to be malformed or not what you expect
3. Do not make a security decision based on un-trusted inputs
4. Check that all arguments are of the correct type and will not overflow any arrays
5. Use data abstraction to enable the compiler to perform rigorous type checking and to enforce constraints on values and lengths
6. Understand the context in which the program will execute
7. Validate your input stream to ensure that the commands invoked are expected and no other commands are injected
8. When performing input validation take into account how programs invoked with those arguments could interpret them
9. Avoid hard coded passwords and secrets in your program
10. Use well known and accepted cryptographic algorithms and. Don't use obsolete or deprecated cryptographic algorithms or create your own algorithms
11. Use well known and accepted cryptographic random number generation. Don't use obsolete or deprecated cryptographic algorithms or create your own algorithms
12. Many tools help you create a secure program, please take advantage of them

Somewhat Important ⬦

i. Hide details that users don't need to know about
ii. Avoid side effects in arguments to unsafe macros. If a developer is using a macro that uses its arguments more than once, then the developer must avoid passing any arguments with side effects to that macro
iii. Use parentheses around macro replacement lists. Otherwise operator precedence may cause the expression to be computed in unexpected ways
iv. Minimize the scope of variables and functions. This prevents many unexpected changes to the variables due to programming error
v. When the memory a pointer points to is freed, set the pointer to NULL. Otherwise, these dangling pointers could cause writing to freed memory, and create a double free vulnerability.

Important ▭

A. If you have no reason to trust it, don't trust it. Take greater care with any input you have not generated
B. If it cannot happen, check for it. Someone may modify the program in such a way that it can happen ... or you may be wrong
C. Do not use input or constructor string functions that do not perform any bound checking
D. Do not use input or constructor functions that cannot check the length of the input
E. C and C++ compilers generally do not check types rigorously. A developer can increase this level of checking by turning on compiler warnings, which will often catch more type errors than if they are not used
F. Avoid calls to malloc() with the parameter (number of bytes to be allocated) set to 0. Either the function returns NULL, or it returns a pointer to space that cannot be used without overwriting unallocated memory
G. Control the input values when possible by limiting them to a finite set
H. Calling functions with null parameters for input should be checked for and defended against
I. Type conversion issues especially for cases that may result in integer wraparound and overflows
J. Rules for pointer arithmetic as vulnerabilities can arise when addition or size checks involve two pointer types
K. When performing input validation make sure that any validated path does not allow escaping from a restricted directory
L. Before creating a directory or file, make sure you have set the correct default permission specification
M. Be wary of off by one errors
N. When using format string functions, make sure that the format string can be authenticated/trusted

Fig. 2. The contents of the concept map.

QUESTION: User input can be unpredictable. Which of the following is the best way to avoid problems processing that input?

a. Elevate privileges when processing user-provided input, to ensure the computation can be done.
b. Drop unnecessary privileges when processing user-provided input, to limit the effects of bad user input.
c. Keep privileges constant whenever possible, for more readable code that is easier to maintain without introducing error.
d. Assign elevated privileges to a new process or thread that reads the input and does the computation, so that any malicious side-effects do not affect the primary process or thread.
e. Keep privileges the same but constrain the process execution in a sandbox so that any malicious side-effects are contained.

The approach to answering this question lies in the effects of bad input, which could cause the program to act in unexpected ways. If the program has elevated privileges, this could breach security. The program may also serve as a vector for the attacker to inject malicious code, for example through a buffer overflow. The answers probe what the student is thinking about how to handle this situation.

Answer (a) focuses on the trade-off between security and getting the job done. Here, students selecting (a) are focused on the latter rather than the former. Answer (d) is similar, but here there is an element of isolation by handling the input in a separate thread. This presents an application of a secure programming concept; it is simply the wrong use of that concept. Answers (c) and (e) sound reasonable because no elevation of privileges is involved, but (c) focuses on simplicity and (e) the concept of isolation. The correct answer is (d), as it implements least privilege most effectively.

Most students (43%) got the right answer. The rest generally chose (d) and (e) (18% and 25%, respectively). A few (9%) chose (c), and only 5% chose (a).

The concept of isolation provides a good distractor. Students found that elevating privileges without isolation was obviously wrong, and keeping privileges constant without isolation was less obviously wrong, but generally considered wrong. So from these answers, an instructor can lead a discussion of the role of isolation in secure programming, and how to use it properly.

4.2   Indexing into an Array

Failing to check bounds and indices when manipulating arrays is a common problem. This question deals with the important concept "Check parameters to ensure that all arguments are of the correct type and will not overflow any arrays." It focuses on overflow in the negative direction (really, underflow) that is more subtle than overflow due to numbers that are too big.

QUESTION: Your program accepts parameters x, y, and z to calculate the position of an item in an array relative to the current item indexed by ptr.

```
101  newOffset = (x * colSize) + (y * rowSize) - z
102  ptr = ptr + newOffset
103  newObject = objectArray[ptr]
```

Which of the following is true?

a. I should check that the result in line 101 is not negative.
b. I should check that the result in line 101 is not null.
c. I should check that the result in line 102 is not negative.
d. I should check that the result in line 102 is not null.

This question examines the student's awareness of needing to locate the parameters to check and to validate the index used. Here, the parameters are implicitly of an integer type or a type that would be coerced into the integer type in arithmetic expressions.

Answers (a) and (b) both deal with validating something other than the index. It is tempting to assume checking `newOffset` is enough as that is derived directly from the parameters, but that is not the index; `ptr` is. They speak to locating the right variable to check.

Answers (b) and (d) both deal with the parameter type. The value "null" refers to a pointer that one cannot validly dereference (for example, the NULL pointer in C). As the result in line 102 is used as an index in line 103, it cannot be a pointer, and hence checking for "null" is not appropriate. Also, in many languages, "null" is a synonym for 0, which is a valid index.

When given to students, 38% got the right answer, (c). The rest of the students generally chose (a) (28%) followed by (b) and (d) (both at 17%). Thus, the three distractors effectively cover the most usual student misunderstandings, and resulting failures to index into an array properly in this code snippet.

4.3 Handling Missing Data

This question speaks to the important concept "If you have no reason to trust it, don't trust it. Take greater care with any input you have not generated." Here, the input from a list has some fields that are missing.

QUESTION: You must read a list of user names and starting date: day, month, year. Then your program must sort them in ascending order to create a list of users by seniority. Some start dates are missing the day or month of the start date. This list-sorting function may be used elsewhere, or tweaked in the future. Which statement below is the most robust way to handle the missing data?

a. Initialize the variables for missing information with a random plausible value.
b. Leave the variables for missing information uninitialized.
c. Initialize the variables for missing information with 0.
d. Initialize the variables for missing information with the maximum plausible value.

This question examines how the student handles the missing data. In general, there are four ways to handle such data: ignore it, insert a value (random, 0, or a maximum value), give an error message and discard the rest of the record, or have the program stop. The answers focus on the first two behaviors. The key is that the caller of the sorting function must handle the missing values because the list-sorting function may be used elsewhere, or changed.

Answer (b) ignores the missing data. Answer (a) suggests using random values. The problem with this answer is that the data with the missing values will be randomly scattered throughout the data with all values present. Answers (c) and (d) cause the data with the missing fields to be grouped together, but as we do not know the minimum value for those fields, setting the missing values to 0 may put the data into the middle of all the data. Answer (d) puts all the data at one end of all the data, so it is the most robust.

When given to students, 22% got the right answer, (d). Of the other answers, 57% of the students chose (c). Fewer chose (a) and (b) (7% and 13%, respectively). Thus the incorrect answers provide good distractors to capture the student misconceptions for this question.[2]

4.4   Pointer Validation

This question tests common misconceptions about two important concepts, "Follow the rules for pointer arithmetic as vulnerabilities can arise when addition or size checks involve two pointer types" and "Be wary of off by one errors." Problems with these concepts often occur together.

QUESTION: For a C program you must create an array of size integers. You write:

```
1  unsigned long *start, *end;
2  start = malloc(size * sizeof(unsigned long));
```

Assuming malloc succeeds, the correct value for end can be computed by:

a. end = start + size * sizeof (unsigned long);
b. end = start + size * (sizeof (unsigned long) - 1);
c. end = start + (size - 1) * sizeof (unsigned long);
d. end = start + size - 1;
e. end = start + sizeof (unsigned long) - 1;

This question tests the student's knowledge of the two concepts by asking the student to set a pointer to the last element of an array of unsigned longs. Answer (a) goes past the end of the array by the number of bytes in one unsigned long integer (usually 4 or 8 bytes). Answers (b) and (c) offer the option of subtracting 1 from either the size of the allocated space or the element size, thereby testing the student's understanding of pointers. Answer (d) captures those students who understand the off-by-one problem, but who do not realize that the buffer size and element size are distinct, and answer (e) omits the number of elements in the array. All these are common student errors.

---

[2] The numbers add up to 99%, not 100%, due to roundoff error.

For this question, 31% of students got the right answer, (c). Answers (b) and (e) distracted roughly 16% of students, while (d) attracted 20%. Even the least successful, (a), attracted 10% of the students. Thus the incorrect answers provide good distractors to capture the student misconceptions for this question.

4.5   Input Validation

This question speaks to the very important concept "Assume any input is going to be malformed or not what you expect." The vehicle used is parameters that are pointers.

QUESTION: You must write a function that stores an integer in the destination pointed to by value, and returns an integer indicating success or failure. You start with this function signature:

```
int getSeconds(int * secondsParameter)
```

Which of the following must you do before or instead of any of the others?

a. I must dereference the pointer to get the memory location.
b. I must find the value that the pointer refers to.
c. I must check that the pointer passed in does not already have a value.
d. I must check that the pointer passed in is not NULL.

Here, common misconceptions about pointers lead to confusion about what is and is not possible with input validation in C. The only thing that the programmer can do is to check that the pointer is not NULL, meaning the correct answer is (d). Answer (a) is based on the erroneous belief that dereferencing a pointer gets the address of the location rather than the value stored at the pointed-to location. Answer (b) refers to the value at the location, but does not check that the pointer is not NULL. Answer (c) uses the common misconception among novice programmers that something special must be done with respect to initializing or not initializing a pointer before it can be used.

Most students (69%) got the correct answer. Distractors (a) and (c) were similar in effectiveness, capturing 10% and 13% of the students respectively. Answer (b) got 8% of the students. Hence most of the students understood the idea underlying the concept of input validation.

4.6   Use of Tools

This question deals with the important concept "There are many tools to help you create a secure program, please take advantage of them." The goal of this question is to see if students know the differences between a file descriptor and a file name.

QUESTION: Explain the choice of a file descriptor over the file name as the channel to securely access a file.

a. A file descriptor is a data structure that allows only me to use the file for as long as it is open, while the file name does not.

b. The file descriptor is an abstraction that makes for more understandable code.
c. The file descriptor is a pointer to the file that stays the same regardless of changes to the file name or location.
d. The file descriptor is a data structure that encapsulates the file name.
e. The file descriptor is a data structure that represents the validated file name.

The approach to answering this question lies in the differences between a file descriptor and a file name. A file descriptor designates an open file in a particular process, and a file name is a string that designates a file in a filesystem. One common problem in computer programming is the TOCTTOU (Time Of Check to Time Of Use) race condition. Using a file descriptor to a file allows one to check or change the status on the file without worrying that the file reference has been changed in the meantime.

Answer (a) is wrong because multiple file descriptors can refer to the same file. Answer (b) is not correct because "file descriptor" has nothing to do with making code more understandable. Answers (d) and (e) are wrong because the file descriptor is an integer that the kernel uses as an index into a table containing information about the file. The "file descriptor is a data structure" in answers (a), (d) and (e) is a good distractor. Thus, those selecting (a), (d) and (e) do not understand the underlying mechanism of a file descriptor. The correct answer is (c), because the file descriptor refers to the same file regardless of changes to the file name or location.

When given to students, 54% got the right answer. The rest generally chose (a), (d) and (e) (11%, 14% and 12%, respectively). A few (9%) chose (b). This suggests that an instructor should focus on the underlying mechanism of a file descriptor.

5   Psychometric Analysis

Once students have taken the test, the test question and its distractors are analyzed. We calculate item effect, which is a point biserial correlation coefficient with a possible range of −1.00 to 1.00. Item effect tells us which students with a high overall score also got a particular test question correct. A strong positive correlation suggests that students who get any one question correct also have a relatively high score on the overall exam. For a concept inventory where the main goal is to identify misconceptions, item effect is most useful for identifying questions that are not functioning at all, i.e., those that have a very low correlation or a negative correlation. Such a correlation would indicate that the distractors are so confusing even students who generally know the material are unable to answer correctly. Figure 3 shows the item effect distribution for the 26 questions on the concept inventory.

We then combine the item effect with an analysis of the percent of correct responses for each item distractor. The table in Fig. 4 shows the item effect and distractor analysis for a sample question (with content removed). The correct answer is (c). This test question is functioning fairly well; it is both discriminating knowers from non-knowers, and the distractors are not so easy that students can guess they are not the right answer.

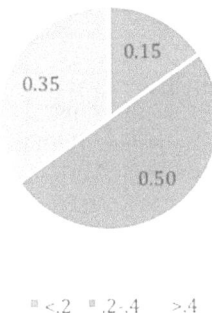

▪ <.2 ▪ .2-.4   >.4

Fig. 3. Item effect distribution for the 26 questions on the concept inventory.

Test Item	% correct response
(a)	27.78%
(b)	17.28%
(c)	38.27%
(d)	16.67%
Item effect	0.363

Fig. 4. Example of distractor analysis and item effect for a sample question.

6   Conclusion

Three schools have used these questions in an evaluation of students in three different classes. The questions here were used to test students' understanding at the beginning of the classes. They could also be used at the end, and the difference will indicate how well the students have absorbed the material on secure programming. A second set of questions has been developed for testing at the end of the classes, using the same concept map and a similar method of evaluating the distractors.

In the future, we hope to involve more academic institutions in this program. The greater the diversity of schools, and hence students, involved in the evaluation of these questions, the more effective the distractors under a wide variety of circumstances. This will lead to clearer results in the evaluation of the secure programming clinics, the ultimate goal of these questions.

Acknowledgements. We thank Stephen Belcher for his valuable insights and assistance with this work. This material is based upon work supported by the National Science Foundation under Grant No. DGE-1303211 to the University of California at Davis and Grant No. DGE-1303048 to Purdue University. Any opinions, findings, and conclusions or recommendations expressed in this material are those of the author(s) and do not necessarily reflect the views of the National Science Foundation.

References

1. Abou Halloun, I., Hestenes, D.: The initial knowledge state of college physics students. Am. J. Phys. **53**(11), 1043–1055 (1985)
2. Ausubel, D.P., Novak, J.D., Hanesian, H.: Education Psychology: A Cognitive View. Holt, Rinehart & Winston, New York (1978)
3. Bishop, M., Orvis, B.J.: A clinic to teach good programming practices. In: Proceedings from the Tenth Colloquium on Information Systems Security Education, pp. 168–174, June 2006
4. Bransford, J.D., Brown, A.L., Cocking, R.R.: How People Learn: Brain, Mind, Experience, and School. National Academies Press, Washington, DC (2000)
5. Dark, M., Ngambeki, I., Bishop, M., Belcher, S.: Teach the hands, train the mind... a secure programming clinic! In: Proceedings of the 19th Colloquium for Information Systems Security Education, pp. 119–133, June 2015
6. D'Avanzo, C.: Biology concept inventories: overview, status, and next steps. BioScience **58**(11), 1079–1085 (2008)
7. Garvin-Doxas, K., Klymkowsky, M., Elrod, S.: Building, using, and maximizing the impact of concept inventories in the biological sciences: report on a national science foundation-sponsored conference on the construction of concept inventories in the biological sciences. CBE Life Sci. Educ. **6**(4), 277–282 (2007)
8. Hake, R.R.: Interactive engagement versus traditional methods: a six thousand student survey of mechanics test data for introductory physics courses. Am. J. Phys. **66**(1), 64–74 (1998)
9. Hestenes, D., Wells, M., Swackhamer, G.: Force concept inventory. Phys. Teach. **30**(3), 159–166 (1992)
10. Laws, P., Sokoloff, D., Thornton, R.: Promoting active learning using the results of physics education results. UniServe Sci. News **13**, 14–19 (1999)
11. Mayer, R.E.: Educational Psychology: A Cognitive Approach. Harper Collins, New York (1987)
12. Özdemir, G., Clark, D.B.: An overview of conceptual change theories. Eurasia J. Math. Sci. Technol. Educ. **3**(4), 351–361 (2007)
13. Pellegrino, J.W., Chudowsky, N., Glaser, R.: Knowing What Students Know: The Science and Design of Educational Assessment. National Academies Press, Washington, DC (2001)
14. Streveler, R.A., Miller, R.L., Santiago-Román, A.I., Nelson, M.A., Geist, M.R., Olds, B.M.: Rigorous methodology for concept inventory development: using the 'assessment triangle' to develop and test the thermal and transport science concept inventory (TTCI). Int. J. Eng. Educ. **27**(5), 968–984 (2011)

Studying Formal Security Proofs
for Cryptographic Protocols

Konstantin G. Kogos[✉] and Sergey V. Zapechnikov

The National Research Nuclear University MEPhI (Moscow Engineering Physics Institute),
31 Kashirskoye shosse, Moscow, Russia
{KGKogos,SVZapechnikov}@mephi.ru

Abstract. This paper discusses the problem of teaching provable security in
cryptography when studying information security. The concept of provable
security is one of the most important in modern cryptography, soit is necessary
to integrate it into the syllabus on cryptographic protocols. Now provable security
is not rare thing in basic cryptography courses. However, security proofs for
cryptographic protocols are far more complicated than for primitives. We suggest
the way of embedding Sequence of Games technique, Universally Composability
framework, module design of protocols and other techniques into the cryptography protocols course. Our experience of teaching formal security proofs for
cryptographic protocols brings quite positive effect for students' research and
development.

Keywords: Information security science · Syllabus · Information security
training · Cryptography · Provable security

1 Introduction

The study of any science should base on a solid theoretical foundation. In modern cryptography, such foundation is provable security methodology. Comparing to classical
cryptography, it replaces the empirical approach of proving security with a strict formal
proofs. Nowadays, the concept of provable security becomes prevalent in cryptography.
University courses should present modern science and technology quite adequately. So,
a lot of attention should be paid to provable security in contemporary university courses.
We see that the concept of provable security was included in many cryptography classes
all over the world, but there are still some gaps.

At first, current courses use ideas of provable security just for cryptographic primitives, but the provable techniques for cryptographic protocols not covered in the courses.
At second, security proofs for modern cryptosystems become more and more complicated. So, it becomes quite difficult to introduce such advanced techniques into the
syllabus. At third, a suite of representative examples should be chosen for teaching
purposes, and it is not evident how to make these examples quite didactic, and reachable
for classwork and self-studying.

M. Bishop et al. (Eds.): WISE 10, IFIP AICT 503, pp. 63–73, 2017.
DOI: 10.1007/978-3-319-58553-6_6

The purpose of our work is to suggest a concept of integration provable security into modern university courses on cryptographic protocols for students specializing in the area of information security. Why is it so important? Because there is a growing demand for specialists capable not only to correctly apply the already existing methods, but also to solve new cryptographic problems "on the fly".

The paper is organized according to the tasks we have solved to achieve the goal. Section 2 briefly presents some related works. After discussing main approaches to proving security in modern cryptography in Sect. 3, we observe and analyze existing practices for studying provable security in the current cryptography courses in Sect. 4. In Sect. 5 we discuss in detail how to integrate provable security into the syllabus on cryptographic protocols and preceding courses, taking into account that provable techniques for protocols are different from techniques for primitives. In Sect. 6 we suggest how to optimally embed so-called Sequence of Games approach for proving security of cryptographic protocols. Section 7 is devoted to problems of embedding so-called Universal Composability (UC) approach and some more advanced related techniques. In Sect. 8 we outline our experience of teaching formal security proofs for cryptographic protocols and conclude that it brings some positive effects. Finally, we identify main results and future directions of the work.

2   Related Works

Of course, there is a number of research focusing on optimizing syllabus on modern cryptography. Some wide-known massive open online courses (MOOCs) and university courses include provable security foundations. In our mind, the best examples are Cryptography course on Coursera [1], MIT course [2], Stanford course [3], UC Davies course [4] and some others. However, we are essentially interested not in the courses themselves, but in teaching methods.

We have carefully analysed a lot of textbooks and scientific papers used in teaching practice. In our opinion, the best textbooks based on provable security approach are [5–7]. Also, we used some well-written papers on advanced proving techniques, such as UC framework by Canetti [8], guides on Sequence of Games techniques by Shoup [9] and Pointcheval [10], reactive security concept [11], an idea of modular design of UC-composable protocols by Camenisch et al. [12]. It is worth noting that most of these papers require essential adaptation to be used effectively in teaching.

3   Provable Security in Cryptography

We have investigated many approaches to proving security of cryptographic algorithms and protocols in modern cryptography. Here we are going to outline briefly our view on a landscape of proof techniques (Fig. 1).

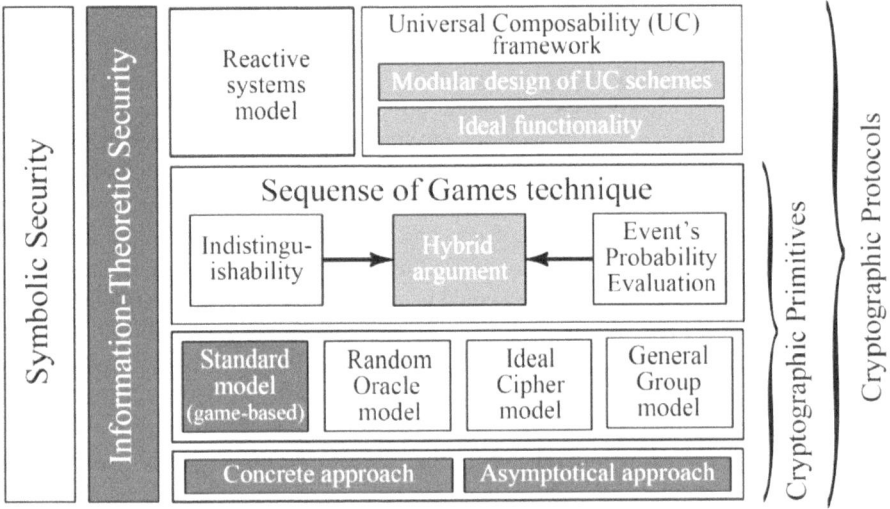

Fig. 1. A landscape of modern provable security methods

There are three fundamentally different approaches to reasoning and proving security of cryptographic constructions: information-theoretic security, computational security, and symbolic security.

Information-theoretic approach is the oldest one. Shannon introduced it in the middle of 1940s [13]. It is well known, that the main idea of this approach is to provide a method of constructing cryptosystems secure against the computationally unlimited adversary. However, it is also well known, that the main drawback of such perfectly secure cryptosystems is its impracticality. For example, implementation of perfectly secure symmetric cipher must have key length no less than the plaintext length. But in some other applications perfectly secure cryptosystems are far more practical. Good examples are Shamir's secret sharing scheme [14] and Pedersen's verifiable secret sharing and commitment schemes [15], which play an important role in modern cryptographic constructions.

Computational security is the leading approach in modern cryptography. Goldwasser and Micali introduce it in the middle of 1980s [16], and Goldwasser, Micali and Rackoff extended it to cryptographic protocols soon [17].

At first, such proof requires a definition of secure cryptographic construction (primitive, protocol, scheme). Secondly, some suggestion about the computationally infeasible problem has to be made. Next, a construction solving the task is offered and a mathematical proof that the construction satisfies the definition must be outlined assuming existence of the infeasible problem. As a rule, the proof makes sure that only chance to violate the security of such a construction is to solve the above-mentioned infeasible task.

We believe it is convenient to allocate some "layers" in modern computationally secure proving techniques.

The lowest layer complies of two basic definitional concepts of security measuring – concrete approach and asymptotical approach. The first one was developed by Goldwasser [7], the last one – by Goldreich [18].

The second level is composed of some proving models using certain definitional approach. They bring a "mechanics" of proving assuming some agreements. Well-known examples are standard model (game-based), random oracle model, ideal cipher model, generic group model (we do not discuss here the specificity of each model).

The next level is Sequence of Games technique. When a proof becomes too complicated, it should be presenred as a series of steps replacing security against ideal adversary to security against real one. Each step could be performed based on indistinguishability argument or event's probability evaluation. If both arguments are combined, this is so called hybrid argument. Sequence of Games technique with hybrid argument is one of the main tools for proving security of cryptosystems.

All three levels are necessary for proving security of cryptographic primitives and relatively simple cryptosystems. However, such levels are not sufficient for complicated cryptosystems composed of many building blocks such as zero-knowledge proofs, commitments and so on. Some kind of simulating cryptosystem's behavior model is desirable for such systems. That is why the forth level of computational security proofs goes on stage. The most known examples are Canetti's UC model [8] using ideal functionalities and reactive systems model [11] simulating dynamically interactive communities. However, when using all these techniques, the monolithic proofs obtained for complicated cryptographic constructions, are very difficult for synthesis and verification. Recently, some techniques to manage this complexity have been offered, for example, UC commitments for modular protocol design [12].

Currently, *symbolic security* approach has a limited scope in cryptography, but it is quite efficient for some protocols, such as key establishment. The first such technique – so-called BAN-logic was invented in 1990 [19]. Some other techniques were introduced in subsequent years, i.e. GNY-logic [20]. Tamarin is one of the currently evolving tools [21]. The main advantage of symbolic techniques is their easy automation. The drawback is that only special types of protocols can be analysed this way.

4   Provable Security in Current Cryptography Courses

As we noted earlier, provable security is an important part of many MOOC and university cryptography courses. Most of them include only historical Shannon's approach and basic computational security techniques. Of course, Shannon's perfect security idea is inavoidable element of cryptography syllabus. It should be emphasized to students, that Shannon was the first to find strong mathematical evidence of information security. His approach became the reference for all subsequent ones.

Computational security is the most usable approach, so it should be represented fully enough in the course. Existing practices mostly include definitional concepts and standard (game-based) model, in other words, first and second level of our landscape (Fig. 1). These are the most fundamental techniques, which ware used for analyzing security of basic symmetric and asymmetric cryptoschemes.

Of course, it is difficult to have enough time to combine both concrete and asymptotical approaches in one course, so just one definitional approach is used in every course. Examples of courses based on concrete security are [4, 7], and courses based on asymptotical security are [5, 6]. According to our research, asymptotical-based courses are far more common. More than 60 universities use it according to [22].

The second element of typical cryptography course is standard game-based model of proving security. The main idea of game-based security model is simulation of interaction among the adversary and responder (prototype of real-world party). It allows to prove that any supposed adversary can get an advantage over the responder if and only if she is able to solve some computationally infeasible problem (i.e., discrete logarithm, Diffie – Hellman, integer factorization etc.).

Symbolic security is rarely used in modern cryptography courses.

Thus, the main conclusion from the analysis of currently taught courses is the following. Currently, just basic methods of provable security are represented in cryptography courses. Evidently, the knowledge of them may be incomplete for construction and analyzing modern crypto algorithms and protocols. So, it is necessary to integrate advanced provable security techniques and tools into the syllabus not only on foundations of cryptography but also on cryptographic protocols.

5 Integrating Provable Security into the Syllabus on Cryptographic Protocols

One of the main factors to expand provable security techniques in research and in training courses is a complication of cryptosystems' structure. Our view on the architecture of modern cryptosystems is shown on Fig. 2. There are several levels in every complicated cryptosystem:

- basic mathematical facts;
- cryptographic primitives, including engineering (confucion/diffusion) and algebraic/combinatorial;
- cryptographic algorithms (functions), including one-key (symmetric), two-key (asymmetric) and no-key algorithms;
- building blocks of cryptographic protocols, such as zero-knowledge proofs, key management infrastructure etc.;
- cryptographic protocols, including two-party and multi-party protocols;
- cryptographic schemes (security mechanisms);
- cryptographic systems (security services);
- security systems, including cryptographic and non-cryptographic security services.

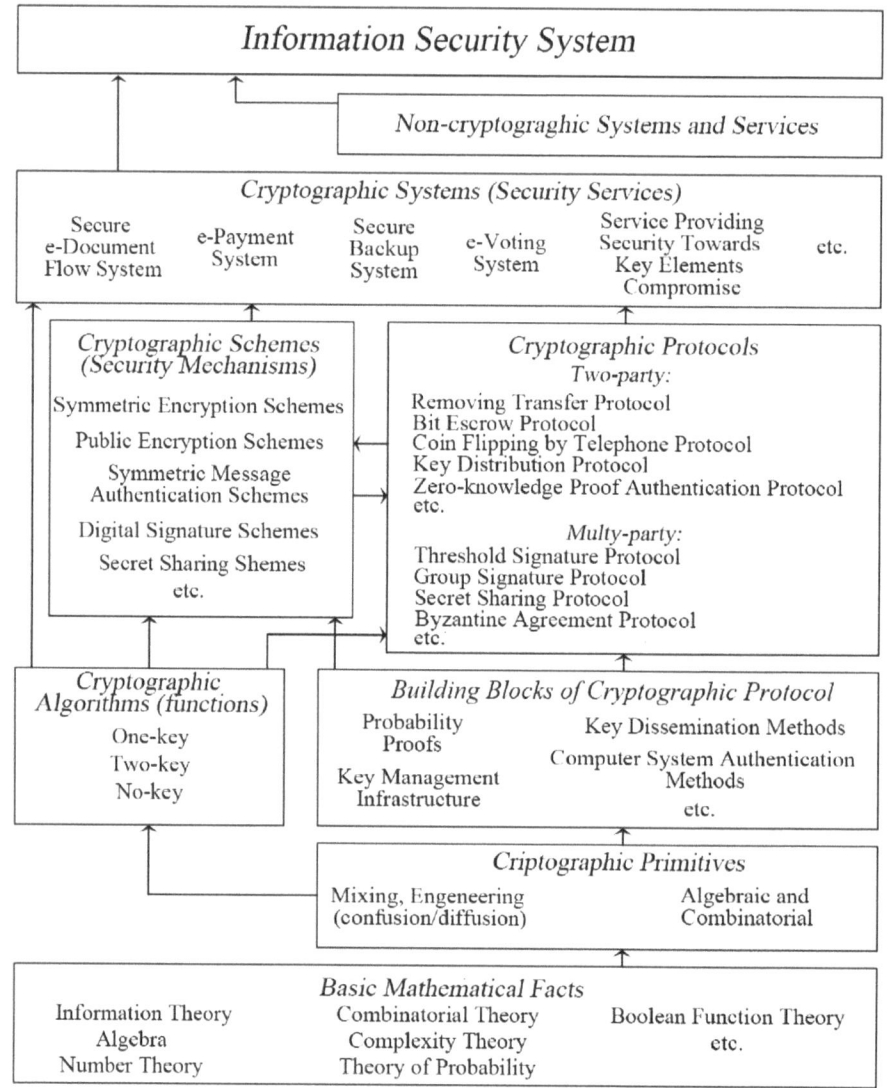

Fig. 2. Architecture of modern cryptosystems

We do not comment this scheme in details, so it is confirmed by wide analysis of numerous modern cryptosystems. We use this scheme as a framework for "Cryptographic protocols" course.

It is easy to notice that architecture on Fig. 2 is quite well correlated with the landscape on Fig. 1. Thus, the above-mentioned levels of proving techniques can be projected on the levels of cryptosystems' architecture. We identify on Fig. 1 a subset of proving techniques that is now included in typical cryptography course (dark grey blocks) and that we recommend including in the syllabus additionally (light grey blocks). Briefly, we recommend to add in syllabus the following:

- Sequence of Games technique, more precisely, hybrid argument method;
- Universal Composability framework and its extensions.

We will analyze special aspects of integrating of these techniques in next sections.

6   Embedding Sequence of Games Technique

Sequence of Games is a popular tool for structuring security proofs for cryptographic protocols and schemes. The purpose of this technique is to tame the complexity of security proofs that otherwise is so difficult as to repeat and verify is nearly impossible [9]. It is not a silver bullet, of course. As Shoup righteously notes, it is only a tool for organizing actual ideas for cryptographic constructions and security analysis.

The essence of this approach is as follows. To prove security one constructs a sequence of N games among the adversary and cryptographic primitive or protocol. The first game in the sequence is the original adversary's attack on the construction. Changes between successive games are minor, so probabilities of events connected to adversary's success or failure, differ very slightly. So, the last game in the sequence is ideal and a target probability of an event is typically either 0 or 1/2 (i.e. probability that an adversary can guess, which of two plaintexts corresponds to given ciphertext).

This is quite powerful method. However, we stress that it was developed in scientific environment for research purposes, so it has to be adapted for teaching purposes. So, we note that for pedagogical purposes two aspects are necessary: inevitable simplifying of the technique and carefully selected examples.

To simplify the explanation of Sequence of Games technique for students we recommend limiting the types of possible transitions among games to transitions based on indistinguishability of 2–3 computationally infeasible problems (preferably, the discrete logarithm nad the Diffie – Hellman problems, integer factorization and the RSA problems, and, may be, the Bilinear Diffie – Hellman problem for advanced students), and also transitions based on failure events that students should be able to evaluate (i.e., probability to find collisions of hash functions).

As regards the examples, we select the following:

- some variants of Luby – Rackoff construction for building a pseudo-random permutation family and one of authenticated encryption modes for "Symmetric cryptography" course;
- El Gamal public key encryption scheme without message hashing and with it and also FDH-RSA scheme for "Asymmetric cryptography" course;
- chosen ciphertext secure symmetric encryption (prototype of TLS protocol), one of the provably secure group key establishment protocols (we used protocols from TDH1 family [23]) and oblivious transfer (we used protocols from [24]) for "Cryptographic protocols" course.

The above-mentioned examples of proofs for cryptographic protocols are quite tricky, so the tutor should explain them as clearly as possible. But we insist that so non-trivial examples should be presented in university courses because of their importance and representativeness.

7 Embedding Universal Composability Framework

Universal Composability is one of the most powerful techniques of provable security in cryptography invented by Canetti in 1990s [8].

The essence of the approach is in its ability to simulate cryptographic protocol properties when many sessions of analyzed protocols along with other protocols are executed in parallel. The UC framework allows specifying the security requirements of most of cryptographic tasks in a unified manner. The advantage of this technique is the possibility of designing complex protocols from relatively simple building blocks. The security of separate protocols is preserved under a composition. The kernel of protocol analysis under UC approach lies in the specification of protocol's ideal functionality and comparison it with execution in the real-world environment to prove that difference among real and ideal executions is negligible. This approach is widely used in research. It is not always used strictly in Canetti's form [25], but many of its elements can be composed with other techniques, such as above-mentioned Sequence of Games and other modular design techniques.

The UC approach also requires adaptation for teaching purposes. We think, it is sufficient to inform students about main ideas of UC approach, without unnecessary details. The main things are Canetti's Composition theorem (proof is unnecessary) and technique for constructing ideal functionality based on virtual trusted third party.

We recommend the following well-documented examples for using during the studying the UC approach in classwork and homework: universally composable symmetric encryption [26], universally composable undeniable signatures [27], universally composable key management [28], universally composable role-based access control [29]. How to work with such examples? We recommend to analyze one of them in details in class and set analyzing slightly modified variant of one of the other schemes as a homework. It will require to make changes in the proof in many places of ideal functionality model, real protocol, game between the adversary and party of protocol and so on. Thus, students will learn how to construct proofs by themselves.

8 Experience of Teaching Formal Security Proofs for Cryptographic Protocols

Our ideas were embedded into the "Cryptographic protocols" course for graduate students in MEPhI. To measure an effect of changing the syllabus we have tested our students (60 people) studied on old and new syllabuses. In particular, the students had to solve some tasks when they passed all three courses:

- to prove the security of some simple RSA modifications;

- to prove the security of some variants of Luby-Rackoff construction;
- to prove the security of universally composable symmetric encryption scheme [26].

The result of students studying courses before their changing is as follows. 80% of students dealt with the first task, 20% of students got through the second task and nobody was successful with the third task. Such a result was not surprising, so the first task is easily solvable by most students with basic mathematical background, the second task is quite complicated for students not familiar with advanced provable security techniques, the third task is actually unsolvable by students without high-level qualifications in provable security.

Students studying courses after our changings showed significant improvement. 80% of students were still successful with the first task, but 60% of students got through the second task and about 25% of students were successful with the third task. It was predictable that the number of students dealt with the first task would not change (it is not a difficult task). But the rate of students that were successful with the second and the third tasks has essentially increased.

9   Conclusion

Summarizing the results of our work, we conclude with the following.

1. A new pedagogical idea was formed. Its essence is to integrate modern provable security techniques into the "Cryptographic protocols" course and improve basic cryptography courses to harmonize them with the provable security based cryptographic protocols course.
2. Views on a suite of current provable security techniques and architecture of modern cryptosystems are offered. Proposals on embedding some proving techniques in the curriculum on cryptographic protocols were formulated.
3. New techniques of teaching cryptographic protocols based on constructing and proving security of prototypes or slightly modified real-life protocols were offered. A set of examples and use cases on proving techniques was selected.

Most of our findings are original, and they were tested on the graduate students specializing in the area of information security. Our experience indicates that integrating our approach has some positive effect, including improving students' competences and more active participation in research and innovations. We plan to improve our crypto syllabuses to monitor the leading crypto tracks.

Acknowledgement. This work was supported by Competitiveness Growth Program of the Federal Autonomous Educational Institution of Higher Professional Education National Research Nuclear University MEPhI (Moscow Engineering Physics Institute).

References

1. Boneh, D.: Cryptography I. https://www.coursera.org/learn/crypto. Accessed 28 Jan 2017
2. Cryptography and Cryptanalysis: MIT Open Courseware. https://ocw.mit.edu/courses/electrical-engineering-and-computer-science/6-875-cryptography-and-cryptanalysis-spring-2005/. Accessed 28 Jan 2017
3. Maurer U. Cryptography Foundations (2016). http://www.crypto.ethz.ch/teaching/lectures/Crypto16/. Accessed 28 Jan 2017
4. Rogaway P. Cryptography course. http://web.cs.ucdavis.edu/~rogaway/classes/127/spring16/. Accessed 28 Jan 2017
5. Katz, J., Lindell Y.: Introduction to Modern Cryptography, 2nd edn., 598 pp. CRC Press, Boca Raton (2015)
6. Boneh, D., Shoup, V.: A graduate course on applied cryptography, 400 pp. (2015). https://crypto.stanford.edu/~dabo/cryptobook/. Accessed 28 Jan 2017
7. Goldwasser, S., Bellare, M.: Lecture notes on cryptography, 289 pp. (2008). https://cseweb.ucsd.edu/~mihir/papers/gb.pdf. Accessed 28 Jan 2017
8. Canetti, R.: Universally composable security: a new paradigm for cryptographic protocols (2001). http://eprint.iacr.org/2000/067.pdf. Accessed 28 Jan 2017
9. Shoup, V.: Sequences of games: a tool for taming complexity in security proofs (2004). http://eprint.iacr.org/2004/332.pdf. Accessed 28 Jan 2017
10. Pointcheval, D.: Contemporary cryptology provable security for public key schemes. In: Advanced Courses CRM Barcelona, pp. 133–189, June 2005. ISBN: 3-7643-7294-X
11. Backers, M., Pfitzmann, B., Waidner, M.: The reactive simulatability (RSIM) framework for asynchronous systems. Inf. Comput. 205(12), 1685–1720 (2007)
12. Camenisch, J., Dubovitskaya, M., Rial, A.: UC commitments for modular protocol design and applications to revocation and attribute tokens. http://eprint.iacr.org/2016/581. Accessed 28 Jan 2017
13. Shannon, C.: Communication theory of secrecy systems. Bell Syst. Tech. J. 28(4), 656–715 (1949)
14. Shamir, A.: How to share a secret. Commun. ACM 22, 612–613 (1979)
15. Pedersen, T.P.: Non-interactive and information-theoretic secure verifiable secret sharing. In: Feigenbaum, J. (ed.) CRYPTO 1991. LNCS, vol. 576, pp. 129–140. Springer, Heidelberg (1992). doi:10.1007/3-540-46766-1_9
16. Goldwasser, S., Micali, S.: Probabilistic Encryption. J. Comput. Syst. Sci. 28(2), 270–299 (1984). Academic Press, New York
17. Goldwasser, S., Micali, S., Rackoff, C.: The knowledge complexity of interactive proof-systems. SIAM J. Comput. 18(1), 186–208 (1989). Society for Industrial and Applied Mathematics, Philadelphia
18. Goldreich, O.: Foundations of Modern Cryptography, vol. 1 – Basic Tools, vol. 2 – Basic applications. Cambridge University Press, Cambridge (2004)
19. Burrows, B., Abadi, M., Needham, R.: A logic of authentication. ACM Trans. Comput. Syst. 8(1), 18–36 (1990)
20. Gong, L., Needham, R., Yahalom, R.: Reasoning about belief in cryptographic protocols. In: Proceedings of the IEEE Computer Society Symposium on Research in Security and Privacy, pp. 234–248 (1990)
21. Meier, S., Schmidt, B., Cremers, C., Basin, D.: The TAMARIN prover for the symbolic analysis of security protocols. In: Sharygina, N., Veith, H. (eds.) CAV 2013. LNCS, vol. 8044, pp. 696–701. Springer, Heidelberg (2013). doi:10.1007/978-3-642-39799-8_48

22. Katz, J., Lindell, Y.: Introduction to Modern Cryptography. http://www.cs.umd.edu/~jkatz/imc.html. Accessed 28 Jan 2017
23. Manulis, M.: Provably secure group key exchange. Ph.D. theses, 225 pp. (2007). http://manulis.eu/papers/psgke.pdf. Accessed 28 Jan 2017
24. Dubovitskaya, M.: Cryptographic protocols for privacy-preserving access control in databases. Ph.D. theses, 213 pp. (2014). http://e-collection.library.ethz.ch/eserv/eth:14431/eth-14431-02.pdf. Accessed 28 Jan 2017
25. Canetti, R., Cohen, A., Lindell, Y.: A simpler variant of universally composable security for standard multiparty computation. https://eprint.iacr.org/2014/553.pdf. Accessed 13 Mar 2017
26. Kuesters, R., Tuengerthal, M.: Universally composable symmetric encryption. http://eprint.iacr.org/2009/055. Accessed 28 Jan 2017
27. Kurosawa, K., Furukawa, J.: Universally composable undeniable signature. http://eprint.iacr.org/2008/094. Accessed 28 Jan 2017
28. Kremer, S., Kunnemann R., Steel, G.: Universally composable key-management. http://eprint.iacr.org/2012/189. Accessed 28 Jan 2017
29. Liu, B., Warinschi, B.: Universally composable cryptographic role-based access control. http://eprint.iacr.org/2016/902. Accessed 28 Jan 2017

Introducing Mobile Network Security Experiments to Communication Technology Education

Stig F. Mjølsnes and Ruxandra F. Olimid[✉]

Department of Information Security and Communication Technology, NTNU,
Norwegian University of Science and Technology, Trondheim, Norway
{sfm,ruxandra.olimid}@ntnu.no

Abstract. We describe a new viable lab assignment that enhances the theoretical study of wireless network security in our master-level communication technology education with hands-on mobile access network experimentation for the students. This new part is added to a well established student lab on wireless network security, by making use of low cost software defined radio devices and readily available open source software for experiments with one-cell GSM mobile access networks. The students can use their own smartphones. The overall objective of the lab is to support the students' practical understanding of the technical problems of building and managing wireless network security mechanisms. We report our findings and experiences from designing, constructing, testing and managing this lab assignment in the autumn semester of 2016.

Keywords: Education · Communication technology · Wireless · Mobile networks · Information security · GSM · Software defined radio

1 Introduction

1.1 Motivation

Cellular mobile access networks (GSM, UMTS, and LTE) have become a ubiquitous part of the world-wide communication systems and are used in both personal and professional everyday life now. Access authorization and authentication, confidentiality, integrity, and location and tracking privacy are some of the highly important communication security properties. The topic of mobile network security has been included in university level curricula at some engineering and computer science programs. Typically, however, the teaching is theory-only with no provision for lab work with real wireless setups.

We propose that gaining experience by a process of doing hands-on experimentation will significantly improve the intuition and understanding of mobile network security concepts and theory, and ought to be an essential component

© IFIP International Federation for Information Processing 2017
Published by Springer International Publishing AG 2017. All Rights Reserved
M. Bishop et al. (Eds.): WISE 10, IFIP AICT 503, pp. 74–83, 2017.
DOI: 10.1007/978-3-319-58553-6_7

of teaching network security. It should make students skilled in both practical attacks, and the best practice of security mechanisms and protocols. As a consequence, a natural question arises: *"How to introduce mobile network security experiments to network engineering education?"*. We describe our recent work of designing, constructing, testing and managing a lab assignment for mobile network security included in a master level course in wireless network security.

1.2   Our Contribution

For many years, the student assignment associated with our Wireless Network Security course within the Master's Programme in Communication Technology has helped students explore the security mechanisms and protocols used in wireless LANs. Useful open source software and inexpensive equipment for this communication technology have been easy to acquire and set up. During the autumn semester of 2016, we have successfully extended this lab assignment with realistic mobile network security experiments based on software-defined radio devices controlled by readily available open source software. The students are able to explore mobile network security protocols by building a one-cell mobile access network and run tests with their own smartphones. For a start, the students can analyze live radio communication protocols, authentication, encryption, and anonymity mechanisms for the GSM mobile system. Equipment and devices useful for setting up such experimental mobile wireless networks are now available at affordable cost, and this creates exciting new possibilities for communication security engineering education. Let this new part of the lab assignment be referred to as the *Mobile Access Network Security section*. This paper describes both the technical details of the lab equipment and tools, and the pedagogical experiences that we have gained so far. Finally, we indicate possible directions for further developments that we plan to take.

2   The Course

The Wireless Network Course is part of the first year master's program in Communication Technology. It builds upon our basic Cryptography, Computers, and Network Security course. Other recommended prerequisites are courses in Access and Transport Networks, Mobile Networks and Services. In general, the scope of the course is functions, protocols, and configurations for realizing authentication, key distribution, integrity, confidentiality and anonymity in wireless access networks for mobile users. Mobile forensics has been included too. The course presents and analyses security techniques employed in existing systems, including WPAN, WLAN, GSM/UMTS/LTE, IMS. In addition, we may present proposed solutions for new wireless technologies, such as ad-hoc and sensor networks. One of the main learning objectives is to acquire analytical skills for information security assessment of communication systems that provide services for mobile users by wireless access networks.

The lab assignment is 20% of the total course. The content of the assignment has steadily evolved since the start in 2006. The original inspiration for creating the course and the lab assignment did not come from similar teaching at other universities. It is our perception that there have been, and still are, few courses on wireless *security* in university level curricula. A major part of our early inspiration came from open source network tools and WiFi hacker tools that were developed and emerged at that time, such as `wireshark`, `kismet`, and the `aircrack-ng` suite of tools [1–3]. Note that the first cryptanalytic results on WEP were published a few years earlier, in 2001. Note also that around that time the term *ethical hacking* became a professional security testing skill sought after by big corporations and governments, which spawned a heated discussion at universities whether computer engineering students ought to be taught attacker/hacker skills. Retrospectively, we are now able to find that Hartpence paper from 2005 describes some of the same considerations that we started out with [4].

This same sort of practical impetus that we had for creating the lab in the first place also holds for our newly added *Mobile Access Network Security* part. Our inspiration here is the availability and low cost of USRP devices, together with open source software [5–8]. After having constructed and conducted this new part, we found out that similar labs exist at some very few other universities, suggesting that the approach starts to gain momentum [9].

3   The Lab Organisation

3.1   Structure

A total of 40 students enrolled in the course for the autumn semester of 2016, whereof 31 males and 9 females. The course attracts a significant number of international exchange students (9 students in 2016). Over the years, the total number of students have fluctuated around 50 students.

Table 1. Student grouping

No. of students per group	No. of groups
3	11
2	3
1	1

For 2016: 40 students divided into 15 groups

We measure that the entire assignment will nominally require at most one full week effort for a group of three students sharing the work load. We advice cooperation on problems both within the group and across groups, and commend self-organised designation of roles and responsibilities within each group. We allow flexibility in establishing the groups (student driven), and Table 1 shows the numbers for the groups last year (2016).

We allocate two calendar weeks due to limitation in lab space and for various other reasons, such as computer resources, noise level, course staff availability. This allows some flexibility for the students or groups to pick a preferred week, thus eliminating absence problems that might be caused by personal circumstances or conflicts with other courses and activities. The groups are granted access to the laboratory room for the week they are registered for.

One week before the lab work, the course staff will give an introductory talk on the lab objectives, description, deliverables and grading criteria. The complete lab assignment description becomes available well in advance for the students to understand the theoretical background needed and to organize their work.

The lab assignment is a mandatory 20% portfolio of the course, and consists of two main tasks over two weeks' time:

(1) Carry out the lab experiments, and demonstrate the results after each milestone to a teaching assistant. All milestones must be passed and approved by a teaching assistant by the end of the first week (pass or fail).
(2) Prepare and submit a written lab report for grading and the end of the following week. We encourage the students to record their progress in a lab journal. The submitted lab report is graded by the course staff.

3.2 Content

The work plan for the mobile network security part contains four main tasks:

1. Set up a one-cell GSM network.
2. Enable 'Open Registration'.
3. Enable 'Cached Authentication'.
4. Enable link encryption.

First task aims to become familiar with the hardware and software tools that will be used later in the lab. The main objective is to set up the hardware and the software for the GSM one-cell network, for which they will configure and test security mechanisms.

The next three tasks challenge the students to experiment with the GSM authentication and access control, (un)linkability, and confidentiality mechanisms. The 2G mobile access networks should issue random strings for TMSI (Temporary Mobile Subscriber Identity), replacing the permanent identity string of IMSI (International Mobile Subscriber Identity). So, students first enable TMSI allocation for their network service, having in mind a purpose for this: to secure their network against passive adversaries (eavesdroppers) that want to break the privacy of a targeted subscriber (identified by a given IMSI).

The access control and authentication protocols of mobile networks are central topics in the course. Hence we ask the students to perform some experiments with two (quite naive) access control mechanisms implemented in OpenBTS: *Open Registration* and *Cached Authentication*. This offers the students a practical environment to reflect on different access control mechanisms. They will analyze the security performance of the mechanisms used, and compare against the real mechanisms in GSM networks. Finally, we ask to enable encryption, keeping in mind the goal of private communication.

Each of the four main tasks corresponds to one milestone. By this, we expect the students to demonstrate the operation, the functionality and their comprehension. We find these milestones to be a good method for the teaching assistants to monitor the progress of each group.

4   Instrumentation

A student group will normally use the following equipment:

- One networked computer.[1]
- One USRP (Ettus B200mini) as in Fig. 2.
- Two smartphones enabled for 2G access (optional).

Universal Software Radio Peripheral (USRP). A USRP is a device used to prototype wireless communication systems. The B200mini is a USRP with size less than a payment card that can be programmed to operate over a wide radio-frequency range (70 MHz - 6GHz) and communicate in full duplex. For instance, it can be used in all of the standard GSM, UMTS, and LTE frequency bands. Figure 1 shows the USRP B200mini board, while Fig. 2 shows the hardware enclosed and with antennas mounted [10], as presented to our students in the lab. More detailed technical specifications on the B200mini can be found at Ref. [11].

Fig. 1. The Ettus Research B200mini USRP board, size 83.3×50.8 mm [11].

Fig. 2. We built our own robust enclosure for the USRP boards and antennas.

---

[1] In fact, each group will use two desktop computers equipped with 802.11 network interface cards required for parts of the lab assignment not reported on here.

OpenBTS. OpenBTS is a Linux-based open source software that can interface to software-defined radio hardware [5]. The OpenBTS implements most of the GSM stack above the radio modem; however, it requires some other distinct applications as prerequisites:

SMQueue (SIP Message Queue) stores and forwards text messages, being a prerequisite for the SMS service between mobile stations using OpenBTS.

Asterisk is a Voice over IP (VoIP) switch that performs call establishment between mobile stations using OpenBTS. Asterisk is an open source framework sponsored by Digium [12].

SIPAuthServe (SIP Authorisation Server) is an application that manages the subscriber database, thus replacing the HLR (Home Location Register) entity found in a conventional GSM network architecture.

The OpenBTS suite and all the prerequisites were installed and configured by the course staff to work with the USRP B200mini before the lab started. More detailed information on OpenBTS is available at Ref. [13,14].

Computers. The computers used in the lab are desktop computers with Intel Core2 Quad CPU Q9400@2.66 GHz running Ubuntu 12.04. The recommendation is to connect the USRP device via a USB3, but we found out that the USB2 transfer speed is sufficient for our lab activities.

Smartphones. Following the BOYD (Bring Your Own Device) policy, we encouraged the students to switch their own mobile phones to 2G and use them for the experiments. Nevertheless, we provided LG Nexus 5X handsets running Android v6 to a few groups that lacked access to the necessary two mobile phone devices. (This was the case for the "one-student group", as well as for some students whose phones disallowed network type selection - e.g.: older versions of iOS).

5   The Lab Tasks

This is a brief description of the tasks in the mobile access network part of the lab. The tasks focus on the security aspects in GSM, as previously explained in Sect. 3.

The course staff have downloaded and built all the necessary software on all desktop computers prior to the lab start. This assures an effective start for the students and avoids much hassle and frustration that can occur with incompatibility of the operating system, drivers, and building the applications. However, the complete installation guidance is given too, say, for or students who want to reproduce the experiments on their personal computers.

The first task is to connect the USRP device to a computer and check if the device is properly connected, by inspecting the LEDs and running specific commands. Each group creates a one-cell mobile network by starting and running the OpenBTS processes. Running several base stations concurrently in the same lab hall must be done with care to avoid radio frequency interferences. There are at least two concerns:

1. Interference with the commercial networks (that use licensed GSM frequency bands) outside the lab hall.
2. Interference among the lab group networks inside the lab hall.

We have put in place the following strategy to avoid these problems: each group is assigned a distinct ARFCN (Absolute Radio Frequency Channel Number) - chosen such that there are no interferences with cells of the other groups—from a frequency band that is not allocated for commercial mobile communication. This avoids interference with the commercial mobile networks [15]. Additionally, the students are asked to configure the USRP devices to a very low transmission power such that the cell radio coverage is effectively restricted to the lab hall.

Further, the lab tasks include the capture, storage, and analysis of network traffic, identify specific messages and parameters in several scenarios, and find and explain particular handset behaviour corresponding to distinct configurations of the network.

As an example, we outline here the procedure for the task *Enable link encryption*. The main objective for this is to investigate the confidentiality mechanisms in GSM. The students have to inspect encryption related parameters in the OpenBTS command line interface and enable encryption by setting appropriate values. Students can make calls from one handset to another, capture the traffic, and observe the differences between the situation where encryption is disabled, respectively enabled. Students are asked to compare the encryption behaviour they observe in the lab with the GSM encryption standard, and to give a description of the technical differences.

A similar method is applied for the others tasks:

- Enable TMSI allocation and observe which changes occur in the message flow. Check if the security goal is fulfilled.
- Experiment with the two access control mechanisms implemented in OpenBTS: *Open Registration* and *Cached Authentication*. Note the differences between the two and compare them with the textbook description of GSM authentication.

We aim for communication observations and analyses to be conducted both on the network side and on the user equipment side. The students are asked to observe how the mobile devices operate in different scenarios and to evaluate the security functionality on both sides. For example, we ask questions related to user experience and privacy, such as:

"Which security modes of operation are signalled by the phone's display to the user? In particular, consider various types of registration, authentication, and encryption modes".

6   Experience and Students' Feedback

The Mobile Access Network Security assignment part has been well received by the students so far. We suggest possible improvements in the final section of the paper. We have used two methods for collecting feedback: a question to be answered in the lab report, and direct interviews and report from the student reference group for the course.

Specific Question in the Lab Report. We use one assignment question to probe the students' opinions about the lab, and suggestions for possible improvements.

> *"How can this lab project be improved? (Answering is optional and does not influence your grade.)"*.

The question was optional, so not all groups answered. However, we got feedback from several groups, and overall it was positive indeed. Two of the responses are:

> *"We think that the practical part was very interesting, not too difficult nor too easy, and it is possible to finish within one week."*
> *"The motivation behind the lab project was clear, visible, and comprehensible. The tasks to be performed were interesting and informative. The well-prepared equipment enabled us to work directly 'hands-on' without long installation tasks. . . . All in all, the lab was a great success."*

Reference Group Report. At our university, it is required that three or four students volunteer to become a reference group for the class and course. They shall represent all students in the class, and provide a formal communication channel between the class and the course staff. They write up a short report at the end of the course, which is used as input to the overall evaluation of the course. Their reported feedback for the lab reads very encouraging:

> *"Lab: Very good, interesting and relevant topics. Hard to find information about different modification that you had to do. The description was very helpful, and the lab was well prepared, including the new part.".*

Finally, we present here some of our findings and experiences from the construction, testing and management of the laboratory.

During the development work of the lab, we tested several USRP devices, mostly from Ettus Research [16]. The final decision on the B200mini was due to several factors: compliance to our needs, affordable price, and small enough to be easily stored and transported in one box. Also, we have tested and found that the B200mini are compatible with our not-so-new desktop computers already in use for the lab. As mentioned earlier, we found that we did not need to upgrade to USB3 ports, so the only additional equipment that had to be bought were the antennas [10] and making the encapsulation for the board. Currently, the USRPs are used in other wireless communication courses and in our master thesis research projects, so they have proved to be a good investment.

We encountered some problems with the software during our lab construction. OpenBTS is an open source platform, always under development, so we sometimes had problems with the up-to-date version of the software, which cracked. We solved this by using a functional version of the source code, but changed the drivers to the ones compatible to the B200mini. This and the amount of time required for build the executables (approx. 30 min) made us decide to pre-install all the necessary software on the lab computers, thus allowing the students to focus their activities on the security related issues.

Students encountered a problem with identifying their own access network when more cells were up in the lab hall at the same time. This happens because some handsets always display the network as Test PLMN 1-1 (for default Mobile Country Code and Mobile Network Code), independent of the actual name assigned to the network by the software configuration. To avoid this, we asked the students to set the Mobile Network Code to their group number, which makes each cell directly identifiable.

7   Conclusions and Further Developments

We have succeeded in enhancing the theoretical study of wireless network security in our master-level communication technology education with hands-on mobile access network experimentation. We consider this as our first and exciting step into the learning possibilities that the brave new environment of open source based mobile networks can bring.

We decided to start with the GSM mobile networks, and next we want to move on directly to 4G (LTE). There are open source projects for LTE emerging, which makes this plan feasible [6–8]. At the same time, we want to develop further the GSM part of the lab, by making use of configurable SIM cards and allow the complete GSM authentication mechanism and encryption to take place. For this, we already acquired and tested configurable SIM cards [17], which we can configure for our purposes by using the PySim software [18] and a card reader [19]. These ideas were independently suggested by some of our students in their lab report feedback:

> "It would be a nice feature if we had the possibility to use programmable SIM-cards in order to play with GSM.Cipher. Encryption enabled or disabled and see the difference in the captured traffic in Wireshark."
>
> "Could it be an idea to set up LTE instead of GSM? Obviously LTE have less security vulnerabilities and is probably more time consuming to set up, however the relevance is greater."

Acknowledgements. Many people have contributed to the development and improvement of this wireless security lab assignment and its form and content. Professor Stig F. Mjølsnes started out in the spring of 2006 and set up the framework and the basic content, structure and text. Master student Lars Haukli joined in during the summer of 2006 and made tremendously good progress by testing out and identifying the best WiFi NICs and drivers for this purpose. He collected, tested, and selected a working environment of software tools for the Linux platform, and contributed enthusiastically to the technical content of this lab description. The first course students of TTM4137 carried out the assignment with success in the fall of 2006. Everything went smoothly, much thanks to dedicated supervision by teaching assistant PhD-student

Marie Moe and lab assistant master student Jan Tore Sørensen. Marie continued as teaching assistant in 2007 and made sure that the experience gained was put to good use in supervision and by editing a new version of the assignment text. The challenge of password dictionary attack was worked out by the teaching assistants and PhD-student Martin Eian and PhD-student Anton Stolbunov in 2008. During the summer 2016, professor Stig F. Mjølsnes, post doc Ruxandra F. Olimid, and engineer Pål Sturla Sæther developed, and built the USRP-based student lab. Ruxandra F. Olimid and student assistant Fredrik Skretteberg tested and managed the first student run-through of the lab assignment in the autumn semester 2016.

References

1. Wireshark Foundation: Wireshark. http://www.wireshark.org/
2. Kismet. http://www.kismetwireless.net/
3. Aircrack-ng: Aircrack-ng   suite.   http://www.aircrack-ng.org/doku.php# documentation
4. Hartpence, B.: Teaching wireless security for results. In: Proceedings of the 6th Conference on Information Technology Education (SIGITE 2005), pp. 89–93. ACM, New York (2005)
5. Range Networks: OpenBTS. http://openbts.org
6. OpenLTE: An open source 3GPP LTE implementation. https://sourceforge.net/ projects/openlte/
7. srsLTE: Open source 3GPP LTE library. https://github.com/srsLTE/srsLTE
8. Open Air Interface: 5G software alliance for democratising wireless innovation. http://www.openairinterface.org
9. Iowa State University: Wireless Security Lab & OpenBTS. http://seniord.ece. iastate.edu/dec1314/documents/Dec13-14_FinalPaper_12_09_13.pdfl
10. Pulse Electronics: W1900 antenna. http://www.pulseelectronics.com/products/ old_antennas/products_solutions/antennas_for_wireless_devices/wd_antennas/ w1900_/_w1902_penta_band_right_angle_stubby_antenna
11. Ettus   Research: USRP   B200mini.   https://www.ettus.com/product/details/ USRP-B200mini
12. Digium: Asterisk. http://www.asterisk.org
13. Iedema, M.: Getting Started with OpenBTS. O'Reilly Media Inc., Sebastopol (2014)
14. Range Networks: OpenBTS application suite - user manual (2014). http://openbts. org/site/wp-content/uploads/2014/07/OpenBTS-4.0-Manual.pdf
15. European Communication Office: ECO Frequency Information System. http:// www.efis.dk
16. Ettus Research: A national instruments company. https://www.ettus.com/
17. Sysmocom: SIM+USIM   Card.   http://shop.sysmocom.de/products/ sysmousim-sjs1-4ff
18. Pysim: A python tool to program SIMs. https://github.com/osmocom/pysim
19. Sysmocom: USB CCID reader. http://shop.sysmocom.de/products/scr3310

Information Security Awareness and Culture

A Linguistic Approach to Information Security Awareness Education in a Healthcare Environment

Lynette Drevin[✉], Hennie Kruger, Anna-Marie Bell, and Tjaart Steyn

Computer Science and Information Systems, North-West University,
Potchefstroom, South Africa
{Lynette.Drevin,Hennie.Kruger,AnnaMarie.Bell,
Tjaart.Steyn}@nwu.ac.za

Abstract. It is widely accepted that healthcare information security is extremely important and that security breaches will have serious consequences in many areas. Despite controls, such as legal frameworks, as well as ongoing research projects into healthcare information security and privacy, there is still an alarming number of healthcare information security breaches reported annually. In this paper, a linguistic approach, utilizing a vocabulary test, is proposed as a tool to determine security awareness levels of healthcare workers and to assist in educating them in security awareness aspects. A vocabulary-measuring instrument was developed and distributed to healthcare workers in a large South African hospital group. Results indicated that information security awareness levels are generally acceptable, but that potential problem areas exist between certain language groups, as well as between different business functions (departments). The study also shows that the proposed approach may offer significant advantages in information security awareness campaigns.

Keywords: Information security awareness · Vocabulary test · Healthcare · Linguistics · Behavior · Knowledge · Education

1 Introduction

Healthcare information systems (HIS) play a critical role within healthcare establishments and have become an integral part of all aspects of modern healthcare. These types of systems operate in a connected and networked environment and receive, store, send and process data that are generally deemed to be of an extremely sensitive nature. A healthcare information system is primarily centered towards the patient [1] and examples of electronic resources in HIS may include digital patient records, diagnostic and treatment data, service provider information, financial information (e.g. medical schemes), etc. Security breaches of healthcare information may have serious consequences in many areas. Personal health information is only one of the areas and patients may be exposed to economic threats, mental anguish and possible social stigma should information, such as medical history, test and laboratory results or insurance information leak out [2]. All

© IFIP International Federation for Information Processing 2017
Published by Springer International Publishing AG 2017. All Rights Reserved
M. Bishop et al. (Eds.): WISE 10, IFIP AICT 503, pp. 87–97, 2017.
DOI: 10.1007/978-3-319-58553-6_8

these point towards an increasing need for security and privacy of electronic health records.

The protection of sensitive electronic health records is not only required as a best practice, but should also adhere to legal liabilities. Maseti [3] pointed out that there are well over 30 countries that have enacted information protection statutes at national or federal level. With regard to the protection of health information, the Health Insurance Portability and Accountability Act of 1996 (HIPAA) in the United States of America is probably of the most well-known legislation [4]. The act ensures that consistent standards are maintained with regard to the handling and privacy of medical information records [5]. In South Africa, where this study was performed, a number of acts are in place to address the security and privacy of information. The Promotion of Access to Information Act No 2 of 2000 (PAIA) provides for giving access to a person to his or her information to ensure correctness and accuracy; The Electronic Communications and Transaction Act No 25 of 2002 deals directly with the protection of personal information; and The Protection of Personal Information Act No 4 of 2003 (POPI) regulates how personal information should be handled, stored and secured [6]. This act applies to anyone in South Africa who processes personal information [3].

The importance of healthcare information and the protection of such information are further emphasized by the large number of research projects and research papers on the topic. Examples of related work that investigate various aspects of healthcare information security include the following. Medlin and Cazier [7] explored the use of social engineering techniques and associated password practices of healthcare workers; Van Deursen et al. [8] applied a mixed methods approach to identify information security risks within healthcare; Appari and Johnson [9] surveyed the literature and provided a holistic view of research in information security and privacy in healthcare. They also suggest new areas that may be of interest in healthcare information security; and, Fernando and Dawson [10] performed a case study to suggest a health information system security threat life cycle. An informative overview of the security and privacy of electronic health records, based on a systematic literature review, is presented in Fernandez-Aleman et al. [11]. Earlier studies can also be found in [12–14].

Despite the acknowledgement that healthcare information security is extremely important, as well as the existence of a legal framework to protect healthcare information, and the ongoing research into healthcare information security and privacy, there is still an alarming number of security breaches, which are regularly reported in various reports. The 2015 breach report on protected health information [15] reports that an astonishing more than 113 million patient health records were breached in 2015. This represents an 897% increase in records breached from 2014 to 2015. It is also significant to note that 98.1% of the records breached in 2015 was the result of hacking attacks or other information technology incidents. These statistics are consistent with those reported in other reports [16, 17].

The above introductory comments clearly indicate an ongoing need to educate healthcare workers and to make them aware of information security threats. Information security awareness plays a significant role in combatting undesirable information technology incidents. Ogutcu et al. [18] pointed out that undesirable behavior is closely related to an IS user's level of information security awareness and that every person is obliged to be aware of information security threats in order to protect information. To design and implement effective information security awareness programs requires the identification of appropriate security topics to be included. Katsikas [19], for example, suggested a methodology to determine information security training needs specifically aimed at different personnel groupings within healthcare establishments. In this paper a linguistic approach, utilizing a vocabulary test, is described to identify areas of concern in information security awareness levels of healthcare workers. The study, which was performed within a large hospital group in South Africa, is based on an earlier exploratory study where the use of a vocabulary test in the context of security awareness was tested with students at a university [20].

The remainder of the paper is organized as follows. In Sect. 2, a brief theoretical background of the linguistic approach followed is presented. In Sect. 3, the methodology used in the study is described and in Sect. 4, the results and a discussion of the results are presented. The paper is then concluded with some final remarks in Sect. 5.

2 Theoretical Context

Linguistics is the scientific study of human language and linguistic knowledge is called a grammar [21]. According to Fromkin [21], a grammar includes various concepts, such as a lexicon (vocabulary), morphology (structure of words), syntax (structure of phrases and sentences), semantics (meaning of words) and phonology (sounds). This study proposes a linguistic approach to assess information security awareness and focuses in particular on the lexicon or vocabulary component, as well as, to a certain extent, the semantics of linguistics.

The proposed linguistic framework may be seen as an expansion of the work reported in Kruger et al. [20]. In this initial exploratory project, the feasibility of a vocabulary test as a tool to assess security awareness was investigated. Empirical tests were performed on students at a tertiary institution and results proved to be useful. Utilizing vocabulary tests in information security is not generally practiced and stems from the success of other educational studies (specifically mathematics) where learners' language proficiency in a subject, e.g. mathematics, was measured using vocabulary tests [22, 23].

A detailed discussion of language development, vocabularies and the associated processes to transform linguistic inputs into beliefs and actions is beyond the scope of this paper. Such a discussion will have to include, amongst others, aspects such as cognitive psychology. Details on these topics can be found in [24] and, to a lesser extent, in [20]. For the purposes of this paper, it will suffice to state that cognitive principles (learn, know, understand, process and recall of information) are important in linguistic tests. Van der Walt [25] argues that three key cognitive skills are necessary for successful learning. The three skills are knowledge of facts, processes and concepts, the ability to apply the knowledge, concepts and processes, and the ability to reason. These three cognitive skills are explained in the context of information security in Table 1. Table 1, which was originally adapted from [25], is quoted directly from [20], as both the original study and this current study are based on the same cognitive skills.

Table 1. Cognitive skills [20]

Cognitive category	Cognitive action
Knowledge of facts, processes, procedures and concepts (what someone needs to know)	Recall, recognize, calculate, derive information from graphs or tables, measure, classify and sort
Explanation: When people do not have reasonable access to a knowledge- or facts-base in information security, focused information security reasoning becomes difficult. Knowledge of security processes (steps, methods or procedures) forms the link between basic knowledge and the implementation thereof. Knowledge of information security concepts enables people to see the relationship among the different elements of information security and helps to ensure that facts are not seen or treated in isolation	
Understanding and application of knowledge	Choose, suggest, develop a model, solve problems and implement solutions
Explanation: Representation of information security ideas forms the basis of perceptions and communication in information security and is a basic prerequisite for a successful information security environment. When it is expected from someone to apply knowledge in the information security area, the type of problem should be known in order to execute the required procedures and to choose the best strategy for solving the problem	
Reasoning (focus on solving problems in unknown situations)	Analyze, generalize, integrate, defend solutions
Explanation: Reasoning in information security requires logical and systematically, including intuitive and inductive, thinking processes. People should be able to implement expertise in different contexts	

Based on the above brief comments and the discussion in Sect. 1, it was decided to perform a comprehensive vocabulary test exercise on the staff of a large hospital group in an effort to determine information security awareness levels. The study was motivated by the importance of medical information and the associated risks and threats that occur in healthcare environments (see Sect. 1). Choosing a linguistic approach is justified by the success of the initial study to use a vocabulary test in the context of information security awareness [20]. This approach is of particular interest to South Africa where the study was performed. South Africa is a multilingual (11 official languages) country where information is often presented in only one language and a real danger of misunderstanding or misinterpreting information and messages exists. Furthermore, it is assumed that information system users may be more susceptible to security breaches if they do not have a basic understanding and comprehension of information security concepts and terminology. An additional advantage of using a vocabulary test is the opportunity it creates to identify suitable topics for inclusion in an information security awareness program as well as the identification of appropriate techniques to conduct awareness campaigns. It should, however, be noted that a linguistic approach may produce unreliable results in some instances, e.g. normal ethical behavior may prevent users from revealing confidential information without knowing what the concept "social engineering" entails. To address this type of problem the measuring instrument also provides for scenario-type questions to test a user's behavior. Details on this and the general methodology followed are highlighted in the next section.

3   Methodological Approach

The general methodology followed in this study was based on a vocabulary-measuring instrument. A questionnaire, consisting of two sections, was developed to assess the security awareness levels of information technology users in a large hospital group. The aim of the first section was to test specific information technology-related knowledge, while the second section focused on the evaluation of expected information security behavior.

To compile the knowledge section of the questionnaire, an extensive Internet search was conducted to identify a list of appropriate information security-related words or concepts. This resulted in a list of 45 concepts that were categorized in four main categories, namely social engineering, viruses, spam, and unauthorized access. Following a rigorous review of these concepts and performing small pilot studies, it was decided to use 20 of the 45 words in the final measuring instrument. An example of a vocabulary-type question to test a respondent's information security knowledge is given below.

Example 1. Vocabulary-type question

A computer virus is a:
  (a) Computer program that is designed to replicate itself by copying itself into other programs in a computer. It may be benign or have a negative effect, such as causing other programs to operate incorrectly or corrupting a computer's memory
  (b) Term used to describe any computer program that functions incorrectly
  (c) Computer program that will influence your computer's performance and which can be bought at any reputable computer dealer
  (d) Group of unsolicited bulk email messages creating havoc
  (e) I do not know

The second section of the questionnaire contained 10 scenario-type questions. The purpose of these questions was to establish whether users really understand a specific information security concept or whether behavior was merely a result of normal under-lying ethical principles. The scenario-type questions were based on appropriate examples in the literature [20, 26], as well as information obtained during pilot studies. Example 2 indicates a scenario-type question.

Example 2. Scenario-type question

> *When you receive a recorded phone call requesting you to call a toll-free telephone number that purports to be that of a well-known financial institution and you are asked to punch in any personal information, what would you do?*
> *(a) Ignore the request*
> *(b) End the telephone call*
> *(c) Phone the toll-free number and supply the information*
> *(d) None of the above*
> *(e) I do not know*

In addition to the Internet searches and literature reviews, the measuring instrument was also subjected to a number of pilot studies. The initial questionnaire was handed to eight staff members of an IT department at a university for comments. Certain changes were suggested and the improved questionnaire was then tested with another 31 respondents. This sample of respondents represented a mix of senior students and lecturers from the same university. The questionnaire was again adjusted according to the feedback of the respondents. A final pilot study was then conducted with the hospital group where the actual study was performed. A total of 46 staff members of the hospital group participated in this pilot study. During the process of constructing and refining the measuring instrument, basic statistical tests were also performed to ensure validity and reliability of the questions included in the final instrument. A limited number of these statistical test results will be highlighted in the next section where the results are presented.

The final questionnaire was made available electronically for two months to information technology users within a large South African hospital group. The hospital group consists of 55 hospitals and 48 retail pharmacies with over 29 000 employees. A total of 3 577 staff members across different departments (e.g. Finance, Marketing, Information Technology, Production, Purchasing, Customer Services, etc.) received the questionnaire by means of their management structure. From this population, 1 039 respondents completed the questionnaire. The questionnaire is not included due to confidentiality reasons. A summary of some of the results are presented in the next section.

4   Results and Discussion

Due to space considerations not all results can be reported here and it was decided to present two sets of results that are of particular interest. The first set of results pertains to the different language groups of the hospital's workforce, while the second set highlights some of the results linked to the different business activities.

The main demographic details of the 1 039 respondents are shown in Table 2.

Table 2. Demographic details of respondents

Gender		Main function or activity	
Female	**77.3%**	Management	**33.5%**
Male	22.7%	Other	27.1%
		Clerical	24.1%
Age		Patient Care	11.3%
Younger than 20	0.3%	Auditing	3.9%
21 - 30	21.4%	**Home language**	
31 - 40	**33.9%**	Afrikaans	**44.2%**
41 - 50	26.8%	English	37.9%
Older than 50	17.5%	Other	17.9%

Basic statistical tests were performed on the complete data set to ensure that valid and reliable results have been obtained. Reliability (accuracy of the measuring instrument) was assessed by calculating the well-known Cronbach Alpha coefficient [27]. The resulting coefficient was 0.71 and based on this, the results were accepted as reasonable. To test for statistical significance (and significant differences between groups of people, e.g. first language groups or business activity groups), it was decided to make use of the Cohen's d-value – also known as an effect size [28]. The d-value is defined as a standardized difference between the means of two populations (groups in this study) and gives the importance of the effect in practice. The standard interpretation of the d-value is given by Cohen [28] as 0.8 = large effect; 0.5 = medium effect; and 0.2 = small effect. This statistic was used to test whether there are significant differences between the information security awareness knowledge of the different language and business function groups. Table 3 presents the d-values of information security awareness knowledge per language group.

Table 3. Effect size (d-values) – Knowledge per language group

Effect size (d-values)		
Afrikaans with English	Afrikaans with Other	English with Other
0.13	0.49	0.61

It should be noted that there are 11 official languages in South Africa. For reporting purposes and due to the number of respondents (per language group), it was decided to group all languages, other than Afrikaans and English, together as "Other". The reported d-values indicated that there is a medium effect (d = 0.49), or medium difference, between the information security knowledge of Afrikaans-speaking health-care workers and those who speak one of the other official languages. There is, however, a more significant difference (d = 0.61) between the knowledge of English-speaking workers and those classified as other. This finding is of particular interest as the measuring instrument is focused on linguistic aspects. The differences in knowledge from the different language groups may indicate that language is probably a barrier in security

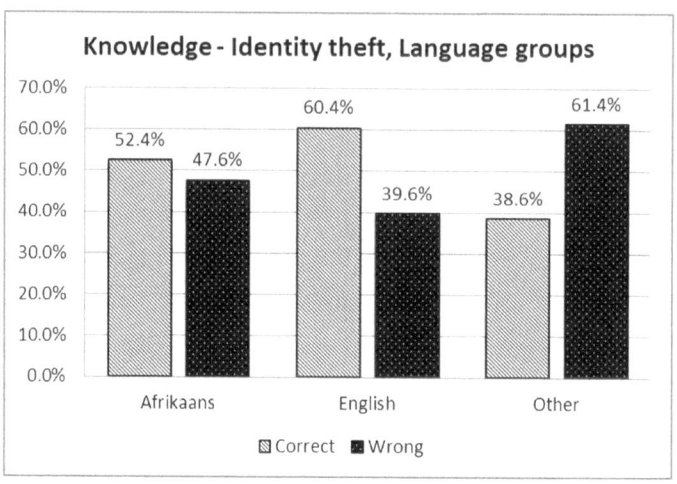

Fig. 1. Vocabulary-type question

awareness programs where information security concepts are explained. To further illustrate this finding, consider the graph in Fig. 1. Figure 1 graphically displays the result of a typical knowledge question where respondents had to explain the meaning of the term "identity theft".

It follows from Fig. 1 that 52.4% of Afrikaans-speaking workers responded in the correct way, 60.4% of English-speaking workers were correct and only 38.6% of the other language groups answered correctly. Overall just over half (53.2%) of respondents knows what "identity theft" is.

In terms of different business functions there were only medium differences recorded in knowledge. Medium effect sizes were noted between the business functions Clerical and Management (d = 0.37); Auditing and Management (d = 0.40); and Patient Care and Management (d = 0.41). What is of significance here is that Management seems to be the common denominator when it comes to knowledge differences in information security concepts. Management have consistently scored higher than the other groups. This may be an indication that information security awareness material should be different for different business function groups. As an additional example to this finding, consider the results of a scenario-type (behavior) question per business function as depicted in Fig. 2.

Respondents had to react to an Income Tax scam scenario. Although 71% of respondents indicated that they would behave in an acceptable and secure manner, it is significant that there are notable differences between business functions, e.g. Patient Care (64.4%) versus Management (78.4%).

The results presented in this section represent only a small extract of the total results of the study. There were also other examples where differences and poor knowledge were recorded. Conversely, there were also a number of results that indicated that healthcare workers do have good knowledge of specific information security concepts and appropriate behavior. The aim was to show that a linguistic approach does offer advantages and that it is possible to use such an approach to collect important

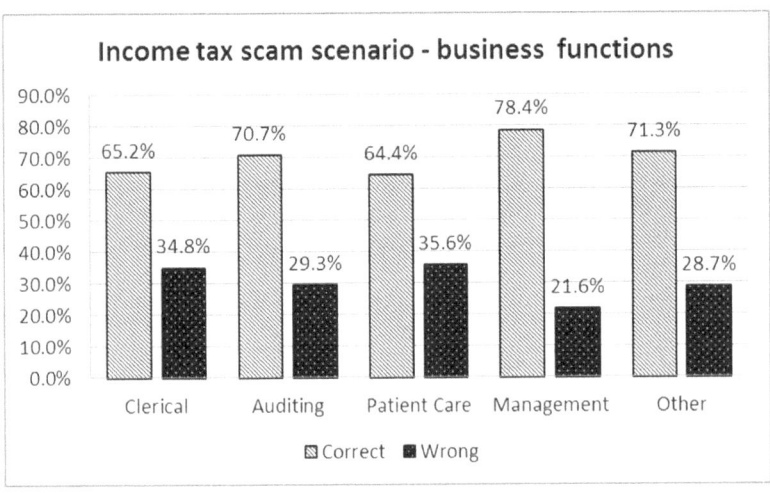

Fig. 2. Scenario-type question

management information pertaining to information security awareness. This study indicates that specific terms and concepts, as well as behavior need to be clarified and should focus on an information security awareness program for at least those healthcare workers who participated in the study. Furthermore, home language and type of work (business function) play a definite role. Certain groups are more prone to risky behavior and certain groups have less information security knowledge. This information is helpful to focus on specific information security topics and concepts, as well as on security-related behavior.

5   Conclusions

Cyberattacks on healthcare organizations are now a fact of life [17]. Healthcare workers depend more and more on healthcare information systems and information security and privacy have become issues of growing importance. This clearly indicates an ongoing need for information security education, and particularly for ensuring high levels of information security awareness among healthcare workers.

This paper presents a linguistic approach, utilizing a vocabulary test, to evaluate healthcare workers' information security levels and to identify possible areas of concern. A vocabulary-measuring instrument was developed and made available to a large South African hospital group with over 29 000 employees. Although positive results were recorded in many instances, the study has shown that potential problem areas exist in terms of different language groups and different business functions. Based on the results it was also concluded that the use of a linguistic approach does offer advantages in information security awareness programs.

Future work may include updating the questionnaire with recent and new threats as the security landscape has a dynamic nature. This survey can also be conducted in other industries for comparative studies.

References

1. Haux, R.: Health information systems – past, present, future. Int. J. Med. Inform. **75**, 268–281 (2006)
2. Appari, A., Johnson, M.E.: Information security and privacy in healthcare: Current State of Research. Center for Digital Strategies Tuck School of Business Dartmouth College (2008)
3. Maseti, O.: A model for role-based security education, training and awareness in the South African healthcare environment. Unpublished M dissertation. Nelson Mandela Metropolitan University (2008)
4. Win, K.T.: A review of security electronic health records. Health Inform. Manage. **34**(1), 13–18 (2005)
5. Meingast, M., Roosta, T., Sastry, S.: Security and privacy issues with health care information technology. In: Proceedings of the 28th IEEE EMBS Annula International Conference, New York City, USA (2006)
6. South Africa.: Protection of Personal Information Act No 4 of 2013. Government gazette, 581:37067, 26 November 2013
7. Medlin, B.D., Cazier, J.A.: Social engineering techniques and password security: two issues relevant in the case of health care workers. IGI Glob. **3**(2), 58–70
8. Van Deursen, N., Buchanan, W.J., Duff, A.: Monitoring information security risks within health care. Comput. Secur. **37**, 31–45 (2014)
9. Appari, A., Johnson, M.E.: Information security and privacy in healthcare: current state of research. Int. J. Internet Enterp. Manage. **6**(4), 279–314 (2010)
10. Fernando, J.L., Dawson, L.L.: The health information system security threat lifecycle: an informatics theory. Int. J. Med. Informatics **78**, 815–826 (2009)
11. Fernandez-Aleman, J.L., Senor, I.C., Lozoya, P.A.O., Toval, A.: Security and privacy in electronic health records: a systematic literature review. J. Biomed. Informatics **46**, 541–562 (2013)
12. Cavalli, E., Mattasoglio, A., Pinciroli, F., Spaggiari, P.: Information security concepts and practices: the case of a provincial multi-specialty hospital. Int. J. Med. Informatics **73**, 297–303 (2004)
13. Janczewski, L., Shi, F.X.: Development of information security baselines for healthcare information systems in New Zealand. Comput. Secur. **21**, 172–192 (2002)
14. Smith, E., Eloff, J.H.P.: Security in health-care information systems – current trends. Int. J. Med. Informatics **54**, 39–54 (1999)
15. Redspin. Breach report 2015: Protected Health Information (PHI). Redspin (2016)
16. Munro, D.: Data breaches in healthcare totaled over 112 million records in 2015. Forbes (2015). http://www.forbes.com/sites/danmunro/2015/12/31/data-breaches-in-healthcare-total-over-112-million-records-in-2015/#1996c0557fd5
17. HIPAA. Major 2016 healthcare data breaches: midyear summary. HIPAA J. (2016). http://www.hipaajournal.com/major-2016-healthcare-data-breaches-mid-year-summary-3499/
18. Ogutcu, G., Testik, O.M., Chouseinoglou, O.: Analysis of personal information security behavior and awareness. Comput. Secur. **56**, 83–93 (2016)
19. Katsikas, S.K.: Health care management and information systems security: awareness, training or education? Int. J. Med. Informatics **60**, 129–135 (2000)
20. Kruger, H.A., Drevin, L., Steyn, T.: A vocabulary test to assess information security awareness. Inform. Manage. Comput. Secur. **18**(5), 316–327 (2010)
21. Fromkin, V.A. (ed.): Linguistics: An introduction to linguistic theory. Fromkin, V.A. Wiley-Blackwell (2001)

22. Jansen van Vuuren, N.: 'n Ondersoek na die gebruik van wiskunde-woordeskat en metakognitiewe strategieë tydens probleemoplossing by Graad 7-leerders. Unpublished M dissertation, North-West University, Potchefstroom (2014)
23. Van der Walt, M.S., Maree, K., Ellis, S.: A mathematics vocabulary questionnaire for use in the intermediate phase. South Afr. J. Educ. **28**, 489–504 (2008)
24. Robinson-Riegler, G., Robinson-Riegler, B.: Cognitive Psychology. Applying the Science of Mind. Pearson, Boston (2008)
25. Van der Walt, M.S.: Aanpassing van die studie oriëntasievraelys in Wiskunde vir gebruik in die intermediêre fase. Unpublished PhD dissertation, North-West University, Potchefstroom (2008)
26. Furnell, S.M., Bryant, P., Phippen, A.D.: Assessing the security perceptions of personal Internet users. Comput. Secur. **26**(5), 410–417 (2007)
27. Kerlinger, F.N.: Foundations of Behavioral Research, 3rd edn. CBS Publishing, Japan (1986)
28. Cohen, J.: Statistical power analysis for the behavioral sciences, 2nd edn. Lawrence Earlbaum Associates, Hillsdale (1988)

Cybersecurity Culture: An Ill-Defined Problem

Noluxolo Gcaza[1,2(✉)] and Rossouw von Solms[1]

[1] Nelson Mandela Metropolitan University, Port Elizabeth, South Africa
S208045801@live.nmmu.ac.za, rossouw@nmmu.ac.za
[2] CSIR, Pretoria, South Africa

Abstract. Cybersecurity necessitates the development of a solution that encourages acceptable user behaviour in the reality of cyberspace. Nowadays, users are considered to be the weakest link in the security chain – due to their insecure behaviour and their lack of awareness. However, even users who possess more cybersecurity awareness are reported to behave no differently from those who lack any form of cybersecurity awareness. Therefore, cultivating a cybersecurity culture is regarded as the best approach for addressing the human factors that weaken the cybersecurity chain. Research focusing on defining and measuring the cybersecurity culture is considered to be lacking. Additionally, there is an apparent lack of widely accepted key concepts that further delimits the culture. Both these assertions suggest that cybersecurity culture is an ill-defined problem. Therefore, this paper will attempt to confirm that cybersecurity culture is an ill-defined problem by means of content analysis. Classifying cybersecurity culture as an ill-defined problem can guide future researchers in what problem-solving processes to employ when addressing the problem of cybersecurity culture.

Keywords: Cybersecurity · Culture · Content analysis · Ill-defined problems

1 Introduction

Cybersecurity needs the development of a cybersecurity culture that encourages acceptable user behaviour in the reality of cyberspace [1]. Cultivating a cybersecurity culture is regarded as the best approach for addressing the human factors that weaken the cybersecurity chain [2]. It has been found that even users who possess more cybersecurity knowledge can behave no differently from those who lack any form of cybersecurity awareness [3]. Regardless, of the fact that the awareness level of the user positively affects the user behaviour, there is still an apparent gap between the user awareness levels and their respective practices and behaviour [4]. Thus, according to van Niekerk [5], in order for a culture to effectively counter the effects of the human factor, user knowledge (awareness and education) and behaviour need to be addressed. Thus, it can be accepted that two of the pillars of cybersecurity culture are awareness and education [6].

While the role of cultivating a culture in pursuing cybersecurity is well-appreciated, research focusing intensely on defining and measuring cybersecurity culture is still in its infancy [7]. Furthermore, studies conducted by Reid and van Niekerk [8, 9] revealed

© IFIP International Federation for Information Processing 2017
Published by Springer International Publishing AG 2017. All Rights Reserved
M. Bishop et al. (Eds.): WISE 10, IFIP AICT 503, pp. 98–109, 2017.
DOI: 10.1007/978-3-319-58553-6_9

that there are no widely accepted key concepts that delimit a cybersecurity culture. Nevertheless, due to the relationship between information security and cybersecurity, it is reasonable to make the assumption that what describes an information security culture should also apply to the cybersecurity culture [10].

It should be noted that there is profound difference information security and cyber-security. However some authors use cybersecurity interchangeably with information security. Ried and Van Niekerk [8] argue that the fundamental difference is that infor-mation security aims to ensure the continuity of business and to limiting the impact of security incidents, in order to minimize business damages. As such, information security is primarily concerned with preserving the information in an organizational context. Cybersecurity, however, extends far beyond the borders of a business, considering that information is shared and disclosed in cyberspace. Therefore, even though a close asso-ciation exists between information security and cybersecurity, there are aspects that fall outside the scope of information security [8].

Nevertheless, Schein [11] defines information security culture as a "pattern of shared basic assumptions that the group learned; as it solved its problems of external adaptation and internal integration, which have worked well enough to be considered valid; and therefore, to be taught to new members, as the correct way to perceive, think, and feel in relation to those problems". Similarly, in information security, Schlienger and Teufel [12] refer to the culture within the organization as that which "should support all [the] activities, in such a way that information security becomes a natural aspect in the daily activities of every employee. Security culture helps to build the necessary trust between the different actors." Both the latter and former information security culture definitions deal with altering the behaviour of users, by instilling a certain way to "naturally behave" in daily life, a way that conforms to certain information security assumptions.

The assertion that research focusing on defining and measuring cybersecurity culture is lacking, as well as a lack of the apparent widely accepted key concepts that delimit the culture, both suggest that cybersecurity culture is an ill-defined problem. With ill-defined problems, the following is true: The information needed to solve the problem is often incomplete or inconsistent; no standard criteria exist to confirm the solutions; and it is uncertain which elements make up the problem, or the solution to the problem [13, 14].

This paper seeks to test the claims that imply that cybersecurity culture an ill-defined problem. In doing so, future researchers addressing cybersecurity culture can be guided in the selection of the problem-solving processes. Hence, this paper reviews the existing literature, focusing specifically on cybersecurity culture, in order to determine the following:

- Does the existing literature acknowledge the need for a cybersecurity culture?
- Does a generally accepted definition of cybersecurity culture exist?
- Does a widely accepted approach for cultivating a cybersecurity culture exist?
- What are the elements that describe a cybersecurity culture?

This paper will attempt to address these questions by means of content analysis. The following section provides a discussion on ill-defined problems. Thereafter, a section entailing the research methodology employed to conduct the content analysis can be found. The section following the research methodology will provide an account of the content analysis on cybersecurity culture; and this is followed by a discussion on the findings. Finally, concluding remarks will be provided.

2 Ill-Defined Problems

The terms "ill-defined" and "ill-structured" are used interchangeably in the literature. To eliminate confusion, this study will adopt the term "ill-defined". Problems are regarded as ill-defined, when "essential concepts, relations, or solution criteria are unspecified or under-specified, open-textured, or intractable, requiring a solver to frame or re-characterize it. This re-characterization, and the resulting solution, [is] subject to debate" [15]. Re-characterization is the process of decomposing the problem into sensible representations. Notably, re-characterization is often inherent in ill-defined problems [15]. In addition to re-characterization, a criterion exists to determine the 'defined' level of a problem [14, 15]. It includes vaguely defined number of goals; incomplete and inaccurate or ambiguous uncertain information; inconsistent relationship between concepts, rules, and principles among cases based on context; multiple solutions, solution paths, or no solution at all; and no one universal agreement on the appropriate solution.

A vaguely defined number of goals relates to the fact that ill-defined problems do not have defined end-states. Moreover, it is often challenging to find all the necessary information that is needed to solve the problem. Ill-defined problems exhibit inconsistency, when considering the concepts and principles that delimit the problem and the rules govern the problem-solving process. Often, there is no standard solution for such problems. Perhaps that is due to the fact that each problem solver re-characterizes the problem from his own unique standpoint and suggests a solution based on that unique perspective. Hence, ill-defined problems lack a single universal solution.

The task of designing a house can be used as an example of an ill-defined problem, particularly in a scenario were the architect is required to be creative and not to use a pre-existing design. In this scenario, the architect is not informed on what the client wants the house to look like on completion. The problem space is ill-defined (referring to the structural elements of the house), the specification of the elements that make up the problem space are unknown (referring to the type of structural elements). Nevertheless, the task of designing a house can easily move to the well-defined end of the problem continuum; if the client makes known the desired end-state of the house. Specifications, such as the number of rooms, the structural specifications, such as a wooden house or brick garage. In this scenario, it can be seen that based on the information that is available, the problem can be rendered ill-defined or well-defined. Thus, an analysis of the existing information can confirm that the cybersecurity culture can be seen as an ill-defined problem.

It can be gathered that what is true for ill-defined problems is in contrast to that of well-defined problems. On the contrary, well-defined problems exhibit characteristics that include a known goal state; a well-defined initial state; and a constrained logical state; constraint parameters; and single correct, convergent answer to reach a satisfactory final solution [14]. Unlike ill-defined problems, well-defined problems have a known end-state. Consequently, a problem-solver approaches the problem with a clear end-goal in mind. Additionally, a well-defined problem has an elaborate initial stage; since all the information about the problem is available to the problem-solver. Furthermore, there is a constraint in all the concepts, rules and cases that form part of the problem space. Lastly, a well-defined problem has a widely acceptable solution [14].

The pursuit to identify a problem as well-defined, or ill-defined, is crucial; because the problem-solving process differs for problems on the different ends of the continuum [16]. According to Voss and Post [17] as well as Sinnott [18] in solving ill-defined problems, a unique problem-solving process is used, compared with that used to address well-defined problems. Simon [14] seems to disagree with this notion; and this author suggests that the question of being ill-defined does not lie on the problem, but rather in the problem-solver. Simon [14] adds that it is the experience of a problem-solver that leads to a problem being deemed well-defined or ill-defined. On the contrary, many authors [17–19] support Reitman [16] in the notion that ill-defined problems require a unique problem-solving process. Generally, when solving a well-defined problem the best solution is selected by anticipating the logical consequences of each [20, 21]. On the contrary, with ill-defined problems the selection of the best solution is guided by the solver's perception of the problem constraints. Thus when solving problems from opposite ends of the continuum – is different the problem solving process differs. Additionally, different techniques are used to solve ill-defined and well-defined problems. For well-defined problems, the techniques are quantitative in nature; whilst for ill-defined problems, the techniques are rather qualitative [22]. Therefore, it is essential for the problem-solver to know the type of problem s/he is dealing with, in order to follow the correct problem-solving process [22].

This section has provided a discussion on ill-defined problems. Additionally, it has contrasted ill-defined and well-defined problems. It has motivated why it is important to categorise a problem as either ill-defined, or well-defined. The following section discussed the methodology that will be used to confirm that cybersecurity culture is indeed an ill-defined problem.

3 Methodology

A content analysis is defined as "a research technique for making replicable and valid inferences from texts (or other meaningful matter) within the context of their use" [23]. Downe-Wambolt [24] describes content analysis as a "research method that provides a systematic and objective means to make valid inferences from verbal, visual, or written data, in order to describe and quantify specific phenomena". The purpose of content analysis is to establish and gather meaning from the text, in order to draw realistic conclusions from the data collected. In the context of this paper, the nature of the analysis will be qualitative; because the data will be presented in words; and the interpretation thereof will be drawn solely from the words [25]. Generally, a three-step process is followed, when conducting a qualitative content analysis. This process includes planning, a data collection, and the data analysis [25].

The qualitative content analysis on cybersecurity culture was carried out in a manner that aligns with the process explained above, with the application thereof being discussed as follows.

Planning. Five elements should be taken into consideration in the planning phase. In the context of the cybersecurity culture analysis, these elements were applied as follows:

Aim. The aim of this content analysis is to confirm that cybersecurity culture is an ill-defined problem.

Sample and unit of analysis. This paper reviewed the literature that explicitly focuses on the cybersecurity culture. For a qualitative content analysis, one to thirty sources are considered sufficient [26]. However, the information needs of the study should govern the number of sources [27]. In the case of this study, however, only thirteen articles were deemed relevant.

The choice of data collection method. The data were collected from online digital libraries. Table 1 has an exhaustive list of the databases that were used.

Table 1. Search strategy

List of sources searched	Search strategy used, including any limits	Total number of results found
1. CSIR worldcat	"cyber security culture"	24 *(3 relevant)*
2. Primo central	"cyber security culture"	9 *(information security)*
3. IEEE	cybersecurity culture	30 *(4 relevant)*
4. Scopus/science direct	(TITLE-ABS-KEY (cyber)ANDTITLE-ABS-KEY (security)ANDTITLE-ABS-KEY (culture))	3
5. Emerald	("Cyber security"W/5culture)	2
6. Springer	("Cyber security"W/5culture)	8
7. EbscoHost	"cyber security culture"	3

Method of analysis. A qualitative content analysis was performed because of the nature of the problem addressed in the paper, namely, a cybersecurity culture.

Ethical considerations. The choice of the data collection method determines whether ethical issues should be considered. This is most likely in methods, such as interviews, focus group and questionnaires. However, in the case of freely available literature, the ethical aspects are not a concern. As such, this issue is not applicable in this inquiry.

The Data Collection. The data were collected from online digital libraries that include CSIR worldcat, Primo central, IEEE, Scopus, Emerald, Springer and EbscoHost. Table 1 contains the search strategies were employed to gather the information.

From the results recorded in the table, in total, only thirteen articles were deemed relevant; because some were duplicated in the sources that were searched. Previously, it was mentioned that only literature that explicitly focuses on cybersecurity culture would be considered. The literature on information security culture, or other related studies were ignored; because if the related studies were included, the sample unit would give a false impression regarding the extent of knowledge that currently exists on the topic at hand. Only peer-reviewed journals and conference articles were considered. The year of publication was not constrained because the aim was to retrieve as much existing information on the topic to date. Additionally, no disciplines were eliminated because the aim was to get information from different contexts.

Data Analysis. This study was deductive in nature; since it is based on a predetermined hypothesis. The hypothesis is that cybersecurity culture is an ill-defined problem. Additionally, the analysis will be based on what is written by the authors – instead of the underlying meaning in the text; thereby, it becomes a manifest analysis.

Report Findings. Sections 4 and 5 provide an account of the findings.

This section discussed the research methodology, the following section provides a review of the existing literature on cybersecurity culture.

4 Cybersecurity Culture Content Analysis

da Veiga [7] focuses on defining cybersecurity culture, in order to be able to measure and quantify the culture. The paper suggests that a cybersecurity culture should ideally be fostered in all levels, including individual, organizational, national and international levels. The author draws insight from the IT discipline, together with industrial psychology, to define cybersecurity culture as "the intentional and unintentional manner, in which cyberspace is utilized from an international, national, organizational or individual perspective in the context of the attitudes, assumptions, beliefs, values, and knowledge of the cyber user.

The cybersecurity culture that emerges becomes the way things are done when interacting in cyberspace; and this can either promote or inhibit the safety, security, privacy, and civil liberties of individuals, organizations or governments." This definition features the description of organizational culture, which is "the way things are done here". Additionally, the paper proposes a cybersecurity culture research methodology (CSeCRM) with the aim to ensure that the culture can be measured. According to the author, the proposed methodology can be potentially used to assist in identifying which actions need to be taken, in order to change and direct a cybersecurity culture.

Malyuk and Miloslovsaya [28] focus on integrating cybersecurity culture in IT professional training courses. The authors argue IT professionals can no longer be predominantly centred on technical cybersecurity measures. According to Malyuk and Miloslovsaya [28] human factors necessitate the integration of cybersecurity culture in the IT profession. Although the paper focuses on the 'cybersecurity' culture, the authors attempted to define 'information' security instead.

Banks [29] studied the impact of leadership on cybersecurity practices in an organizational setting. The paper identifies leadership from senior management as the key to implementing a culture of cybersecurity amongst employees. Banks [29] argues that poor leadership is the weakest link of the cybersecurity chain in organizations; therefore, senior management should be an example and "practise what they preach". According to Banks [29], senior management can demonstrate their leadership by means of security policies and cybersecurity awareness and education programs.

Tziarras [30] focuses on cultivating cybersecurity culture on a global level through multi-levelled collaboration. The paper argues that for a global cybersecurity culture to be formed, there is a need for a multi-levelled management of cybersecurity. As such, Tziarras [30] proposes a framework for the multi-levelled management of cybersecurity culture. The study goes into great depth to evaluate the international cybersecurity implementation. It furthermore attempts to define cybersecurity culture from the concept of strategic culture. According to Tziarras [30], strategic culture only implicates members of a specific nation; therefore it is limited when compared with cybersecurity culture. Even so, the paper draws principles from strategic culture to describe a culture of cybersecurity as "a body of collective – i.e., non-state, sub-national, and national attitudes, patterns of behavior, beliefs, as well as conceptions of (cyber) security, based on the need to secure multiple referent objects against various cyber threats, which would influence [the] cybersecurity strategies."

Reid and van Niekerk [8] sought to discern information security culture from a cybersecurity culture. A literature review on both domains was done, in order to expose any seeming similarities and differences. The authors reported that cybersecurity culture was under researched. The authors suggest that due to the relationship between information security and cybersecurity, insights from an information security culture could be extrapolated to define a cybersecurity culture. As such, the authors discuss cybersecurity culture by using the same principles that delineate information security. However, Reid and van Niekerk [8] argue that the context of information security and cybersecurity differ; therefore, practical implementation would also differ when applying some of the extrapolated principles.

Kortjan and von Solms [31] focus on establishing a national cybersecurity culture in a South African context. Firstly, the paper discusses what constitutes a cybersecurity culture from international sources that include the ITU and OECD. From these sources, the authors reason that awareness and education are key instruments in establishing the culture. Hence, the study proposes cybersecurity awareness and education guidelines that are drawn from an existing campaign in SA.

Reid and van Niekerk [9] examine how education can be used to foster a cybersecurity culture. The aim of the paper is to establish a standard approach in structuring a culture fostering an education campaign. The authors address the aim by reviewing an existing campaign in SA. The study revealed the following four lessons. Firstly, the manner in which educational material is distributed impacts how/if the message is received. Secondly, the involvement of teachers with the cybersecurity campaign is crucial; as it encourages the participation of learners. Thirdly, for a campaign to be reliable and memorable to its intended target audience, official and age-appropriate branding is necessary. Finally, the content of the campaign should be appropriate and continuously improved.

Luiijf, Basseling and Graaf [32] study and compare nineteen national cybersecurity strategies from eighteen different nations across the globe. The paper reveals the differences and the similarities found in how nations address cybersecurity. From the analysis, a list of recommendations are made to assist other nations in developing national cybersecurity strategies. Amongst other things that can be gathered from the analysis, there is the fact that only three national strategies: from Uganda, South Africa and Romania, explicitly list cultivating a cybersecurity culture, as a strategic objective. Primarily, the contribution of the paper is a basic structure for developing a cybersecurity policy.

Hall [33] examines the importance of humans in the cybersecurity process in an organizational setting. This author identifies employees as the "greatest source of weakness in the cybersecurity effort [or] plan". The author emphasizes that in any cybersecurity plan, organizations should take cognizance of the vulnerabilities that employees bring about. The paper advocates a culture of cybersecurity amongst all the employees. According to Hall [33], the culture will, over time, create an environment where employees implement cybersecurity practices without resentment.

Kritzinger and von Solms [34] attempt to address the major cyber safety concerns in the African continent. According to these authors, the major cybersecurity concerns are the lack of focused research on cybersecurity, the lack of a legal framework and policies, the lack of cybersecurity awareness and the lack of technical security measures. With these four concerns in mind, the paper proposes a framework that consists of four dimensions. These dimensions entail a combination of all possible solutions to the cybersecurity concerns. The authors suggest that the proposed framework is crucial in enhancing a cybersecurity culture in Africa.

Ghernouti-Hélie [35] analyses the "characteristics and issues related to the deployment of a national cybersecurity strategy in an interconnected world". The paper reviews the components of cybersecurity national strategies. It emphasizes the importance of operational structures to support the deployment of such strategies. Additionally, the paper stresses the importance of a cybersecurity culture in supporting a cybersecurity strategy. The author identifies education and awareness as "pillars of a cybersecurity culture". From an educational point of view, the paper focuses on formal education to build human capacities. From an awareness point of view, the author focuses on end-users, policy-makers, and on the professionals in various disciplines.

Adelola, Dawson and Batmaz [36] have attempted to establish the need for an Internet security awareness programme in Nigeria. The authors examine Internet security awareness programmes in developed countries for the purpose of deducing principles that can be used by Nigeria in establishing a cybersecurity awareness and education campaign. These countries include the US and the UK; additionally, the authors review the existing guidelines that aid the development of an awareness programme. The paper gives an extensive account of a framework developed by the National Institute of Standards and Technology (NIST). According to the authors, this campaign should enable a cybersecurity culture in Nigeria amongst all the cyberspace users.

Batteau [37] studies safety culture and corporate culture in defining a cybersecurity culture in an organizational context. The article suggests that critical to such a culture is the concept of trust, in relation to identification and authentication. The article goes to great length to motivate that trust is essential in cultivating a culture; because those who subscribe to a particular culture are linked by the perception and belief that "they are in this together". Additionally, the lack of trust amongst people (referring to the confidence in the actions and intentions of others) leads to compromised security in an organization. With trust in mind, the author describes cybersecurity culture as follows: "A culture of cybersecurity is a complex amalgamation of generalized transactional and strategic trust relationships. This culture cannot be designed, in the sense that an engineer designs a complex piece of machinery; but it can be cultivated, in the sense that a gardener cultivates a flower garden".

5   Summary of the Results

This section provides the results of the qualitative content analysis in Table 2. The results are analysed using the research questions stated in Sect. 1. Thus the coding scheme for the analysis is extrapolated from research questions.

Table 2. Content analysis summary

Study	Mentions importance of cybersecurity culture	Provides a definition of cybersecurity culture	Proposes an approach to cultivate cybersecurity culture	Delimits the elements that make up a cybersecurity culture
da Veiga [7]	✓	✓		
Malyuk and Miloslovsaya [28]	✓		✓	
Banks [29]	✓		✓	
Tziarras [30]	✓	✓	✓	
Reid and van Niekerk [8]	✓			
Kortjan and von Solms [31]	✓		✓	
Reid and van Niekerk [9]	✓		✓	
Luiijf, Basseling and Graaf [32]	✓			
Hall [33]	✓			
Kritzinger and S. von Solms [34]	✓			
Ghernouti-Hélie [35]	✓			✓
Adelola, Dawson and Batmaz [36]	✓		✓	
Batteau [37]	✓	✓		

A total of thirteen sources were included as part of the content reviewed in this paper. Table 2 presents a summary of the results. The results show that all of the included sources acknowledge the importance of cultivating a cybersecurity culture. Additionally, only three of the reviewed sources define cybersecurity culture. The definitions all differ; because they are established from different concepts that were deemed fitting for each author, i.e. security culture and/or corporate culture, as well as strategic culture. Only six sources proposed an approach to cultivate cybersecurity culture. The sources regard one, or a combination of the following measures, as the means to cultivate the culture: Awareness Programs; Formal Education; Cybersecurity Policies; Collaboration. Furthermore, only one source delimits the elements that potentially make up a culture. The source identifies Awareness and Education, as the pillars of the culture.

From the results presented above, six observations can be made. Firstly, judging from the number of articles that explicitly focus on cybersecurity culture, it can be confirmed that research in this area is currently lacking. Secondly, the need for a cybersecurity culture is well appreciated. Thirdly, even though there is acknowledgment of the need for a cybersecurity culture, there is no single standard solution for cultivating the culture. Fourthly, no criteria to measure the validity of the proposed approaches can be found. Fifthly, the definition of cybersecurity culture is subject to the authors' context of application; and it is established from a range of relevant concepts, according to the authors' perspective. This approach, when defining a subject, is known as re-characterization, which is inherent in ill-defined problems. Finally, the elements that make up a cybersecurity culture are still to be defined.

According to the primary objective of this paper, the first and last observation confirm the assertions that research focusing on defining and measuring cybersecurity culture is considered to be lacking. Additionally, there is an apparent lack of widely accepted key concepts that delimit the culture. It was suggested that these claims indicate that cybersecurity culture is still an ill-defined problem. The findings from the analysis show that research focusing specifically on cybersecurity culture is currently lacking, this observation relates to incomplete and uncertain information as per the characteristics of ill-defined problems. Additionally, the findings show that there is no single standard solution for cultivating the cybersecurity culture, as such this relates to the lack of a universal agreement on the appropriate solution. Furthermore, the fact that the definition of cybersecurity culture is subject to the authors' perspective and context of application illustrates that there are inconsistent relationships between concepts, rules, and principles among cases based on context. Thus, when contrasting the observations against the characteristics of an ill-defined problem, it may be concluded that a cybersecurity culture can be classified as an ill-defined problem.

6 Conclusion

To effectively ensure cybersecurity, a supplementary method to complement the technical measures is required. Such a method should holistically address the human factors. This approach is recognized as a cybersecurity culture. Cultivating a culture is acknowledged as a paramount effort in ensuring cybersecurity; however, what defines a cybersecurity culture is still unclear in the research community. Thus, this study sought to classify cybersecurity culture as an ill-defined problem by means of qualitative content analysis.

It was said that classifying cybersecurity culture as ill-defined would contribute to future research by guiding future researchers in what problem-solving processes to employ, when addressing the problems of a cybersecurity culture.

The study is limited; in that it does not suggest suitable problem-solving processes for cybersecurity culture. However, it does hint on some qualitative approaches. The study is part of a large research project that ultimately attempts to define the cybersecurity security culture problem space; and it proposes an inclusive approach for cultivating the culture.

References

1. International Telecommunication Union: Global Security Report (2008)
2. Van Niekerk, J.F., Von Solms, R.: Information security culture: a management perspective. Comput. Secur. **29**, 476–486 (2010)
3. Al-shehri, Y.: Information security awareness and culture. Br. J. Arts Soc. Sci. **6**(1), 61–69 (2012)
4. Furnell, S.: End-user security culture: a lesson that will never be learnt? Comput. Fraud Secur. **4**, 6–9 (2008)
5. Van Niekerk, J., Von Solms, R.: Understanding information security culture: a conceptual framework. In: Proceedings of the ISSA 2006, pp. 1–10 (2006)
6. Kortjan, N., Von Solms, R.: A conceptual framework for cybersecurity awareness and education in SA. S. Afr. Comput. J. **52**, 29–41 (2014)
7. da Veiga, A.: A cyber- security culture research philosopy and approach to develop a valid and reliable measuring instrument. In: SAI Computing Conference 2016, p. 10 (2016)
8. Reid, R., van Niekerk, J.: From information security to cyber security cultures organizations to societies. In: Information Security for South Africa (ISSA), pp. 1–7 (2014)
9. Reid, R., van Niekerk, J.: Towards an education campaign for fostering a societal, cyber security culture. In: Proceedings of the Eighth International Symposium on Human Aspects of Information Security & Assurance (HAISA 2014), pp. 174–184 (2014)
10. Gcaza, N., Von Solms, R., Van Vuuren, J.: An ontology for a national cyber-security culture environment. In: Proceedings of the Ninth International Symposium on Human Aspects of Information Security & Assurance (HAISA 2015), pp. 1–10 (2015)
11. Schein, E.: Organizational culture and leadership, 2nd edn. Jossey-Bass, San Francisco (1992). (2nd ed. Jossey- Bass; 1992)
12. Schlienger, T., Teufel, S.: Information security culture – from analysis to change. In: Security in the Information Society, pp. 191–201 (2002)
13. Wood, K.P.: Inquiring systems and problem structure: implications for cognitive development. Hum. Dev. **26**, 249–265 (1983)
14. Simon, H.A.: The structure of ill-structured problems. Artif. Intell. **4**, 181–201 (1973)
15. Lynch, C., Ashley, K.D., Pinkwart, N., Aleven, V.: Concepts, structures, and goals: redefining ill-definedness. Int. J. Artif. Intell. Educ. **19**(3), 253–266 (2009)
16. Reitman, W.: Cognition and Thought. Wiley Publishing, New York (1965)
17. Voss, J., Post, T.: On the solving of ill-structured problems. In: The Nature of Expertise. Lawrence Erlbaum, New Jersey (1988)
18. Sinnott, J.D.: A Model for Solution of Ill-Structured Problems: Implications for Everyday and Abstract Problem Solving. Praeger, New York (1989)
19. Wood, K.P.: A secondary analysis of claims regarding the reflective judgment interview: internal consistency, sequentially and intra-individual differences in ill-structured problem solving. In: Annual Meeting of the American Educational Research Association (1994)
20. Bransford, J., Stein, B.: The IDEAL Problem Solver: A Guide for Improving Thinking, Learning, and Creativity. W.H. Freeman, New York (1983)
21. Newell, A., Simon, H.A.: Human problem solving. **104**(9) (1972)
22. Hong, N.S.: Well-structured and Ill-structured. The Pennsylvania State University (1998)

23. Krippendor, K.: Content Analysis: An Introduction to Its Methodology. SAGE Publications, Thousand Oaks (2004)
24. Downe-Wambolt, B.: Content analysis: method, applications and issues. Health Care Women Int. **13**, 313–321 (1992)
25. Bengtsson, M.: How to plan and perform a qualitative study using content analysis. NursingPlus Open **2**, 8–14 (2016)
26. Fridlund, B., Hildingh, C.: Health and qualitative analysis methods. In: Qualitative Research, Methods in the Service of Health, pp. 13–25. Studentlitteratur, Lund (2000)
27. Patton, M.Q.: Qualitative, Research & Evaluation Methods. SAGE Publications, California (2002)
28. Malyuk, A., Miloslavskaya, N.: Cybersecurity culture as an element of IT professional training. In: 3rd International Conference on Digital Information Processing, Data Mining, and Wireless Communications, DIPDMWC 2016, pp. 205–210 (2016)
29. Banks, N.: Practise what you preach. Comput. Fraud Secur. **2016**(4), 5–8 (2016)
30. Tziarras, Z.: The security culture of a global and multi-levelled cybersecurity. In: Carayannis, E.G., Campbell, D.F.J., Efthymiopoulos, M.P. (eds.) Cyber-Development, Cyber-Democracy Cyber-Defense Challenges, Opportunities and Implications for Theory, Policy and Practice, pp. 319–335. Springer, New York (2014)
31. Kortjan, N., von Solms, R.: Fostering a cyber security culture: a case of South Africa. In: Proceedings of the 14th Annual Conference on World Wide Web Applications, November 2012
32. Luiijf, E., Besseling, K., De Graaf, P.: Nineteen national cybersecurity strategies. Int. J. Crit. Infrastruct. **9**(1–2), 3–31 (2013)
33. Hall, M.: Why people are key to cybersecurity. Netw. Secur. **2016**(6), 9–10 (2016)
34. Kritzinger, E., von Solms, S.: A framework for cyber security in Africa. J. Inf. Assur. Cybersecur. **2012**, 1–10 (2012)
35. Ghernouti-Hélie, S.: A national strategy for an effective cybersecurity approach and culture. In: 2010 International Conference on Availability, Reliability and Security, pp. 370–373 (2010)
36. Adelola, T., Dawson, R., Batmaz, F.: The urgent need for an enforced awareness programme to create internet security awareness in Nigeria. In: Proceedings of the 17th International Conference on Information Integration and Web-based Applications & Services - iiWAS 2015, pp. 1–7 (2015)
37. Batteau, A.W.: Creating a culture of enterprise cybersecurity. Int. J. Bus. Anthropol. **2**(2), 36–47 (2011)

A Study into the Cybersecurity Awareness Initiatives for School Learners in South Africa and the UK

Elmarie Kritzinger[1], Maria Bada[2], and Jason R.C. Nurse[3(✉)]

[1] School of Computing, University of South Africa, Pretoria, South Africa
kritze@unisa.ac.za
[2] Global Cyber Security Capacity Centre, University of Oxford, Oxford, UK
maria.bada@cs.ox.ac.uk
[3] Department of Computer Science, University of Oxford, Oxford, UK
jason.nurse@cs.ox.ac.uk

Abstract. This research reports on a study into the cybersecurity awareness initiatives for school learners in South Africa and the UK, which are supported by government, industry and academia. Furthermore, this article provides an overview of similarities and differences between initiatives across countries, and posits as to the reasons why they may exist. The research concludes by presenting recommendations for both countries to improve school cybersecurity initiatives.

Keywords: Cybersecurity · Awareness · Children · Nation states

1 Introduction

The impact of cyberspace on society is indisputable. These technologies have permeated every area of our lives and are used to support a vast range of activities, from communication to gaming, business and trade. As these technologies have increased in usage, however, so too has their attractiveness to online predators (e.g. criminals, hackers and child groomers) and their use for unethical and illicit activities (e.g. cyber stalking, illegal trade) [1]. This is a significant security and privacy challenge for society in general, but is especially poignant given the number of children using the Web, and the hours that they spend online.

In a recent study for instance, it was found that 7 to 16-year-olds spend about three hours online daily, but this figure rises to almost five hours when the age range 15 to 16-year-olds are considered in isolation [2]. Moreover, the study found that 67% of youngsters owned a tablet device with access to the Internet. Ownership is a key factor here because it raises the question of whether parents check or even have access (e.g. a security code) to the device. Given the high likelihood that young children are unaware of the various threats online,

M. Bishop et al. (Eds.): WISE 10, IFIP AICT 503, pp. 110–120, 2017.
DOI: 10.1007/978-3-319-58553-6_10

they are immediately at an increased risk and highly susceptible to attack. This fact has been emphasised by several studies in practice and across academia [3].

This paper focuses on the topic of children's safety and security online, by reflecting critically on some of the existing cybersecurity awareness initiatives for school learners. The research focuses on the awareness efforts present (or absent) in schools and the reasons for these. Firstly, given that school is compulsory in a majority of countries, it would be one of the best places for awareness training to be provided. There is also the reality that children will be online at school or at home (e.g. browsing or on social media), and as such will be at risk; this is especially true with the vast range of security and privacy risks on the horizon [4].

To set the context for our research, we investigate the cybersecurity awareness initiatives for school learners in South Africa and the United Kingdom (UK). These countries were selected because they would allow us to explore and compare the current state of initiatives in a developed, and a developing, nation. Whilst one would expect developing countries to be more advanced, there is still the question of how much more exactly; also, how do culture, society and industry play a part in these initiatives? Some school awareness research was conducted in respect of these countries separately especially in South Africa [5,6], but efforts were neither aimed at investigating the complete set of initiatives, nor did they attempt to present actionable recommendations for the range of key stakeholders. This current article seeks to add the most value to existing research by focusing on the current state of initiatives in both countries and reflect on how factors such as culture might define that state.

The remainder of this paper is structured as follows. Section 2 reflects on the relevant research and practice in cybersecurity safety for school learners. This section highlights the range of cyber risks affecting school learners, before continuing to identify the main types of awareness initiatives that may be present in schools. Section 3 considers the current situation as it relates to cybersecurity awareness initiatives for school learners in South Africa and the UK respectively. Section 4 first discusses the key similarities and differences across the two countries before then presenting recommendations for parents, schools and government on how to improve awareness initiatives. Finally we conclude the article in Sect. 5.

2 Background

2.1 Cybersecurity/Safety for School Learners

In today's world, school learners grow up within an Information and Communication Technology (ICT) environment and become technology users from their early years. ICTs are integrated in all aspects of their daily lives and are used for the purpose of education, socialising, gaming and information gathering. Recent studies have shown that a growing number of school learners have access to technologies, including devices such as mobile (cell) phones, tablets and desktops [3,7].

The number of ICT users is growing each year due to the decrease in the cost of devices, increase in access to networks and higher network bandwidth. Another factor to consider is the significant growth of users that have access to mobile devices. Currently, there are more mobile phones in the world than people and 40% of the world's population have access to the Internet [8]. One group of ICT users who are becoming cyber citizens in their own right are school learners (i.e. school children between the age of 8 and 18) [9].

On the one hand, access to cyberspace provides school learners with a wide range of advantages and benefits which include socialising, access to information and improving their education. On the other hand, however, cyberspace is an unregulated and dangerous platform and school learners could easily fall victim to a range of cyber risks and attacks [10]. Next, we expand on the dangers that school learners may face and discuss a number of the cybersecurity risks present in the online space.

2.2   Cyber Risks Affecting School Learners/Youth

There are a number of cyber risks and threats connected to cyberspace that may have a short- and long-term impact on the social, physical and emotional well-being of school learners [11]. According to Stone [7], cyber risks for school learners can be divided into three main categories as depicted in Table 1.

Table 1. Main cyber risk categories (according to Stone [7])

Individuals' intention to harm the learner	Learners' exposure to harmful online interactions	Learner places her-/himself in a harmful situation
Cyber bullying: trolling, flaming, excluding, masquerading, mobbing, denigrating, outing, harassing, cyber grooming, impersonation, blackmail, cyber snooping, identity theft, social engineering, online predators	Inappropriate content/material, digital reputation ruin, social platforms and chat rooms, viruses, malware, cookies	Illegal file sharing, plagiarism, inappropriate posting online, free downloads, copyright infringements, non-ethical postings of others' material, sexting

Some research has argued that a more youth-centred approach to cybersecurity is long overdue [9]. It is vital that school learners understand their responsibility in protecting themselves and their information in cyberspace. Other cyber-related issues to be dealt with include: protecting passwords; managing privacy settings; adhering to cyber etiquette; meeting in real life people you initially met online; age-appropriateness and digital footprint. School learners should be encouraged and equipped to take responsibility for their own cybersecurity through effective awareness programmes and education.

Considering this wide range of issues, a consolidated awareness approach is needed to enable school learners to gain the knowledge and skills in order to safely interact while in cyberspace. In the next section, our article progresses from theory to practice, and examines the cybersecurity awareness initiatives that have been developed in two countries to educate and protect school learners.

3   Current Situation in South Africa and the UK

To scope our current study, we have decided to focus on the cybersecurity awareness initiatives in the developing nation of South Africa and the developed state of the UK. Our work seeks to provide an overview of the various types of initiatives and identify the different sectors (government, industry, academia or education/schools) that drive these initiatives. This therefore supplies the foundation for the detailed comparison and the recommendations provided in Sect. 4. The methodology that we adopt for our study involves a thorough search and review of existing initiatives in South Africa and the UK, including those present on the web as well as digital and print media. Following this, we critically reflect on these initiatives, their aims, and the sectors which drive them.

To briefly summarise our study's findings, we discovered that South Africa has an understanding of the relevance and importance of cybersecurity awareness for school learners. There are some clear indications of attempts to raise cybersecurity awareness and to establish an effective cybersecurity culture in South Africa. With respect to the UK, several initiatives and programmes are currently being organised to raise cybersecurity awareness, covering various target groups of society, including school learners. These are generally coordinated by the UK's National Cybersecurity Strategy [12]. When it comes to initiatives focusing specifically on school children, it was noticed that some efforts are

Table 2. Cybersecurity initiatives in South Africa and UK

Initiatives	South Africa	UK
School curriculum	Academia	Government, industry
School workbooks	Academia	Government, industry, academia
Teacher training	–	Government, industry
School ICT policies and procedure	Government, schools	Schools
Incident handling process in schools	–	–
Awareness material (posters, brochures)	Academia, industry	Government, industry
Parent involvement projects	Schools	Government, industry
One-off initiatives (open days, talks, workshops)	Academia, schools, industry	Government, academia
Web presence	Industry, academia, government	Government, industry
Traditional media presence	Government, industry, academia	Government, industry
Legislation, policy or regulation on cybersecurity in schools	Government	Government

in place. Furthermore, the public and private sector, academia as well as the schools, are working to establish a cybersecurity culture for school learners.

In Table 2 we present our findings including the initiatives currently being undertaken and their main proponents in both countries.

4   Reflections and Recommendations

In this section, we reflect on, and present, the key similarities and differences in cybersecurity initiatives in South Africa and the UK. Our approach to this task involved reviewing the data gathered on initiatives and critically comparing the findings from both countries. Based on this reflection, we then sought to identify recommendations for each country on how awareness efforts may be improved.

4.1   Key Similarities and Differences

In reflecting on the initiatives in both countries, several similarities and differences were identified. With respect to the similarities, it was commendable to find that both countries are making noteworthy efforts to increase cybersecurity awareness in schools and institutions nationwide. This demonstrates an understanding of the range of threats and cyber risks that school learners, in particular, and society in general, are facing. The cybersecurity awareness initiatives that were identified cover areas such as learner training and educational materials (e.g. workbooks and posters by SACSAA, Childnet, the Digital Wildfires project), as well as a range of activities (e.g. one-off workshops and talks by academia and industry) intended to highlight the risks of cyberspace [13–15]. A few of these initiatives (e.g. Digital Wildfires) have been targeted at specific age-groups to ensure maximum impact once released.

Our research also found that industry played a crucial part in raising awareness among school learners in both countries. In South Africa, the Internet Safety Campaign (ISC) [16] has developed several online resources, and in the UK a plethora of initiatives have been launched, with the UK Safer Internet Centre, the Mobile Industry Crime Action Forum, and the TechFuture Partnership all being involved. Industry involvement is ideal as they contribute expertise and information on a range of current and future technologies.

School-driven programmes were also encountered in our study. This was significant as it demonstrated schools' keenness on promoting cybersecurity and e-safety, even if it was not an obligatory part of their charters. One slight difference here was that whilst e-safety school policies appear to be popular in the UK, uptake in South Africa seemed limited to schools with greater access to funding. This is somewhat understandable given the context of the two nations (a developed versus a developing state). It is encouraging, however, to witness that whenever funding is available, cybersecurity and e-safety awareness appear to be topics that are considered.

Although there are a number of similarities between South Africa and the UK, there are also several differences. To start, the UK government has made a significantly larger effort to incorporate cybersecurity awareness in all parts of society. Initiatives range from national awareness programmes such as Cyber Aware (formerly Cyber Streetwise) and GetSafeOnline to ensuring that cybersecurity awareness is included in the school curriculum. Overall, the contribution by government is possibly the largest difference between the status of cybersecurity in the two countries. By targeting the curriculum and providing a variety of resources to support school learners and teachers (including specific training), the UK is ensuring that its approach stands the best chance of success.

Some of the awareness efforts from the UK mentioned above can be witnessed in South Africa (e.g. ISC, within industry), but they are not as concentrated, organised or detailed. Also, important areas such as teacher training have not received much attention thus far. While both countries boast a number of initiatives led by industry, the drive by industry-based consortiums in the UK is so substantial that they rival the initiatives of the government in South Africa. This is less than ideal from a government perspective, because contributions by industry often do not last in the long term. There are also questions about the true effectiveness of such programmes if they have not been properly planned or coordinated.

One notable area where South Africa leads the way is in its emphasis on academic research in cybersecurity awareness in schools and in the provision of learning and educational materials. Academics from SACSAA have contributed significantly to the body of research knowledge, and have engaged in the curriculum design for cybersecurity education, workbooks, posters, workshops and school visits. Conversely, academia in the UK does not appear to be involved as much (barring work by the Digital Wildfires group), nor in the efforts towards supporting national awareness campaigns. There is undoubtedly insight from research that could be beneficial in designing and executing such campaigns.

Moreover, the SACSAA workbooks in South Africa are available in multiple languages and through the alliance there are multiple opportunities for outreach in schools and communities. UK academics are involved with outreach (e.g. CAS [17]), but only a few efforts are undertaken towards the creation of workbooks and educational materials. This lack of focus may, however, be the result of the variety of programmes offered by government and industry.

One last point to note about the initiatives adopted by both countries is the influence that culture has had on their design. To consider the UK's GetSafeOnline campaign and the Parents' Corner Campaign in South Africa as examples, it clearly indicates the emphasis on an individualistic approach in the UK (i.e. getting people to think of online security as their own responsibility), whereas in South Africa the emphasis is more on a collective approach (i.e. it is everyone's responsibility to protect one another and society). This is a factor highlighted before (e.g. see [18]), and it can still be noticed in the way that campaigns are designed and conducted. This demonstrates the importance of culture as an overriding factor that should not be ignored.

4.2   Recommendations

From our reflection on the practices of each country, it became clear that both countries have engaged in efforts towards building and enhancing their cybersecurity initiatives within the school environment. There are some areas, however, where improvements can be made and countries can learn from good practice. Below, we present some brief recommendations based on areas where we felt the most value could be added.

Recommendations for South Africa: To consider the case of South Africa first, there is a noteworthy start to the process of ensuring cybersecurity among school learners. Some recommendations for a national plan to improve cybersecurity within the school environment are:

1. Create a national school plan that describes how cybersecurity will be addressed to improve the awareness efforts of all school learners and teachers.
2. Ensure that all schools will implement an ICT policy that includes cybersecurity. This ICT policy must be provided to schools by the relevant government department and must be standardised for all schools.
3. Ensure that all ICT policies in schools are implemented with regular monitoring and evaluation.
4. Provide schools with a clear cybersecurity incident-handling protocol. This protocol should include the details of all the participating organisations that can assist when cyber incidents occur.
5. Provide training for all teachers regarding the following: (a) Cybersecurity awareness for school learners; (b) Age appropriateness for school learners regarding selective topics; and (c) Incident-handling methods if the safety or security of a school learner has been compromised.
6. Collaborate with industry and academia in order to supply the necessary resources for providing cybersecurity education and training for teachers.
7. Establish and implement a parent involvement plan that would allow them to assist with cybersecurity awareness efforts and training.
8. Ensure nationwide exposure to cybersecurity (through social media, traditional media, workshops, open days, posters, and brochures).
9. Create and integrate a cybersecurity curriculum into the national school curriculum. This recommendation aims to incorporate cybersecurity within the "Life Skills" section of the curriculum.
10. Develop awareness-raising programmes, courses and online resources for target demographics, such as school learners, parents and teachers.
11. Involve academia, civil society, and the public and private sector in the development of awareness-raising programmes.
12. Circulate comprehensive and tailored workbooks (including educator guides) that can be used in schools.

For all recommendations mentioned above, the responsibility lies primarily with the government, and particularly the Department of Basic Education, which is ultimately responsible for the school system within the country. Secondary, all schools themselves should be responsible for the implementation and monitoring of policies, procedures and measures set by government departments. It is therefore vital that both the government and schools commit to working together to improve cyber safety. Lastly, industry and academia should provide the requisite assistance to these other sectors to facilitate the transfer of knowledge, skills, tools and research. This would ensure that the recommendations are properly and effectively created, implemented and monitored.

The main focus point to improve cyber safety awareness is to ensure that a national cyber safety skills and capacity building project is provided to all role-players including government employees and teachers. The starting point to improve cyber safety awareness in schools is to "teach the teachers".

Recommendations for the UK: To enhance the existing efforts of the UK, the following steps are recommended:

1. Maintain and expand the existing awareness programmes (and campaigns) to identify and cover specific target groups.
2. Ensure a strong link between awareness efforts and the national cybersecurity strategy.
3. Enact evaluation measurements to study the effectiveness of the awareness programme in schools at a level where they inform future campaigns (taking into account gaps or failures).
4. Continue to promote a high multi-stakeholder engagement in the design of awareness campaigns, including in academia and civil society.
5. Encourage the private sector to also provide awareness education in order to promote the safe use of their offered services.

A key positive in the UK is that education offerings in cybersecurity range from primary to postgraduate. The Programmes of Study for Primary and Secondary education were published by the Department for Education in 2013 [19]. Internet safety is included in the Programmes of Study for all Key Stages to help ensure that young people are using technology safely. The various projects have been developed in collaboration with key industry partners who provide business cases and ideas for each, and supply industry resources and software for students to use. That being said, concerns have been expressed about whether these offerings are aligned with practical cybersecurity and operational challenges [20]. The government promotes partnerships with various sectors in order to enhance the education of teachers, but still not all teachers are trained in cybersecurity issues. To improve the level of capacity, we also recommend the following:

1. Create compulsory cybersecurity modules for students and teachers.
2. Develop effective metrics to ensure that educational investments meet the needs of the cybersecurity environment.
3. Cultivate partnerships for the development of interfaces to research and innovation and for interaction between universities and the local economy.
4. Develop a centralised platform to share guidance with teachers and parents.

The findings of this research indicate that through the take-up of these recommendations, the state of cybersecurity awareness of school learners in particular and of the UK in general, will be greatly enhanced. Both the Government of the UK and industry already collaborate to establish programmes for enhancing skills and capability in cybersecurity, while national education and skills priorities are informed by broad multi-stakeholder consultation. However, in order to enhance the existing capacity cybersecurity awareness needs to be engrained through all stages of education not only for school learners but also for teachers.

Furthermore, investments should be made both by the public and private sector but also by academia into effective metrics that will ensure that educational offerings meet the needs of the cybersecurity environment. An important step towards this goal would be forming working groups comprised by stakeholders from the public and private sector, academics as well as law enforcement representatives, exploring metrics of effectiveness. Currently, the effectiveness of such existing measurements is often limited due to difficulties in reporting cybercrime. Finally, as mentioned above, the development of a central platform for sharing information and requirements for cybersecurity training provided to teachers and parents can lead to better coordination of the existing efforts.

5   Conclusion

While cyberspace has provided society with a range of opportunities, several risks are associated with it. This is especially the case for younger individuals who may be unaware or too naive to recognise the seriousness of the threat. In this paper, we focused on the topic of school learners' safety and security online, and reflected critically on the existing cybersecurity awareness initiatives. The scope of our work was limited to South Africa and the UK, as we aimed to understand the state of initiatives in a developing and a developed country. This allowed us to assess the levels of maturity in these countries in terms of their awareness programmes, but also to consider the impact of culture and society.

Through our in-depth analysis of South Africa and the UK, we found numerous awareness efforts in play. Both countries boast initiatives launched by the main national sectors (government, industry, academia and schools), with the main difference in the maturity of these initiatives. Given the status of the countries, in some instances this was understandable as the UK government has taken greater effort with awareness in schools. However, in other cases, our findings were unexpected (e.g. in South Africa, academia was considerably more involved in supporting awareness efforts).

Having reflected on the initiatives in each country, this paper set about providing recommendations on how to enhance cybersecurity awareness efforts among school learners. In South Africa, these recommendations concentrated on building capacity for awareness in each sector, whilst in the UK the goal was more towards ensuring concerted awareness efforts that were ingrained and measurable. The conclusion of the research proposes the crucial steps in going forward to ensure that school learners are prepared for the cyber risks and threats that they face on a daily basis. Implementing the proposed recommendations will also have follow-on benefits for the country's economy, given that these learners are the next generation of workers. Future research should focus on similar analysis in different cultural environments in order to identify best practice when it comes to achieving cybersecurity awareness for school learners. Moreover, quantitative work could be conducted to determine the efficacy of the various aspects of these awareness initiatives.

References

1. Symantec Corporation: Internet security threat report (2016). https://www.symantec.com/security-center/threat-report
2. BBC: Time spent online 'overtakes TV' among youngsters (2016). http://www.bbc.co.uk/news/education-35399658
3. Livingstone, S., Smith, P.K.: Annual research review: harms experienced by child users of online and mobile technologies. J. Child Psychol. Psychiatr. **55**(6), 635–654 (2014)
4. Nurse, J.R.C.: Exploring the risks to identity security and privacy in cyberspace. ACM XRDS: Crossroads Mag. **21**(3), 42–47 (2015)
5. Reid, R., Niekerk, J.V.: Snakes and ladders for digital natives: information security education for the youth. Inf. Man. Comput. Secur. **22**(2), 179–190 (2014)
6. Kritzinger, E.: Enhancing cyber safety awareness among school children in South Africa through gaming. In: Science and Information Conference (SAI), pp. 1243–1248. IEEE (2015)
7. Stone, K.: Keeping children and young people safe online: balancing risk and opportunity. Key Messages (2013). http://withscotland.org/download/keeping-children-and-young-people-safe-online-balancing-risk-and-opportunity
8. Boren, J.: There are officially more mobile devices than people in the world (2014). http://www.independent.co.uk/life-style/gadgets-and-tech/news/there-are-officially-more-mobile-devices-than-people-in-the-world-9780518.html
9. Miles, D.: Youth protection: digital citizenship-principles & new resources. In: 2011 Second Worldwide Cybersecurity Summit (WCS), pp. 1–3. IEEE (2011)
10. Furnell, S.: Jumping security hurdles. Comput. Fraud Secur. **2010**(6), 10–14 (2010)
11. Byron, T.: Safer children in a digital world: the report of the Byron review: be safe, be aware, have fun (2008). http://childcentre.info/robert/extensions/robert/doc/6f4474a71e4794a8c119a0c8fb8ab8ef.pdf
12. HMG: National cyber security strategy 2016 to 2021 (2016). https://www.gov.uk/government/publications/national-cyber-security-strategy-2016-to-2021
13. SACSAA: South African Cyber Security Academic Alliance (2011). http://www.cyberaware.org.za
14. Childnet International: E-safety in the computing curriculum (2015). http://www.childnet.com/resources/esafety-and-computing
15. Digital Wildfires Project: (Mis)information flows, propagation and responsible governance (2016). http://digitalwildfire.org
16. ISC Africa: Internet Safety Campaign (ISC) (2016). http://iscafrica.net
17. Computing At School (CAS): Events (2017). https://community.computingatschool.org.uk/events

18. Bada, M., Sasse, A., Nurse, J.R.C.: Cyber security awareness campaigns: why do they fail to change behaviour? In: International Conference on Cyber Security for Sustainable Society, pp. 118–131 (2015)
19. HMG Department for Education (HMG-DE): National curriculum in England: computing programmes of study (2013). https://www.gov.uk/government/publications/national-curriculum-in-england-computing-programmes-of-study
20. Global Cyber Security Capacity Centre: Cybersecurity capacity of the UK (2016). https://www.sbs.ox.ac.uk/cybersecurity-capacity/content/cybersecurity-capacity-uk

South African Computing Educators' Perspectives on Information Security Behaviour

Thandolwethu Mabece[✉], Lynn Futcher[✉], and Kerry-Lynn Thomson[✉]

Nelson Mandela Metropolitan University, Port Elizabeth, South Africa
{s213258919,Lynn.Futcher,Kerry-Lynn.Thomson}@nmmu.ac.za

Abstract. With the growing dependency of users on computers, technology and the internet, the protection of information and information systems is of utmost importance. Current computing graduates will become tomorrow's users and protectors of information and information systems. It is, therefore, essential that higher education institutions provide adequate information security education to enable these graduates to protect information and related information systems. This information security education should, preferably, be a part of their formalized studies. This paper discusses the opinions and experiences of computing educators regarding the extent to which information security is currently integrated within computing curricula and the current information security behaviour of computing students and educators. A total of twenty educators, from six South African higher education institutions, all universities, voluntarily participated in this study. Results indicated that there was limited information security integration within computing curricula at these higher education institutions. This could potentially negatively impact the information security behaviour of computing graduates. However, since behaviour is complex in nature, this paper briefly suggests various factors that could positively influence the information security behaviour of computing students and should be taken into consideration by computing educators.

Keywords: Information security education · Information security behaviour · Computing curricula · Computing students · Pervasive information security

1 Introduction

User behaviour accounts for the majority of security breaches experienced by organisations, although often not with malicious intent to cause harm [1, 2]. Users who have not been educated with regard to information security could be easy targets for hackers because of their ignorance. Therefore, educated and trained users could be a critical success factor in order to mitigate threats within organisations [3, 4]. Once computing graduates leave higher education institutions, many become employees within organisations with various responsibilities including; designing and developing software, maintaining networks and information systems. Computing in this context refers to Computer Science (CS), Information Systems (IS) and Information Technology (IT).

© IFIP International Federation for Information Processing 2017
Published by Springer International Publishing AG 2017. All Rights Reserved
M. Bishop et al. (Eds.): WISE 10, IFIP AICT 503, pp. 121–132, 2017.
DOI: 10.1007/978-3-319-58553-6_11

Various Association for Computing Machinery (ACM) curricula guidelines [5–7] describe what characteristics computing graduates should have once they have completed their degrees. The ACM CS guidelines [5] explain that a graduate *"needs a set of general principles, such as sharing a common resource, **security**, and concurrency.* The ACM IS guidelines [7] refer to Information Assurance and Security (IAS) as IT security and risk management. The ACM IT guidelines [6] specifically state that an IT graduate should have an *"understanding of professional, ethical, legal, **security** and social issues and responsibilities"*. Furthermore, the IT guidelines [6] describe IAS as an integrative knowledge area that should be pervasive throughout other knowledge areas. Pervasive, in this context, is defined as *"existing in all parts of a place or thing; spreading gradually to affect all parts of a place or thing"* [8]. In order for information security to be pervasively integrated into a computing curriculum, it must be formally planned and integrated across various modules within each knowledge area. The CS, IT and IS computing guidelines [5–7] suggest that graduates from these disciplines should be conscious of information security, particularly when they become employed within organisations. It is important that they stay abreast of industry trends, as these graduates need to be able to solve current real world problems. If the curriculum does not offer the necessary tools needed to solve these real world problems, then the higher education institution has failed [6].

Education is often the only way to convince users of the need to do things differently [9]. Schneider [10] argues that an educated workforce is essential to building trustworthy systems. In the same way, computing graduates who are conscious of information security could design and build systems that protect information. According to Schein [9], people will often refuse to accept the need for new, responsible behaviour patterns until they have acquired the relevant information security knowledge, skills and insight.

According to Hu et al. [11], information security culture shapes and guides information security behaviour. Similarly, an organisation's information security culture is cultivated by the information security behaviour of its employees [12]. If an information security culture does not exist within an organisation, the behaviour of new employees, for example computing graduates, coming into the organisation could influence the cultivation of an information security conscious culture [13, 14]. As information security threats continue to be a grave concern, the importance of information security education cannot be stressed enough in computing curricula [15].

In terms of this paper, it is important to determine the perspectives of computing educators with regard to information security education and behaviour. Section 2 discusses information security behaviour, while Sect. 3 explains the purpose of this study. Section 4 describes how this research was conducted including the interview process, participants and the structure of the questionnaire. Section 5 highlights the results and findings, while Sect. 6 provides a discussion of the survey results. Section 7 briefly suggests various factors that could possibly influence the information security behaviour of students, while Sect. 8 concludes the paper.

2 Information Security Behaviour

Information security is not solely a problem of technology, but more often than not, it is a human problem. The greatest threat to information security could be employees who are not information security conscious [16, 17]. Information security behaviour refers to the behaviour of employees when they engage with information systems, including hardware, software and network systems. Such security-related behaviours have major implications for information security [18]. Depending on its nature, employee behaviour may either pose a risk or reduce threats to information assets. Information security behaviour is classified into four broad categories, according to Guo [18]. These categories include security assurance behaviour, security compliant behaviour, security risk-taking behaviour and security damaging behaviour.

Security Assurance Behaviour (SAB): SAB refers to intentional behaviours that employees carry out actively to protect information assets and information systems. In other words, this behaviour refers to employees that are information security conscious. This is the most desirable behaviour from an information security management perspective. Examples of SAB include identifying and being aware of threats and implementing the necessary security measures to counteract those threats. A significant characteristic of SAB is that it implies conscientious action, which means that employees make an effort to behave securely [18].

Security Compliant Behaviour (SCB): SCB refers to intentional or unintentional behaviours that adhere to organisational information security policies. According to Guo [19], SCB may be intentional in that employees make a conscious effort to avoid infringing security policies. It may also be unintentional in that employees may do something without thinking about security issues in mind, although their behaviour might still be adhering to security policies. Employees in the SCB group can be viewed as doing what they are required to do [18].

Security Risk-taking Behaviour (SRB): SRB refers to intentional behaviours that may put information systems at risk, although not with the intentional motive to cause damage. In other words, employees may put organisations at risk unintentionally by, for example, writing down passwords, leaving sensitive documents lying around or visiting websites that are not secure. This behaviour can be likened to that of a non-malicious security violation [20]. Employees in this group are not doing what they are supposed to do [18].

Security Damaging Behaviour (SDB): SDB refers to intentionally damaging behaviours that can cause significant damage to information systems. These behaviours are malicious and deliberate, and can be subject to punishment under the laws and regulations of the society rather than policies [18]. Examples of SDB include industrial espionage, fraud and information theft. Essentially, employees that are categorised in this group are intentionally doing what they are prohibited from doing.

Based on this discussion regarding the different security-related behaviours, it is evident that SAB is the ideal behaviour to ensure information security. When computing students graduate from higher education institutions, they are likely to be employed by organisations. As such, they will be expected to protect organisational information systems and related information assets. Therefore, they need to be educated on how to provide the required protection. Ideally, this should be done before graduating. Higher education institutions are responsible for producing computing graduates who are information security conscious and who meet industry needs with regards to information security [21].

Computing students who have not been educated with regards to information security could typically fall into the SRB category. This is mainly due to the fact that they may not be aware that their actions or inactions, pose a risk to information assets and information systems. The ideal situation would be one where computing students demonstrate SAB before graduating and becoming employees. Over time, information security education could lead to an information security culture where the normal behaviour is SAB.

3   Purpose of the Study

It is currently not known to what extent information security is integrated into undergraduate computing curricula in South African higher education institutions. In addition, the information security behaviour demonstrated by computing students and educators is unknown. The purpose of this study was, therefore, to address two main objectives. The first objective was to determine the perspectives of computing educators regarding the extent to which information security is currently integrated into computing curricula. The second objective was to determine the current information security behaviour of computing students and educators as perceived by computing educators. In order to meet these objectives, this study gathered opinions and experiences from computing educators at six South African higher education institutions. In addition, this paper suggests various factors that could influence the information security behaviour of computing students.

4   Research Process

This section explains the process that was followed in order to collect data from the participants. It must be noted that this is an initial study to gather the perspectives of computing educators with regard to information security education and behaviour. These computing educators were from the CS, IS and IT disciplines to gather a general perspective. However, the purpose was not to do a comparative study across these disciplines. In addition, this section describes the semi-structured interview process, the participants, as well as the design of the questionnaire that was used as a basis for the interviews conducted. This study used a mixed method approach, including both quantitative and qualitative data.

Interview Process: A semi-structured interview was conducted with twenty participants with the aid of a questionnaire to gather the opinions of the participants. Participation in this study was voluntary and participants remain anonymous.

Participants: The participants were selected from six South African higher education institutions, all universities. Three were from CS, eight from IT and nine from IS.

Questionnaire Design: The questionnaire was divided into two sections with each section focusing on a single objective. The primary aim of Sect. 1 was to ascertain the opinions of the participants on whether information security was currently integrated within their undergraduate computing curriculum and their general views on the pervasive integration of information security. The purpose of Sect. 2 was to determine the opinions and observations of participants with regard to the information security behaviour of their students, as well as their colleagues. Sections 1 and 2 consisted of closed (yes/no) and open-ended questions thereby gathering both quantitative and qualitative data. The following section provides the results and findings of this initial study.

5 Results and Findings

The purpose of this section is to provide the results and findings of the semi-structured interviews based on the questionnaire briefly described in the previous section.

Section 1 - **To determine computing educators' perspectives regarding the extent to which information security is currently integrated within computing curricula:** Table 1 represents the number of participants who answered "yes" or "no" to the closed questions for the first objective. It is important to note that the table does not show the complete list of questions for this section, as some were open-ended questions. However, answers to both the closed and open-ended questions are discussed in this section.

Table 1. Section 1 closed questions and responses

Section 1 closed questions		Yes	No
1.1	Do you teach any security-related modules?	9 (45%)	11 (55%)
1.3	Is information security pervasively integrated within other modules?	14 (70%)	6 (30%)
1.5	Do you think information security should be an important part of your discipline?	19 (95%)	1 (5%)
1.8	Do you think that your colleagues share the same views with regards to pervasively integrating information security?	19 (95%)	1 (5%)
1.10	Do you foresee any perceived challenges with regards to pervasively integrating information security?	18 (90%)	2 (10%)

As shown in Table 1, 11 (55%) of the participants indicated that they did not teach any specific security-related modules (Question 1.1). In response to Question 1.2, the 9 (45%) participants who answered "yes" to Question 1.1 indicated they taught security-related modules ranging from 1st year through to the 5th year of study.

For Question 1.3, it must be noted that even though the question asked if information security was pervasively integrated, on further enquiry most participants misinterpreted the term *pervasive*, as they perceived the ad hoc discussion of information security concepts in some modules as being pervasive. For example, 14 (70%) of the participants indicated that there are certain modules that include a few aspects of information security (Question 1.3). Therefore, these participants misinterpreted this as being pervasive. Examples of the modules where information security aspects were mentioned include: project management, databases, application development and forensics (Question 1.4). 19 (95%) of the participants agreed that information security should be an important part of their discipline (Question 1.5). In response to Question 1.6, one participant indicated that people interact with information and information systems on a daily basis; thus they should be able to protect those information systems. Other participants indicated that it is important for everyday life as information security is a real world problem. The participants' perceptions on the pervasive integration of information security is that it is important to integrate information security. However, many participants mentioned that it should be contextualised within the applicable modules (Question 1.7).

19 (95%) participants indicated that they thought their colleagues shared the same views as they did with regard to pervasively integrating information security (Question 1.8). Others indicated that only those colleagues with some information security background knowledge shared the same views with regard to the integration of information security (Question 1.9). However, 18 (90%) of the participants indicated that they foresaw challenges with regard to the pervasively integration of information security into their modules. In answer to the open-ended Question 1.11, some of the perceived challenges they foresaw included: not enough time within their existing modules to include information security; information security is too technical; and educators do not know *how* to integrate information security within their respective modules. These were the predominant challenges indicated by participants.

Section 2 - To determine the current information security behaviour of computing students and educators as perceived by computing educators: Table 2 represents the number of participants who answered "yes" or "no" for each closed question.

Table 2. Section 2 closed questions and responses

Section 2 closed questions		Yes	No
2.1	Do you think that your students behave in a secure manner?	6 (30%)	14 (70%)
2.3	Are you aware of any information security behavioural policies within your institution?	0 (0%)	20 (100%)
2.4	Are students aware of any ICT-related policies?	9 (45%)	11 (55%)
2.5	Are there any consequences for "insecure" behaviour?	17 (85%)	3 (15%)
2.7	Does an information security culture exist in your department amongst colleagues?	14 (70%)	6 (30%)

As can be seen in Table 2, 14 (70%) of the participants indicated that their students do not behave securely (Question 2.1). In relation to Question 2.2, examples provided by the participants indicated that their students did not behave in a secure manner as they tend to share passwords and accounts. They also do not log off their computers and they do not scan their USB sticks.

All of the participants (100%) indicated that they were not aware of any specific information security behavioural policies that exist at their respective institutions. Upon further investigation, participants mentioned that their higher education institutions had ICT usage policies that students had to comply with (Question 2.3). 9 (45%) of the participants indicated that their students were aware of the ICT usage policies (Question 2.4). Furthermore, 17 (85%) of the participants indicated that there were consequences for "insecure" ICT usage policy behaviour (Question 2.5). Consequences provided by participants for "insecure" ICT usage behaviour (Question 2.6) include: disciplinary hearings; disabling accounts; community service; and banning students from computer laboratories.

14 (70%) of the participants specified that an information security culture does exist within their department amongst colleagues (Question 2.7). However, it was indicated by participants that the security culture that does exist within their department seems to be limited to locking office doors, protecting examination papers with passwords when sent via email and logging off unattended computers (Question 2.8).

Some examples highlighted by participants with regards to how they would influence students and colleagues to behave more securely included (Question 2.9): increased information security knowledge, education and awareness; contextualised information security examples; information security scenarios and scare tactics.

6 Discussion

The various ACM computing curricula guidelines [5–7] clearly present IAS as an integrative knowledge area that should permeate other knowledge areas. However, results from the survey show that there is limited information security integration within the computing curricula of the universities surveyed. The possible reason for the limited integration could be the challenges as perceived by computing educators. Participants indicated that possible challenges for pervasive integration could be that educators did not know how to integrate security; they do not have enough time within their modules; and that information security is too complex. More focus should be placed on ways to incorporate information security practically within these modules so that it permeates throughout the curriculum. There needs to be a conscious effort from computing educators in this regard.

Participants generally acknowledged the importance of information security as being an integral part of any ICT practitioner's daily life. The participants from the IS discipline in particular emphasised that information was at the core of what they did within their discipline.

The majority of the participants were willing to consider the integration of information security into their modules. The participants indicated that they would prefer small, contextualised information security examples that are applicable to each of their specific modules. In addition, many indicated that they were not equipped with any guidelines on *how* to integrate information security concepts into their modules. This poses a great challenge since the ACM states that information security should be a pervasive theme, but they do not suggest ways in which this can be done.

The majority of participants indicated that their students did not act in a secure manner, since they shared accounts and passwords, remained logged onto their computers when unattended and did not scan USB sticks. This result suggests that the behaviour of many students falls into the SRB category and that there is a significant need for change in their information security behaviour.

Most of the participants indicated that a limited information security culture existed within their work environment amongst colleagues. If an information security culture does not exist within computing departments, it is possible that computing students will not act in a secure manner.

As discussed in Sect. 2, intentional SAB is the desired information security behaviour that computing graduates should demonstrate. It cannot, however, be expected that SAB will evolve naturally. There should be a conscious effort by computing educators to integrate information security into their modules, which could positively influence the conscientious behaviour of computing graduates. However, from this study, it can be concluded that many computing educators in South Africa are not *consciously* doing enough to positively influence the information security behaviour of their computing graduates. In order to address this, future research could be conducted to help educators consider the various factors that could influence the information security behaviour of their students. The following section suggests possible factors to be considered in future research.

7 Factors Influencing Information Security Behaviour

Many behavioural theories exist in an attempt to explain why humans behave the way they do. Each theory focuses on different factors in order to explain the behaviour of people. While many behavioural theories exist, the theories briefly referred to in this paper include the Theory of Planned Behaviour, Protection Motivation Theory and the Social Cognitive Theory.

The **Theory of Planned Behaviour** explains the links between various concepts that could influence behaviour. As the name suggests, this theory helps to predict the deliberate behaviour of people because behaviour can be planned [22]. The Theory of Planned Behaviour has been widely used in investigating ethical behaviours when using information systems and the decisions of individuals to adopt acceptable computer or information security measures [23]. According to this theory, attitude, subjective norms and perceived behavioural control all influence a person's intention, which ultimately could determine their behaviour.

The **Protection Motivation Theory** is considered to be one of the leading theories in the area of health behaviour motivation. However, it has been extended to various other fields of research. It is widely used as an explanatory theory to predict individual intentions to take precautionary or protective measures when faced with threats [24–26].

The **Social Cognitive Theory** explains how people acquire and maintain certain behavioural patterns. According to the theory, evaluating behavioural change depends on personal factors, behavioural factors and environmental factors [27].

In order for computing students to demonstrate the desired security assurance behaviour (SAB), factors that could influence such behaviour need to be addressed. Table 3 indicates some factors from the above-mentioned theories that could influence the behaviour of computing students.

Table 3. Factors that could influence information security behaviour

Influence	Factor	Theory
Personal and Behavioural	Attitude	Theory of Planned Behaviour
	Perceived behavioural control and self-efficacy	Theory of Planned Behaviour Protection Motivation Theory
	Perceived vulnerability and perceived severity	Protection Motivation Theory
	Outcome expectancy	Social Cognitive Theory
Environmental	Subjective norms, Modelling, Identification and Culture	Theory of Planned Behaviour Social Cognitive Theory Social Cognitive Theory

Attitude - computing students with a positive attitude towards information security are more likely to adhere to the required SAB, while those with a negative attitude are less likely to adhere to the required SAB.

Perceived behavioural control and self-efficacy - computing students with a high perceived behavioural control and self-efficacy are more likely to execute the required behaviour as opposed to computing students with a low perceived capability. When it comes to information security and the protection of information assets, it is important for computing students to have high perceived behavioural control and self-efficacy so that they could demonstrate the desired SAB.

Perceived vulnerability and perceived severity - computing students should be educated about the various threats that they are susceptible to in order for them to protect themselves from those threats. If computing students do not know that they are susceptible to information security threats, they are less likely to behave in a secure manner with regard to information assets and information systems. In addition, computing students should be aware of the potential impact that information security threats can have on information assets and information systems.

Outcome expectancy - if computing students do not adhere to an ICT usage policy in laboratories, they could be denied access. Therefore, the outcome expectancy of the computing students would be that if they do not adhere to the ICT usage policy, they would be denied laboratory and internet access. This negative consequence could influence computing students to demonstrate SAB.

Subjective Norms, Modelling, Identification and Culture - it is important that higher education institutions have a positive information security culture. The information security culture could be influenced by subjective norms, modelling and identification – all of which are ways in which people learn through social pressure and observation. Furthermore, it is important that higher education institutions provide computing students with an environment where SAB is the norm. It could be argued that if computing students have role models they can identify with, for example their educators, they too could be influenced to display the desired SAB.

Further considerations, not directly linked to behavioural theories, include policies and education.

Policies - information security policies are important within organisations as they dictate the appropriate behaviour of employees [28, 29]. Similarly, an information security policy within higher education institutions should provide guidance to computing students on how to behave with regard to information security.

Education - information security education is important as it could provide computing graduates with the necessary knowledge, insight and skills they need to protect information assets within organisations. As discussed, the ACM specifically states that information security should be an integrative knowledge area that should permeate other knowledge areas.

Acceptable information security behaviour combined with technological and physical security measures could help to protect organisations effectively against malicious attacks [23, 30]. In the same way that organisations should focus on the information security behaviour of their employees, higher education institutions should focus on influencing the information security behaviour of computing students.

8   Conclusion

In order to adequately protect the information assets of an organisation, it is important for computing students to acquire the necessary information security knowledge through education. The results from the semi-structured interviews suggest that participants generally accepted that information security is an important part of everyday life and thus should be taught in computing curricula. However, there is limited conscious effort from some computing educators to do this. It is believed that if computing students were exposed to information security through formal planning and integration across the curriculum, this could positively influence the information security behaviour of these students. However, for this to be effective, various factors need to be taken into consideration, as suggested in this paper.

Acknowledgements.   The financial assistance of the National Research Foundation (NRF) towards this research is hereby acknowledged. Opinions expressed and conclusions arrived at, are those of the authors and are not necessarily to be attributed to the NRF.

References

1. Tajuddin, S., Olphert, W., Doherty, N.F.: Relationship between stakeholders' information value perception and information security behaviour. In: AIP Conference Proceedings (2014)
2. Tu, Z., Yuan, Y.: Critical success factors analysis on effective information security management: a literature review. In: Information Systems Security, Assurance, and Privacy Track (SIGSEC), pp. 1–13 (2014)

3. Al Awawdeh, S., Tubaishat, A.: An information security awareness program to address common security concerns in IT unit. In: Proceedings of the 11th International Conference on Information Technology (ITNG 2014). New Generations (2014)
4. Cox, J.: Information systems user security: a structured model of the knowing-doing gap. Comput. Hum. Behav. **28**(5), 1849–1858 (2012)
5. ACM. Computer Science Curricula 2013: Curriculum Guidelines for Undergraduate Degree Programs in Computer Science (2013)
6. Lunt, B.M., Ekstrom, J.J., Lawson, E.: Information technology 2008 curriculum guidelines for undergraduate degree programs in information technology (2008)
7. Topi, H., Valacich, J.S., Wright, R.T., Kaiser, K., Nunamaker, J.F., Sipior, J.C., de Vreede, G.J.: IS 2010: curriculum guidelines for undergraduate degree programs in information systems (2010)
8. Oxford Dictionaries. Oxford Dictionaries - Language matters. Oxford online dictionary (2015). http://www.oxforddictionaries.com/definition/learner/pervasive. Accessed 1 Dec 2016
9. Schein, E.H.: The corporate culture survival guide: sense and nonsense about culture change. Jossey-Bass, San Francisco (1999)
10. Schneider, F.B.: Cybersecurity education in universities. IEEE Secur. Priv. **11**, 3–4 (2013)
11. Hu, Q., Dinev, T., Hart, P., Cooke, D.: Managing employee compliance with information security policies: the critical role of top management and organizational culture. Decis. Sci. **43**(4), 615–660 (2012)
12. Da Veiga, A., Eloff, J.H.P.: A framework and assessment instrument for information security culture. Comput. Secur. **29**(2), 196–207 (2010)
13. Van Niekerk, J., Von Solms, R.: A holistic framework for the fostering of an information security sub-culture in organizations. In: Information Security South Africa (2005)
14. Von Solms, R., Von Solms, B.: From policies to culture. Comput. Secur. **23**, 275–279 (2004)
15. Yoon, C., Hwang, J.-W., Kim, R.: Exploring factors that influence students' behaviors in information security. J. Inf. Syst. Educ. **23**(4), 407 (2012)
16. Öğütçü, G., Testik, Ö.M., Chouseinoglou, O.: Analysis of personal information security behavior and awareness. Comput. Secur. **56**, 83–93 (2015)
17. Shropshire, J., Warkentin, M., Sharma, S.: Personality, attitudes, and intentions: predicting initial adoption of information security behavior. Quat. Geochronol. **49**, 177–191 (2015). http://doi.org/10.1016/j.cose.2015.01.002
18. Guo, K.H.: Security-related behavior in using information systems in the workplace: a review and synthesis. Comput. Secur. **32**(1), 242–251 (2013)
19. Guo, K.H.: Revisiting the human factor in organizational information security management. ISACA J. **6** (2013)
20. Guo, K.H., Yuan, Y., Archer, N.P., Connelly, C.E.: Understanding nonmalicious security violations in the workplace: a composite behavior model. J. Manage. Inf. Syst. **28**, 203–236 (2011). http://doi.org/10.2753/MIS0742-1222280208
21. Talib, M.A., Khelifi, A., Ugurlu, T.: Using ISO 27001 in teaching information security. In: 38th Annual Conference on IEEE Industrial Electronics Society (IECON 2012). IEEE, Montreal (2012). http://doi.org/10.1109/IECON.2012.6389395
22. Ajzen, I.: The theory of planned behavior. Organ. Behav. Hum. Decis. Process. **50**, 179–211 (1991). https://doi.org/10.1016/0749-5978(91)90020-T
23. Ifinedo, P.: Understanding information systems security policy compliance: an integration of the theory of planned behavior and the protection motivation theory. Comput. Secur. **31**(1), 83–95 (2012). https://doi.org/10.1016/j.cose.2011.10.007

24. Safa, N.S., Von Solms, R.: An information security knowledge sharing model in organizations. Comput. Hum. Behav. **57**, 442–451 (2016). https://doi.org/10.1016/j.chb.2015.12.037

25. Siponen, M., Adam Mahmood, M., Pahnila, S.: Employees' adherence to information security policies: an exploratory field study. Inf. Manage. **51**(2), 217–224 (2014). https://doi.org/10.1016/j.im.2013.08.006

26. Yoon, C., Hwang, J.-W., Kim, R.: Exploring factors that influence students' behaviors in information security. J. Inf. Syst. Educ. **23**(4), 407–416 (2012). http://www.scopus.com/inward/record.url?eid=2-s2.0-84880826819&partnerID=40&md5=4a3c2d7fe56348029208741e54be814c

27. Bandura, A.: Organisational applications of social cognitive theory. Aust. J. Manage. **13**(2), 275–302 (1988)

28. Höne, K., Eloff, J.H.P.: What makes an effective information security policy? Netw. Secur. **2002**, 14–16 (2002). https://doi.org/10.1016/S1353-4858(02)06011-7

29. Von Solms, R., Von Solms, B.: From policies to culture. Comput. Secur. **23**, 275–279 (2004). https://doi.org/10.1016/j.cose.2004.01.013

30. Furnell, S., Clarke, N.: Power to the people? The evolving recognition of human aspects of security. Comput. Secur. **31**(8), 983–988 (2012). https://doi.org/10.1016/j.cose.2012.08.004

Training Information Security Professionals

ISO/IEC Competence Requirements for Information Security Professionals

Natalia Miloslavskaya$^{(\boxtimes)}$(ID) and Alexander Tolstoy

The National Research Nuclear University
MEPhI (Moscow Engineering Physics Institute),
31 Kashirskoye Shosse, Moscow, Russia
{NGMiloslavskaya, AITolstoj}@mephi.ru

Abstract. In the modern interconnected world, the requirements for compe-
tencies for information security (IS) professionals are needed as never before.
The peculiarities of the European approach to the development of IS professional
competencies are discussed using the example of the European e-Competence
Framework e-CF 3.0. Bases on this, two short content predictions for new
ISO/IEC 27021 and ISO/IEC 19896 international standards are proposed.

Keywords: Information security · Competence · Information security
professionals · ISO/IEC standards

1 Introduction

The ever-growing need for information security (IS) professionals in this fast-moving
field is currently understood worldwide as never before. A professional in any field of
activity (including the IS area) must have specific qualifying characteristics. The
modern approach to determining them is based on the definition of a set of professional
competencies demonstrating a professional's capacity to solve given problems and to
perform specific work within his sphere of activity.

We distinguish "competence" from "competency" [1]. Competence refers to the
ability to apply knowledge and skills to achieve intended results and to do something
well: the quality or state of being competent. It enables a person to function effectively
in a job or situation and demonstrate the ability to apply knowledge and/or skills. In
turn, competencies support definitions of job classifications/occupational group profiles, roles and responsibilities, position descriptions, duty statements, etc. A competency is traditionally defined as a combination of observable and measurable
knowledge (K), skills (S), and abilities (A) (KSA all together) as well as individual
attributes and work experience that contribute to enhanced employee performance and
ultimately result in organizational success. Knowledge is the cognizance of facts, truths
and principles gained from formal training and/or experience. A skill is a developed
proficiency or dexterity in mental operations or physical processes that is often
acquired through specialized training; using these skills results in successful performance. Ability is the power or aptitude to perform physical or mental activities that are
often affiliated with a particular profession. The ability to apply knowledge and skills in

M. Bishop et al. (Eds.): WISE 10, IFIP AICT 503, pp. 135–146, 2017.
DOI: 10.1007/978-3-319-58553-6_12

a productive manner, which can be characterized by such attributes of behavior as aptitude, initiative, enthusiasm, willingness, communication skills, team participation, leadership and others, shows the professional's effectiveness.

The efforts to develop a common approach to vocational training's Common Body of Knowledge (CBK) and requirements to the IS professional competencies are underway worldwide for a long time. A CBK is "a collection of information and a framework that provides a basis for understanding terms and concepts in a particular knowledge area" [2] and it relates only to the first competency's component. The first attempts to create a common point of view on the subject in general were in the World International Conferences on IS Education (WISEs) in the late 1990's and early 2000's [3–5]. About the same time, some CBKs for security professionals were initiated by the industry for certification purposes (like CISA, CISSP, GIAC, etc.).

At present, we can say that three key views – American, Australian and European (analyzed in [6]) – have been formed:

- "Information Technology Security Essential Body of Knowledge: A Competency and Functional Framework for IT Security Workforce Development" by the National Cyber Security Division of the U.S. Department of Homeland Security [7] and the more specialized National Initiative for Cybersecurity Education (NICE), led by the National Institute of Standards and Technology [8];
- "Cyber Security Capability Framework & Mapping of IS Manual Roles" [9] by the Australian Government Information Management Office;
- e-Competence Framework 3.0 (e-CF 3.0) by the European Commission [10].

e-CF 3.0 will include four new ISO/IEC standards, as yet uncompleted: 27021 "Information technology – Security techniques – Competence requirements for information security management systems professionals"; and three parts of 19896 "Information technology – Competence requirements for information security testers and evaluators": (1) "Introduction, concepts and general requirements"; (2) "Knowledge, skills and effectiveness requirements for ISO/IEC 19790 testers"; (3) "Knowledge, skills and effectiveness requirements for ISO/IEC 15408 evaluators".

The main goals of this paper are to analyze e-CF 3.0 as a potential source of additional IS professional requirements beyond those of the current ISO/IEC standards on IS professional competence. It is organized as follows. e-CF 3.0 is analyzed in detail in Sect. 2. In Sects. 3 and 4 we discuss possible contents of the ISO/IEC 27021 and ISO/IEC 19896-1 standards respectively. Key findings conclude the paper.

2 The European e-Competence Framework

e-CF 3.0 is a result of nine years' continuing effort and commitment by multi-stakeholders from the European ICT sector, with the encouragement of the European Commission and strongly backed by the CEN ICT Skills Workshop community. This 53-pages document defines competence as a demonstrated ability to apply knowledge, skills, and attitudes for achieving observable results.

Compared to the four IS functions (Manage, Design, Implement and Evaluate) from [7] and the seven Specialty areas (Securely Provision; Operate and Maintain; Protect and Defend; Investigate; Collect and Operate; Analyze; Oversight and Development) from [8], e-CF 3.0 is structured with four dimensions reflecting different levels of business and human resource planning requirements in addition to job/work proficiency guidelines. Dimension 1 covers five e-Competence areas derived from the ICT business processes, namely Plan (A) – Build (B) – Run (C) – Enable (D) – Manage (E). Dimension 2 reflects a set of reference e-Competences (40 in total) for each area. Dimension 3 describes proficiency levels for each e-Competence. Dimension 4 is a sample of knowledge (K) and skills (S) but not abilities (A) related to e-Competences in Dimension 2.

The main shortcoming of e-CF 3.0 is that it distinguishes e-Competences only for two types of IS professionals – ICT Security Manager and ICT Security Specialist. Table 1 allows us to compare them very easily.

Table 1. General description for ICT Security Manager and ICT Security Specialist (e-CF 3.0)

ICT security manager	ICT security specialist
Manages the ICT security policy (ICTSP)	Ensures the ICTSP's implementation
Mission: Defines the ICTSP. Manages security deployment across all Information Systems. Ensures the provision of information availability. Recognized as the ICTSP expert by internal and external stakeholders	...Proposes and implements necessary IS updates. Advises, supports, informs and provides IS training and awareness. Takes direct action on all/part-of a network/system. Recognized as the ICT technical IS expert by peers
Deliverables: accountable: ICTSP; responsible: Knowledge or Information base, IS strategy; contributor: Risk Management policy, New technology integration proposal, ICT Strategy & Implementation	...accountable: Knowledge or Information base (Security); responsible: New technology integration proposal (Security); contributor: Risk Management policy & plan; ICTSP
Main tasks: defines and implements procedures linked to ICT security; contributes to the development of the organization's IS policy; establishes the prevention plan; informs and raises awareness among general management; ensures the promotion of the IS charter among users; inspects and ensures that IS principles and rules are applied.	...ensures security and appropriate uses of ICT resources; evaluates risks, threats and consequences; provides security training/education; provides technical validation of security tools; contributes to definition of security standards; audits vulnerabilities; monitors security developments to ensure ICT resource data and physical security
Key performance indicators: ICTSP effectiveness	...Security measures in place

e-Competences for the ICT Security Manager and Specialist are shown in Tables 2 and 3 respectively. As can be seen, they have only one common e-Competence (E.8 IS Management), but with different proficiency levels (PLs). E.8 e-CF 3.0 contains seven K and seven S examples (only examples are given, not the full lists):

- K1-K7: the organization's IS management policy and its implications for engagement with customers, suppliers and subcontractors; the best practices and standards in IS management; the critical risks for IS management; the ICT internal audit approach; IS detection techniques, including mobile and digital; cyber attack techniques and counter measures for avoidance; computer forensics;

- S1-S7: document the IS management policy, linking it to business strategy; analyze the company critical assets and identify weaknesses and vulnerability to intrusion or attack; establish a risk management plan to feed and produce preventative action plans; perform IS audits; apply monitoring and testing techniques; establish the recovery plan; implement the recovery plan in case of crisis.

Table 2. e-Competences for ICT Security Manager (e-CF 3.0)

A.7 Technology Trend Monitoring – Investigates latest ICT technological developments to establish understanding of evolving technologies. Devises innovative solutions for integration of new technology into existing products, applications or services or for the creation of new solutions	PL 4: Exploits wide ranging knowledge of new and emerging technologies, coupled with a deep understanding of the business, to envision and articulate solutions for the future. Provides expert guidance and advice, to the leadership team to support strategic decision-making
D.1 IS Strategy Development – Defines and makes applicable a formal organizational strategy, scope and culture to maintain IS from external and internal threats, i.e. digital forensic for corporate investigations or intrusion investigation. Provides the foundation for IS Management, including role identification and accountability. Uses defined standards to create objectives for information integrity, availability, and data privacy	PL 5: Provides strategic leadership to embed IS into the culture of the organization
E.3 Risk Management – Implements the management of risk across information systems through the application of the defined risk management policy and procedure. Assesses risk to the organization's business, including web, cloud and mobile resources. Documents potential risk and containment plans	PL 3: Decides on appropriate actions required to adapt security and address risk exposure. Evaluates, manages and ensures validation of exceptions; audits ICT processes and environment
E.8 IS Management – Implements IS policy. Monitors and takes action against intrusion, fraud, IS breaches or leaks. Ensures that IS risks are analyzed and managed. Reviews IS incidents, makes recommendations for IS policy and strategy to ensure continuous improvement of IS provision	PL 4: Provides leadership for the integrity, confidentiality and availability of data stored on information systems and complies with all legal requirements

(continued)

Table 2. (*continued*)

E.9 IS Governance – Defines, deploys and controls the management of information systems in line with business imperatives. Takes into account all internal and external parameters such as legislation and industry standard compliance to influence risk management and resource deployment to achieve balanced business benefit	PL 4: Provides leadership for IS governance strategy by communicating, propagating and controlling relevant processes across the entire ICT infrastructure

Table 3. e-Competences for ICT Security Specialist (e-CF 3.0)

C.2 Change Support – Implements and guides the evolution of an ICT solution. Ensures efficient control and scheduling of software or hardware modifications to prevent multiple upgrades creating unpredictable outcomes. Minimizes service disruption as a consequence of changes and adheres to defined service level agreement (SLA). Ensures consideration and compliance with IS procedures	PL 3: Ensures the integrity of the system by controlling the application of functional updates, software or hardware additions and maintenance activities. Complies with budget requirements
C.3 Service Delivery – Ensures service delivery in accordance with established SLA's. Takes proactive action to ensure stable and secure applications and ICT infrastructure to avoid potential service disruptions, attending to capacity planning and to IS. Updates operational document library and logs all service incidents. Maintains monitoring and management tools (i.e. scripts, procedures). Maintains IS services. Takes proactive measures	PL 3: Programmes the schedule of operational tasks. Manages costs and budget according to the internal procedures and external constraints. Identifies the optimum number of people required to resource the operational management of the IS infrastructure
D.9 Personnel Development – Diagnoses individual and group competence, identifying skill needs and skill gaps. Reviews training and development options and selects appropriate methodology taking into account the individual, project and business requirements. Coaches and/or mentors individuals and teams to address learning needs	PL 3: Monitors and addressees the development needs of individuals and teams
D.10 Information and Knowledge Management – Identifies and manages information and considers information distribution policies. Creates information structure to enable exploitation and	PL 3: Analyses business processes and associated information requirements and provides the most appropriate information structure

(*continued*)

Table 3. (*continued*)

optimization of information. Understands appropriate tools to be deployed to create, extract, maintain, renew and propagate business knowledge in order to capitalize from the information asset	
E.8 IS Management – Equal to those for ICT Security Manager	PL 3: Evaluates IS management measures and indicators and decides if compliant to IS policy. Investigates and instigates remedial measures to address IS breaches. PL 4: Equal to those for ICT Security Manager

The IS competencies are mentioned throughout e-CF 3.0 and incorporated within the relevant dimensions in several places (e.g., K8-security and S4-contribute to the development of ICT strategy and policy, including ICT security and quality for A.1 Information System and Business Strategy Alignment; K6-ICT security standards for A.2 Service Level Management; K2-systems architecture requirements performance, maintainability, extendibility, scalability, availability, security and accessibility for A.5 Architecture Design; K14-security for B.1 Application Development; and K5-best practices and standards in IS management for C.2 Change Support and C.3 Service Delivery, etc.).

3   What to Expect from ISO/IEC 27021

The ISO/IEC 27000 family of standards is a globally accepted world leading for managing IS in organizations and will be broadened by the new ISO/IEC 27021 "…Competence requirements for information security management systems profes-sionals". Its development started in fall 2013 and final publication is planned for October 2017. In March 2017, ISO/IEC 27021 is at the 40.20 "Draft international standard ballot initiated" stage) (see Fig. 1).

By providing a required Body of Knowledge (BoK) in the area of IS management (ISM) only, this standard combines with ISO/IEC 27001 [11] to produce a logical continuation of the that standard. It is expected to specify the minimum competence requirements and to provide guidelines for setting the BoK for ISM system (ISMS) professionals required for leading or establishing, implementing, maintaining and continually improving ISMS according to the Plan–Do–Check–Act (PDCA) cycle. In the worst case, only elements of the BoK will be given in the standard.

Clause 7.2 of ISO/IEC 27001 supports ISMSs by ensuring that people are com-petent. For that purpose, the following activities should be performed: identify the competence requirements for those who have an impact on IS performance within an organization; acquire the necessary competence whenever current personnel fail to meet the organization's IS competence requirements; and evaluate the effectiveness of any actions taken to acquire the IS competence that the organization needs to have.

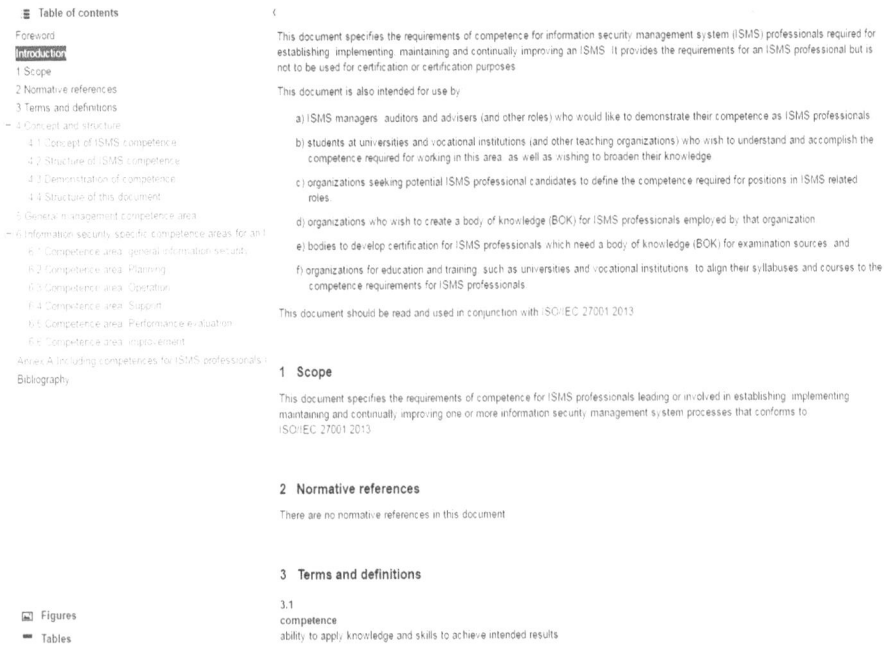

This document specifies the requirements of competence for information security management system (ISMS) professionals required for establishing, implementing, maintaining and continually improving an ISMS. It provides the requirements for an ISMS professional but is not to be used for certification or certification purposes

This document is also intended for use by

a) ISMS managers, auditors and advisers (and other roles) who would like to demonstrate their competence as ISMS professionals

b) students at universities and vocational institutions (and other teaching organizations) who wish to understand and accomplish the competence required for working in this area, as well as wishing to broaden their knowledge

c) organizations seeking potential ISMS professional candidates to define the competence required for positions in ISMS related roles,

d) organizations who wish to create a body of knowledge (BOK) for ISMS professionals employed by that organization

e) bodies to develop certification for ISMS professionals which need a body of knowledge (BOK) for examination sources, and

f) organizations for education and training, such as universities and vocational institutions, to align their syllabuses and courses to the competence requirements for ISMS professionals

This document should be read and used in conjunction with ISO/IEC 27001:2013

1 Scope

This document specifies the requirements of competence for ISMS professionals leading or involved in establishing, implementing, maintaining and continually improving one or more information security management system processes that conforms to ISO/IEC 27001:2013

2 Normative references

There are no normative references in this document

3 Terms and definitions

3.1
competence
ability to apply knowledge and skills to achieve intended results

Fig. 1. ISO/IEC 27021 preview at http://www.iso.org

The audience of ISO/IEC 27021 includes, but is not limited, to the following categories: organizations seeking ISMS professionals, to define the competence required for positions in ISMS related roles; educational institutions, to align their syllabi for training ISMS professionals; ISMS professional certification bodies, to use the BoK for examination sources; all ISMS related roles (such as managers, auditors, advisers and others), to prove their competence as ISMS professionals; and students, to understand and attain the competence required for working in the area.

As can be seen in the ISO/IEC 27021 preview, an ISMS professional refers to a person who establishes, implements, maintains and continuously improves one or more ISMS processes. And competence is the ability to apply knowledge and skills to achieve intended results [12].

ISO/IEC 27001 leads to dividing the KSA competencies of ISMS professionals (see Fig. 2) into two groups:

(1) *General or domain-independent*, including managerial; and
(2) *Professional or domain-specific* for IS and ISMS Planning – Operation – Support – Performance evaluation – Improvement (particularly for the IS and ISMS areas like Risk Management, Incident Management, Auditing, Security Controls, Business Continuity, Forensics, Access Control, Data Protection, Intrusion Prevention, Vulnerabilities Assessment, Physical and Environmental Security, Cryptography, etc.).

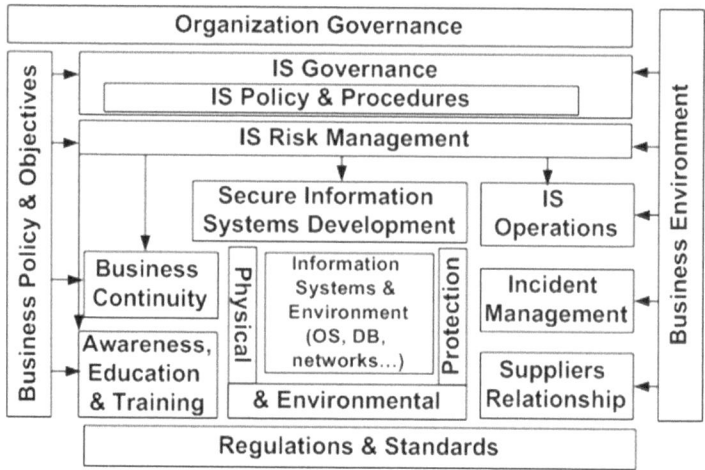

Fig. 2. ISMS competencies areas

Some examples of general competence are: organisation design, culture and business, Project Management, Leadership, Governance, Strategies and Policies, IT and Information Systems, Human Resources, Communication, Problem management, Analytical Methods, Efficiency and Effectiveness Measurement, Finance and Budgeting, Compliance, and Supplier Management.

The IS domain-specific competences include but are not limited to knowledge and skills required in the following areas:

(1) IS governance within a business governance framework: the organization's business context, IS governance concepts, strategies, standards (such as ISO/IEC 27014) and policies, ISMS-specific legal and regulatory issues, IS assessment methodologies, business continuity, asset management, etc.;

(2) IS risk management: IS risk assessment and treating, and their application within the ISMS scope (on ISO/IEC 27005 basis);

(3) IS incident management: IS incident detection, reporting, assessment and response, and their application within the scope of ISMS (based on ISO/IEC 27035);

(4) IS auditing: internal and external IS audit, monitoring and self-assessment, their application within the scope of ISMS (based on ISO/IEC 27006-27008); and

(5) IS controls: IS policy implementation, access control, cryptography, operations and communication security, human resources security, physical and environmental security, system security, compliance, etc.

The ISMS domain-specific competences include but are not limited to knowledge and skills required in the following areas:

(1) ISMS Planning: ISM strategy and policies, ISMS scope, objectives, structure, roles, all subprocesses, resources, reporting, communication, etc. with such key

knowledge terms as Business impact analysis, assets, IS risk acceptance criteria, IS controls, IS threat modelling, vulnerabilities, etc.;

(2) ISMS Operation: ISM subprocess design, implementation, efficient and effective operation and documentation, etc. with such key knowledge terms as security measures, IS monitoring, insider IS threats, IS threat analysis, vulnerability analysis, intrusion detection and prevention system, access control, antivirus software, system log, SIEM, configuration and patch management, etc.;

(3) ISMS Support: ISMS subprocess life cycle, documentation, awareness, education and training, information protection tools, etc. with such key knowledge terms as end users' IS training, IS curriculum and training programme, learning objectives, testing, learning management system, etc.;

(4) ISMS Performance Evaluation: IS auditing, monitoring, measurement and analysis, as well as determining compliance with external/internal relevant regulation on a periodic basis, etc. with such key knowledge terms as IS monitoring and measurement, control, IS internal and external audits, IS audit programme, scope and criteria, IS effectiveness, vulnerability assessment, etc.; and

(5) ISMS Improvement: constant strategic and tactical improvement of all key aspect of ISMS in a timely manner in accordance with the most recent technological innovations and corresponding methodologies and frameworks.

We hope to see more advanced lists in ISO/IEC 27021 than those specified here, with detailed descriptions for each competence.

4   What to Expect from ISO/IEC 19896-1

Compared to ISO/IEC 27021, the first two parts of ISO/IEC 19896 are at the 30.60 "Close of voting/comment period" stage in March 2017, while the third is at the 10.99 stage (new project approved). Their audience includes IS and IS product evaluation and conformance testing specialists (testers and evaluators), validators, certifiers and approval authorities, testing laboratories, vendors and technical providers as well as organizations offering professional credentialing.

We expect that ISO/IEC 19896-1 will provide an overview of the definitions, the fundamental concepts, and a general description of the framework used to communicate the competence requirements for IT product security evaluations and conformance testing as well as the minimum competence requirements for IT product security evaluators and testers to conduct its testing/evaluation using standards established by the ISO committee CASCO.

Without any doubt, all parts of the ISO/IEC 19896 series will be based on ISO/IEC 17025:2005 "General requirements for the competence of testing and calibration laboratories" [13], which was also prepared by CASCO. ISO/IEC 17025 is frequently specified as a basis for conformity testing amongst security assurance conformance-testing and evaluation laboratories. It addresses the general requirements for the competence of testing and calibration laboratories (a broad range of laboratories, and not only in the field of IT product security assurance testing and evaluation).

Clause 5 of ISO/IEC 17025 requires two important controls: (1) laboratory management, to ensure the competence of all who operate specific equipment, perform tests and/or calibrations, evaluate results and sign test reports and calibration certificates; and (2) personnel performing specific tasks to be qualified on the basis of appropriate education, training, experience and/or demonstrated essential skills. Thus, in order to support conformity in evaluating or conformance-testing IT security products, one of the key factors is the competence of the individuals performing this work.

As for any other professional activity, a minimum competence is needed to support achieving conformity and repeatability of the results. The main elements of competence are the minimum necessary knowledge, skills, experience and qualifications relevant to the target IT product security assurance standard. The CBK is formed from a knowledge of IT product architecture and design in relevant technology areas, all relevant standards, policies and procedures, any associated testing or evaluation methods, typical vulnerabilities, which may occur in that product or technology, etc.

Skills are the ability to understand the evaluation and testing scope (including its boundaries), to analyze various documentation, to understand the source code used in specifying and implementing products, to develop and perform functional and special IS testing, to use specialized testing tools, to interpret testing results and to write reports detailing these results, etc. Additional skills to communicate effectively and to perform project management are needed at the higher competence's levels.

An experienced individual should have a deep understanding of the accreditation body's requirements and policies, have already performed evaluations or testing, and perhaps have taught or mentored others.

The specification of particular educational qualifications can help determine an individual's ability to follow a formal program or work independently. In some cases, it may be acceptable to substitute appropriate and relevant experience for education or qualifications.

These main elements of competence can be extended by additional elements such as leadership, teamwork, initiative, aptitude, willingness, etc.

All competence elements must assume their measurability. Knowledge tests may include an examination of professional qualifications gained through third parties or through testing by approval authorities or the laboratory itself. Methods for skills measurement should demonstrate the mastery of all necessary skills. They can be based on a specific laboratory's proficiency testing programme or on the use of previous training records. Experience is measured not by the number of years of experience, but by the number of projects in which a person participated before (considering project complexity, technologies and test methods used). An individual's education can be measured by referring to the educational certification issued by accredited and recognized authorities/university and checked by the laboratory.

It will be reasonable to include in ISO/IEC 19896-1 a few competence levels, to distinguish different levels of professional capability and define professional roles within the organizations with respect to competence. For example, the first one is usually a technician, supporting another's activities and performing testing or evaluation under supervision. An evaluator/tester is competent to work unsupervised in many areas, but may require supervision in a few testing and evaluation areas. A senior evaluator/tester is competent to work unsupervised in most areas and is able to supervise the work of two previous persons. A lead evaluator/tester is competent to work unsupervised in all areas of testing or evaluation according to the defined standards and methods, to provide project management, to supervise the work of three other persons and to communicate with stakeholders.

We estimate this standard will be ready for publication not earlier than 2018.

5 Conclusion

Our dynamic life has put us in the forefront of the need to develop the specialized professional competencies for the very popular field of IS in the short term. While waiting for them, it is very hard to predict the new ISO/IEC 27021 and ISO/IEC 19896-1 international standards' content, even after scrupulously analyzing the ISO/IEC 27000 standard family and ISO/IEC 17025 as their main statements. Our review of the key ideas underlying the European approach to IS professionals' competencies development revealed that e-CF 3.0 as the first all-Europe attempt to begin formulating e-Competencies was not very successful with respect to the IS area because of its very narrow consideration, but it began a very proper and necessary process. Since the description of e-Competencies for IS professionals is not the primary goal of e-CF 3.0, it can be used only as the most basic initial guidance, and requires substantial additions and clarifications. For example, general, business and managerial knowledge and skills, competence in IS area and legal issues, IS operation, auditing and risk management from e-CF 3.0 are completely applicable to ISO/IEC 27021 and ISO/IEC 19896-1. Hence, all European academia, industry and governments hope to see soon mature enough and usable standards.

Acknowledgement. This work was supported by Competitiveness Growth Program of the Federal Autonomous Educational Institution of Higher Education National Research Nuclear University MEPhI (Moscow Engineering Physics Institute).

References

1. Miloslavskaya, N., Tolstoy, A.: Professional competencies level assessment for training of masters in information security. In: Bishop, M., Miloslavskaya, N., Theocharidou, M. (eds.) WISE 2015. IFIP AICT, vol. 453, pp. 135–145. Springer, Cham (2015). doi:10.1007/978-3-319-18500-2_12
2. Bishop, M., Engle, S.: The Software Assurance CBK and University Curricula. In: 10th Colloquium for Information Systems Security Education. University of Maryland, USA (2006)
3. Fischer-Hübner, S., Yngström, L. (eds.): Proceedings of the IFIP WG 11.8 First World Conference on Information Security Education WISE1, 17–19 June, Kista, Sweden (1999)
4. Armstrong, H., Yngström, K. (eds.): Proceedings of the IFIP WG 11.8 Second World Conference on Information Security Education WISE2, 12–14 July, Perth, Australia (2001)

5. Irvine, C.E., Armstrong, H.L. (eds.): Security Education and Critical Infrastructures, IFIP WG11.8 Third Annual World Conference on Information Security Education WISE3, 26–28 June 2003, Monterey, California, USA. Kluwer (2003)
6. Miloslavskaya, N., Tolstoy, A.: State-level views on professional competencies in the field of IoT and cloud information security. In: Proceedings of 2016 4th International Conference on Future Internet of Things and Cloud Workshops. 3rd International Symposium on Intercloud and IoT (ICI 2016), 22–24 August 2016, Vienna, Austria, pp. 83–90 (2016)
7. State Government Information Security Workforce Development Model. A Best Practice Model and Framework. Final Version 1.0, June 2010
8. The U.S. National Cybersecurity Workforce Framework. https://www.dhs.gov/national-cybersecurity-workforce-framework. Accessed 08.11.2016
9. The Cyber Security Capability Framework & Mapping of ISM Roles. Final Report. Australian Government Information Management Office, June 2010
10. The European e-Competence Framework 3.0. A common European Framework for ICT Professionals in all industry sectors. CWA 16234:2014 Part 1. CEN
11. ISO/IEC 27001:2013 "Information technology – Security techniques – Information security management systems — Requirements"
12. ISO/IEC 17024:2012 "Conformity assessment – General requirements for bodies operating certification of persons"
13. ISO/IEC 17025:2005 "General requirements for the competence of testing and calibration laboratories"

Evaluating a Multi Agency Cyber Security Training Program Using Pre-post Event Assessment and Longitudinal Analysis

Erik Moore[✉], Steven Fulton, and Dan Likarish

Center for Information Assurance Studies, Regis University, Denver, CO, USA
{emoore,sfulton,dlikaris}@regis.edu

Abstract. This study presents the context and measured results of cyber security joint cyber defense training exercises. Building on previously published work by the authors that introduced AGILE methodologies, this study analyzes the outcomes of that professional development and laboratory-supported environment. Analysis focuses on the development of specific individual skill levels and generally describes desired multi-agency collaborative capabilities. While all training events do not have sufficient pre-post data to isolate the particular causes of a rise in capabilities, competence in progressively harder levels of capabilities is observed over time in relation to the training components. A comprehensive Personalized Education Learning Environment (PELE) aggregate data of individuals is not presented here, indicators suggest that this would enhance outcomes.

Keywords: Cyber · Security · Defense · Training · Agile · Multi-agency · Collaborative · PELE · Personalized · Education · Learning · Environment · Tabletop · Simulation · Joint · Physical · Exercise

1 Introduction

The purpose of this study is to determine the efficacy of a joint regional cyber defense training exercise using qualitative assessment and quantitative measures. The impetus for developing a joint regional cyber defense training exercises is an acknowledgement of local entities experiencing cyber attacks such as cyber terrorism, hacktivism, and cyber crime in relation to local, regional, and international events. The frequency, motivation, targets, and types of cyber attacks has expanded significantly [1]. In order to respond to that growing range of cyber-based civil disruption, regional response teams will likely become increasingly necessary in order to provide an agile response to disruptive events, to help under-resourced entities achieve business continuity, and to mitigate damage where possible. This is a type of response is in addition to the array of private services, law enforcement agencies, national defense, and security standards bodies.

Regis University (RU), in partnership with the Colorado Army and Air Force National Guard (CONG) and the State of Colorado (SOC), has completed the first phase

© IFIP International Federation for Information Processing 2017
Published by Springer International Publishing AG 2017. All Rights Reserved
M. Bishop et al. (Eds.): WISE 10, IFIP AICT 503, pp. 147–156, 2017.
DOI: 10.1007/978-3-319-58553-6_13

of a multi-phase project to build essential and immediate cyber security expertise capacity within the CONG and its information technology (IT) citizen workforce. Their intended cyber-attack response role is similar to their response to a natural disaster like firefighters parachuting out of an airplane, known as "smokejumpers" to put out a forest fire. Successful participants in this training program will be the smokejumpers of the cyber security world. The CONG's IT workforce employs approximately 2000 citizen members with a variety of IT skills and work experience verified through commercial certification. The results of our first year study indicate that the training methodology developed utilizing AGILE methods has improved the ability of the CONG and SOC to respond to attacks against Colorado's critical infrastructure. Based on AGILE development lifecycle principles, the approach we proposed for the Phase I study under a United States National Security Agency/Department of Homeland Security Annex II capacity building grant delivered an executable training partnership model facilitated by collaboration between Academia, the National Guard, and Government. The specific application of AGILE methodology is discussed previously by two of the authors with another collaborator [2]. The study presented here conducted pre and post self-assessment surveys and skill tests reflecting the effect of a multi-year program involving multiple training components, communications with industry, and advanced study of SOC policy.

Because this program relies intentionally on broadly available resources like certification programs, other governmental entities should be able to adapt this model to develop response teams. The training included multiple physical exercises (immersive cyber simulations) and tabletop exercises (collaborative verbal scenario walk-throughs) designed to give real-world substance to more abstract cyber security concepts and integrate physical world consequences to actions performed by the participants.

Items not measured in this research but very important in terms of response capabilities include establishing transitive trust between organizations, a framework for incident response interaction, capabilities to self-organize teams within that framework, and the capacity in the relationship to sustain the empathy and open communications necessary to work through difficult situations. Various activities were designed to provide dynamic group interactions and a common body of knowledge to support discourse and collaborative activities. The exercises incrementally ramped up technical and logistical requirements with what we generally call a crawl-walk-run approach, i.e. starting with easier tasks and working to harder. In addition, the collaborative training space was neither Department of Defense, nor the State of Colorado, releasing constraints for participants to self-organize into a skill-based team structure through rapid discourse rather than extant hierarchies internal to the participating organizations. The significance placed on these capabilities is based on the notion that incident response is the wrong time to introduce responders to each other exchange business cards. Below are the activities in our joint training events intended to develop individual skills and team capabilities.

A relevant approach to cyber security training includes both simulation and physical exercise represent challenge-based learning [6]. This idea of challenge-based learning is a key factor for stakeholders of the training program for validating the capabilities of the participants beyond what is available in certifications, lectures, and other components.

2   Participant Assessment Methodologies

In assessing individual capabilities, pre and post tests were used in the study where data could be gathered. Unlike methods proposed for forming a perfect case, the trainers were obliged to train all participants, and thus a control group could not be established [7]. Therefore the data is analyzed in relation to the longitudinal progress without fully establishing attribution of progress to specific training components over long periods of time. However, general progress of the population can be established by the tests while understanding that there were several factors in the participants' lives that contributed to their development in capabilities, including requirements for professional certification, continued work activities at their civilian employers, and other National Guard training. The quantitative longitudinal data is therefore represented as general progress of the population and not particularly efficacy of the particular training program. Understanding the professional context of the training clarifies multiple mutually reinforcing technical activities taking place in the lives of the participants.

The analysis presented herein uses what Creswell and Clark refer to as "two phase explanatory design mixed methods research" where quantitative data is used to identify change in a group and qualitative analysis is used to understand that change [8]. The authors conducted pre and post event surveys and interviews characterizing the multi-year regime of physical exercises, lectures and certification exams, all of which advanced the study participants domain knowledge, awareness of SOC policy, and communication level with industry. The joint training leadership included multiple simulation challenges, physical exercise scenarios, and tabletop exercises designed to give real-world substance to more abstract cyber security concepts and integrate physical world consequences to actions performed by the participants.

3   Experiment Structure

To achieve an increase in cyber defense capabilities, the joint training leadership team planned joint events with a set of activities specifically designed to inform participants, exercise their skills, and also facilitate inter-organizational collaboration to validate working capabilities, described in Table 1. This study focuses on measuring of the exercising of skills of the participants.

During information sessions where vendors or organizations presented exercise related materials, participants were encouraged to be interactive in order to move towards functional understanding of the scenario. During physical exercises, participants split up into teams purposefully composed of members from disparate institutions to increase inter-institutional interaction. In addition to addressing the content areas and application usage, the exercise design required participants to practice self-organizing, to close gaps and resolve issues across institutional boundaries in the face of each new challenge. During tabletop exercises, participant teams involved in inter-institutional activity and technical leads walked through scenarios that would require broad multi-institutional cooperation. Specific cases suggesting the need for inter-institutional cooperation included: response to a persistent intrusion at a public utility company, a recurring denial of service attack at a state agency, or a targeted attack against online government services where the local support team is overwhelmed. Each of these scenarios require that inter-institutional teams jointly address the policies of each institution and develop working relationships and methods to achieve functional capabilities while maintaining local responsibilities and adhering to relevant security and operations policies.

Table 1. Teaching activities

Teaching activities	Definition
Simulation	A hands-on immersive scenario which permits instant "reset" of computers, networks, etc. to initial conditions, allows for compression of long term activity into short periods, often provides for lower cost than utilizing real computers, networks, software, protocols, etc., permits ease of scalability, creation of scenarios too risky for "real world" testing [3]
Physical exercise scenario	Activity employing actual technology to engage in a technical challenge in order to develop skill, increase familiarity, and develop team capabilities in relation to a particular active scenario or specific static situation requiring action. This can be "staged" phases with assistance, or timed with measured performance to clarify capabilities. These are immersive experiences that include various levels of social and psychological components to create increasing degrees of validity in relation to the expected real-world events for which one trains
Tabletop exercise	Focuses on a primarily verbal walk through team activity of a scenario [4]. Typically, participants role play to review all aspects of a scenario in order to discover challenges to address within the scenario, develop standard operating procedures, identify appropriate team structures, formulate communications plans, and develop default practice. Usually, this does not involve hands-on use of technologies that actual situations would employ.
Lectures	An instructor provides detailed material and students are the receiver of the information. Often, the student is seen as a passive learner, dependent upon the teach to impart what is to be learned [5]

During time between joint events, the supervisors of each participating group encouraged participants to work in three areas: (1) Certifications such as CISSP and GIAC, (2) Security applications and relevant procedures, and (3) Rules of engagement based on jurisdictions and inter-institution policies. This study does not definitively separately attribute the sources of skill growth between these directed areas of study and the actual training events. Table 2 shows the categories of content and concepts, along with specific applications and utilities that were identified as warranting usage during physical exercises at the joint events. The research team further divided these categories into specific questions on surveys and tests.

Table 2. Application categories and examples

Content area and concepts	Outcomes and assessment	Larger set of example applications
Logging and monitoring	Composite monitor and visualization to maintain stateful awareness of systems and infrastructure	Kiwi syslog/Splunk, Alien Vault, Security Onion, SNARE OSSIM
Coding and scripting	Move from user interface based to command line scripting, programming and tool switch orientation	Python, command line interface, powershell
Network, Infrastructure Analysis and System Vulnerability Testing	Cert preparation and testing, skill building, increased training simulator availability for practice	CISSP (cert), GIA (cert), Wireshark, Kali, Nmap, Metasploit, OpenVAS, Cobalt Strike (Armitage), MobiSEC
Systems audit, compliance and regulation	Audit, compliance	Wapiti, W3A, CISA, CISM (also review of compliance requirements local regulations)
Communication and interpersonal group relationship	Incident handling and involvement of government and commercial stakeholders to better define rights and privileges of citizens, National Guard and state officials	Tabletop exercises, physical exercises, round table discussions with critical infrastructure sectors

In order to determine the efficacy of the multi-year training program, the authors formulated an assessment strategy, first identifying content and concept areas, and based on that designing a set of pre and post event surveys and tests for understanding in addition to qualitative interviews gathered during events. To provide differentiation between the impact of a specific joint training exercise event and the overall progress of participants in the multi-component program, the authors gathered pre and post assessment of a single joint training event, and then longitudinal assessments at the beginning of every event.

The joint training program leadership team members negotiated for their institutions the specific sequence for the delivery of curricular content incrementally, based on an assessment of readiness at each phase of training, and also considered the progression of enabling layers of skill yielded new levels of capability. Once the new curricular content for each event was determined, the particular event was rapidly formulated into a set of challenge exercises covering the categories in the table above. The first event was a network defense challenge similar to the Collegiate Cyber Defense Challenge, with a framework dividing participants into "IT Consultant Teams" required to take over, fix, and defend a mismanaged IT infrastructure as described in an earlier work [2].

The results saw about 10% change from initial population per event (n > 30 for the first two events and n > 13 where participants were in large part the original population for the 3rd). While this definitely affects that relative percentage of any trend within the core population, "skill gap" closure can still be observed in areas discussed below.

The change in population can be explained by invitation of several groups from outside the core Colorado teams to join in the training exercises, including National Guard representatives from another US state and a Jordanian Military security team. Overall, these representative groups integrated rapidly into the self-organizing teams during physical challenges and expressed value in the presentation of new tools, observation of the tabletop exercises, and participation in discussions to exchange challenges and ideas. Initially, the exercises were composed of Colorado state government, Colorado National Guard, and academic institutions, and quickly attracted interest from IT security industry companies and governmental entities outside of Colorado. This suggested that the model for operating this program might have broad value for other regions. A key point of value in these conversations was that the exercises included multiple simulation, physical exercise scenarios, and tabletop exercises designed to give real-world substance to more abstract cyber security concepts and integrate physical world consequences to actions performed by the participants.

4   Findings

Participants completed evaluation surveys and knowledge tests both at the beginning and at the end of only the first joint event. Longitudinal pre event tests measure variance in capability between the start of each event. One observation was the lack of participants' voluntary participation in the post-event assessment for all events. This could be explained by the fact that participants were tired following the event and did not wish to remain long enough to complete the survey.

The overall trend of data goes upwards over the span of years, while we recorded levels of capability fluctuating up and down within the same event and between events. Interpretation of the pre-post event test data must also take into consideration the compounding nature of the skills introduced over time. This may account for some fluctuation in results. Discrete tracking of particular technical skills suggested that "gap filling" was a stronger aspect of the training events rather than the broad acquisition of skills in new areas.

One possible influencing factor outside of the training events is the study and practice that participants were directed to complete by their respective institutions as part of the overall effort to enhance capabilities. This broader longitudinal acquisition of new skills took place between events, by the efforts of individuals at their jobs, in pursuit of professional certification, and in collaborative study teams. Generally institutional requirements were set with their own program customized for each participant, called here Personalized Experiential Learning Environment (PELE) tracking because it tracks independent professional experience, professional development training, and other related activities. PELE is managed at each these institutions using a spreadsheet for tracking activities against needs. There was no comprehensive system coordinating all related activities across all institutions, except for the annual self-assessment and skill testing data gathered in this study.

The results in Fig. 1 suggest that some modest progress was made in most areas with a significant gap being filled in web forensics. The drop in "NMAP - Analysis" score suggests that users became aware of their own skill level as smaller in relation to a larger body of knowledge at this event, likely during the learning challenges.

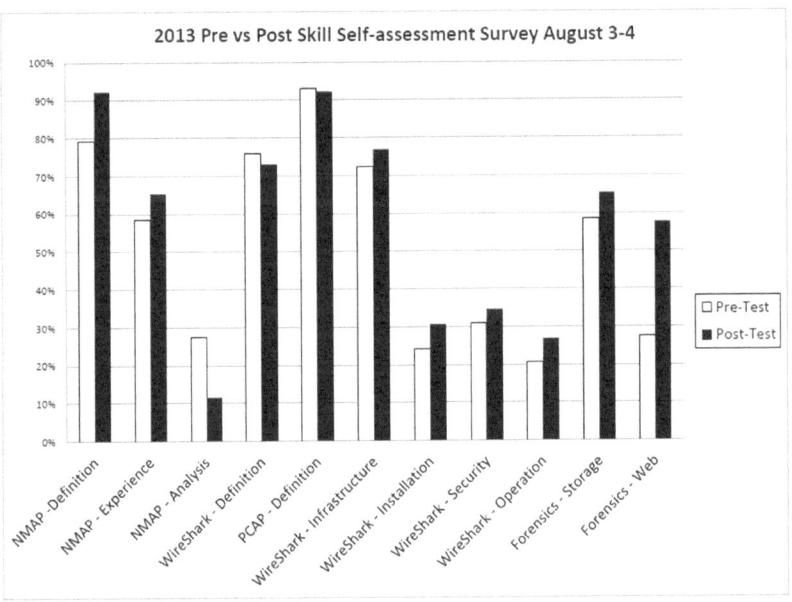

Fig. 1. 2013 User Self Evaluation results plotted an average percentage of self-perceived proficiency across a range of areas (n = 30).

Tested skills in Fig. 2 generally improved over the two-day event, with significant skill gaps improving in relation to a larger body of knowledge. Small changes suggest prior knowledge of the skill at least at the level presented in the challenge event.

Over the span of 2013–2015 as represented in Fig. 3, students' perception of skill levels often significantly shifted as a group average. In examples such as "NMAP - Experience" and "Forensic - Storage", relative confidence is often deflated and then rises up over a span the span of years. Other profiles of progress exist within the data, such as areas where there was significant previous experience like "Wireshark" that exhibited consistent skill levels.

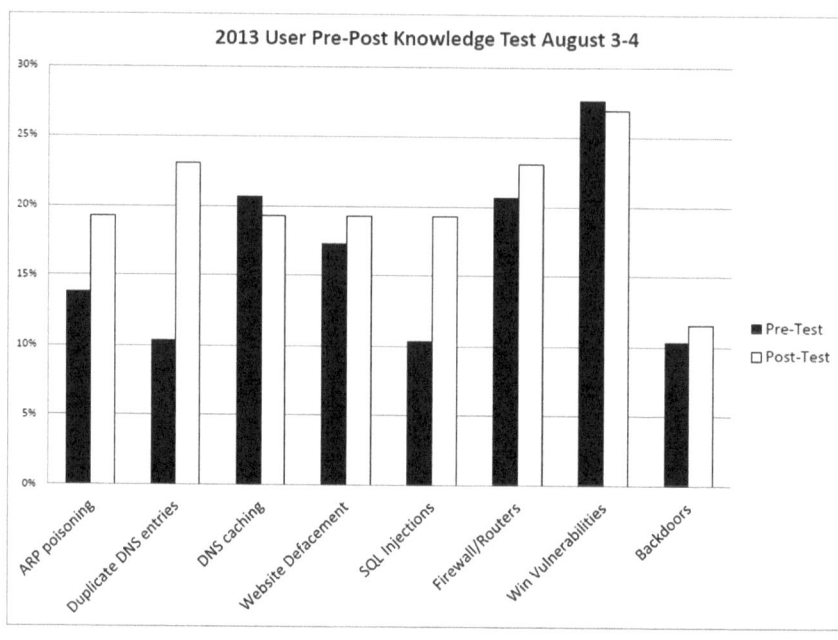

Fig. 2. 2013 Participant knowledge tests prior to and after the challenge event (n = 30).

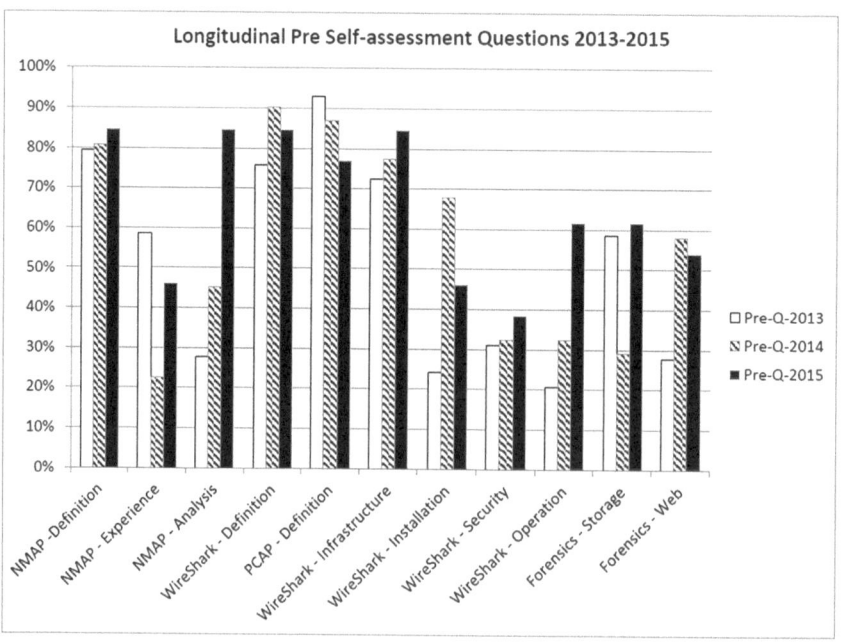

Fig. 3. Longitudinal surveys over three years of self-perceived skills where 2013 (n = 30), 2014 (n = 30), and 2015 (n = 13).

While Fig. 4 shows some skill gap-filling as identified in areas like backdoors, vulnerabilities, and routers, areas like "ARP poisoning" and "Duplicate DNS entries" suggest that skills emphasized early on may have needed continuing attention to achieve retention. Participants completed the pre event tests using pen and paper individually while proctored in a large classroom.

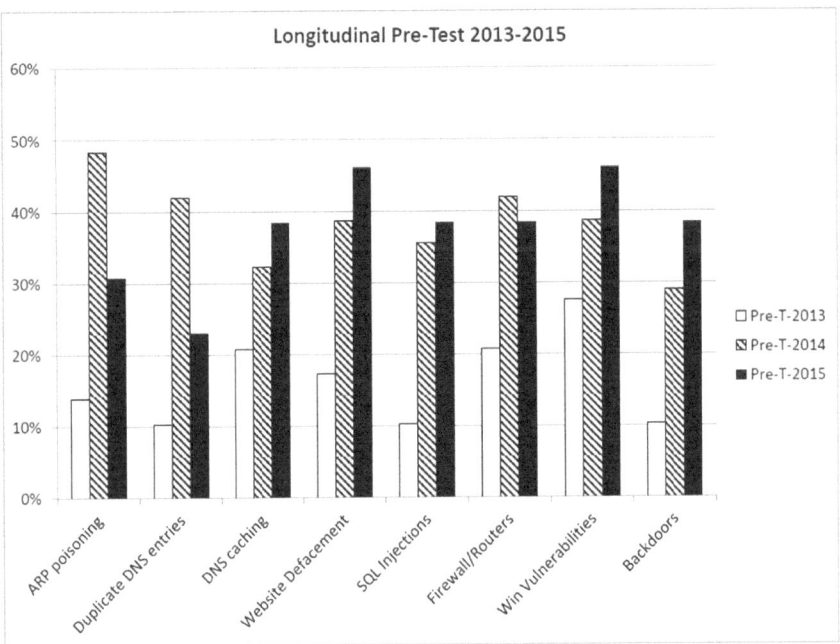

Fig. 4. Longitudinal pre-testing knowledge over the span of three years where 2013 (n = 30), 2014 (n = 30), and 2015 (n = 13).

5 Conclusion

After multiple iterations of surveys and tests we determined through observation of the National Guard working group that an individualized, PELE would benefit the user and manager. The documents that we examined were after action reports, interviews with the managers responsible for the participating institutional team members and a compilation of reports by observers. Not surprisingly the user and manager requirements were similar provide accurate and real-time situational awareness of strengths and weaknesses The managers were primarily interested in how best to respond to an immediate threat given the available workforce and up to date competency data. This is similar to other observations in separate research [9].

High variance in skill growth trends can be explained by some underlying causes. While the self-assessment and test topics remained consistent over the years, the event content emphasis was re-negotiated by the joint training program leadership team prior to each event to maintain relevance for all participant institutions in the face of real world events. The program leaders' rapid modification of the content was essential to achieve high levels of institutional engagement by addressing changing priorities of stakeholders. This deemphasized some skills tracked in the assessment design. The stakeholders often became aware of the new priorities upon review of tabletop and other exercises.

The need for additional types of research became apparent upon review of the data in relation to the events. The PELE approach used by the participating institutions between training events was significant, allowing the individual capabilities to rise between events even though post-surveys did not suggest strong technical advancement in single-weekend events. This is reflected in the significant growth from a longitudinal view. Creating a coordinated PELE should enhance the various agencies ability to both consistently cover identified areas and make agile moves in a more structured way. This research did not cover the PELE systems or processes but merely observed the need to track inter-event progress of participants to fairly attribute the source of skill growth. The authors confirmed this in after-action briefings with joint training program leadership. Additionally, there is a need for more detailed study of each component of this general program to determine what value each is contributing. A behavioral study assessing the specific causes of learning outcomes could lead to better rebalancing the portfolio of activities. Finally, this study did identify significant growth in the participants of the program, particularly over the longitudinal span of years. The general method presented could address skill gaps seen in the measured areas for a range of similar collaborative ventures. Future studies of this method would require better tracking of growth related activity or specific behavioral studies of learning activities.

References

1. Kenney, M.: Cyber-terrorism in a post-stuxnet world. Orbis **59**(1), 111–128 (2015)
2. Moore, E., Likarish, D.: A cyber security multi agency collaboration for rapid response that uses AGILE methods on an education infrastructure. In: Bishop, M., Miloslavskaya, N., Theocharidou, M. (eds.) WISE 2015. IFIP AICT, vol. 453, pp. 41–50. Springer, Cham (2015). doi:10.1007/978-3-319-18500-2_4
3. Saunders, J.H.: Simulation approaches in information security education. In: Proceedings of the 6th National Colloquium for Information System Security Education, Redmond, WA, June (2002)
4. Perry, R.W.: Disaster exercise outcomes for professional emergency personnel and citizen volunteers. J. Contingencies Crisis Manag. **12**(2), 64–75 (2004)
5. Petress, K.: What is meant by "active learning?" Education **128**(4), 566 (2008)
6. Cheung, R.S., Cohen, J.P., Lo, H.Z., Elia, F.: Challenge based learning in cybersecurity education. In: Proceedings of the 2011 International Conference on Security & Management, vol. 1, July 2011
7. Bartel, A.P.: Measuring the employer's return on investments in training: evidence from the literature. Ind. Relat. **39**(3), 502 (2000)
8. Creswell, J.W., Clark, V.L.P.: Designing and Conducting Mixed Methods Research. SAGE Publications Inc., Thousand Oaks (2007)
9. Eckerson, W.W.: Performance Dashboards: Measuring, Monitoring, and Managing your Business. Wiley, New York (2010)

"Network Security Intelligence" Educational and Research Center

Natalia Miloslavskaya[✉][ORCID], Alexander Tolstoy, and Anton Migalin

The National Research Nuclear University MEPhI (Moscow Engineering Physics Institute),
31 Kashirskoye Shosse, Moscow, Russia
{NGMiloslavskaya,AITolstoj,ASMigalin}@mephi.ru

Abstract. The paper presents a recent experience (since 2016) in establishing and running the "Network Security Intelligence" educational and research center (NSIC) in the framework of the new NRNU MEPhI's Institute of Cyber Intelligence Systems (ICIS). The created center is designed to provide training and research on effective network security management based on intelligent approaches and applications, the use of Big Data technologies for processing information security information, the study of the compatibility between different network protection tools, as well as the evaluation of network security. The educational NSIC's basis currently consists of two laboratories with Next-Generation Firewall (NGFW) and Data Loss Prevention (DLP) systems at their cores respectively. Here we discuss the use of the first one. The main areas of further work in expanding NSIC's operation for training and research conclude the paper.

Keywords: Network security intelligence · Educational and research center · NGFW · DLP · Information security

1   Introduction

Intensive development and use of modern information and communication technologies (ICT) has led to serious qualitative changes in the economic, socio-political and spiritual spheres of public life. Nowadays we witness dramatic changes in ICT that are driving current information security (IS) trends and require sophisticated structures and adequate approaches to manage IS on different scales: for individuals, for organizations, for countries and for the entire world. The wide range of new and ever-growing IS threats, especially those related to new ICT, network technologies, services and devices, are all around us.

The "e-Skills for the 21st Century: Fostering Competitiveness, Growth and Jobs" Communication from the Commission to the Council, the European Parliament, the European Economic and Social Committee and the Committee of the Regions says that "There is an important need to address ICT-related skills (e-skills) issues in order to respond to the growing demand for highly-skilled ICT practitioners and users, meet the fast-changing requirements of industry… Shortages of ICT practitioner skills have been endemic due to technological innovation and the fast growth of ICT activity in

© IFIP International Federation for Information Processing 2017
Published by Springer International Publishing AG 2017. All Rights Reserved
M. Bishop et al. (Eds.): WISE 10, IFIP AICT 503, pp. 157–168, 2017.
DOI: 10.1007/978-3-319-58553-6_14

comparison with the relatively low supply and availability of new employees and entrepreneurs with relevant educational qualifications" [1].

In 2015 the World Summit on the Information Society (WSIS) noted that it should explicitly recognize ICT Professionalism because the implementation of WSIS action lines and Sustainable Development Goals requires the services of a skilled, competent, ethical, accountable, and trustworthy ICT workforce [2].

In its 2016 Cybersecurity Skills Gap graphics [3], ISACA has shown that more than 1 in 4 organizations have experienced an APT attack and by 2020 the average cost of a data breach is estimated to be $150 million, while 53% of organizations experience delays as long as 6 months in finding qualified security candidates. A global shortage of 2 million cybersecurity professionals is expected in 2019.

Hence the demand for highly-skilled ICT practitioners ready to act in modern heterogeneous ICT systems, which are vulnerable to various sophisticated attacks, is more obvious than ever before. To meet this challenge, to achieve business objectives, to stay competitive and to operate legally, organizations of all types (e.g. commercial or non-profit organizations, government agencies), sizes and spheres of activity need to have a unified, inclusive, scalable, effective security system with proper security intelligence services in place and "best-in-breed" information protection tools (IPTs), measures, and staff to truly manage IS for their sensitive assets.

The paper describes our experience with the recently established (in 2016) educational and research center for intelligent network security management, called the "Network Security Intelligence Center" (NSIC), within the framework of the new NRNU MEPhI's Strategic Academic Unit called the Institute of Cyber Intelligence Systems (ICIS). At present we only consider educational purposes (because the hardware and software base of the center is still not fully developed for research purposes). Prof. Bart Preneel from the Catholic University of Leuven is NSIC's Scientific Leader.

Our current work is aimed at developing the NSIC concept in general, and our own NSIC in particular, as a world-class educational and research center. The goal of this work is to present a model of NSIC for its study and continuous improvement, taking into account the characteristics of today's networks and the forecast for networks in the not so distant future. For our purposes, our NSIC will be based on three bearing laboratories with Next-Generation Firewalls (NGWFs), Data Loss Prevention (DLP), and Security Information and Event Management (SIEM) systems at their cores respectively. The NSIC can be reasonably used as a basis for creating a trusted educational environment for blended learning with many e-learning components.

Our paper is organized as follows. Section 2 provides a brief review of related work. The general NSIC's description is given in Sect. 3. The use of NGFWs for educational purposes is presented in Sect. 4. The main areas of further work in expanding the NSIC's operation for training and research conclude the paper.

2   Related Work

The world's leading IT research and advisory firm, the Gartner Company, identified the top 10 strategic technology trends that organizations of different sizes and spheres of activities cannot afford to ignore in the next three years (up to 2018) [4]. Gartner highlighted the advent of intelligence everywhere, meaning three wide-spreading trends. First, "Advanced, Pervasive and Invisible Analytics" will take center stage as the volume of data generated by embedded systems increases, and data lakes of structured, semi-structured and unstructured data [5] inside and outside the organization should be analyzed for more informed decision-making. Second, embedded intelligence combined with deep analytics will drive the development of "Context-Rich (and context-aware) Systems" that monitor their rapidly changing surroundings and respond appropriately. And last, but not least, "Deep Analytics" applied to an understanding of context provide the preconditions for a world of smart machines that learn for themselves and act autonomously. Our key task is to teach them to act constructively, not destructively.

Most publications discuss centralized network security management in terms of first generation SIEM systems run from a Security Operations Center (SOC) (e.g. [6], with more detailed analysis in [7]). Cisco Systems in particular contributed to the SOC idea [8]. Subsequent publications focus on either tools for computer network defense [9–11] or on people and processes.

Then people began to talk about a Security Intelligence Center (SIC) with an integrated IS architecture and a 2nd generation SIEM system, providing full visibility and control and context-driven security intelligence in one place to temporarily deal with network-level and more important higher-level IS events. SIC as a separate term exists since 2011 [12], with a few papers on the topic [13–15]. In [16] a short comparison of SOC and SIC is given which was a starting point for our research.

To empower the autonomy of network security management within one organization and to deepen its knowledge of the computing environment, our research is aimed at uniting all the advantages of a SIC and a Network Operations Center (NOC) [17] with their unique and joint toolkits and techniques in a unified NSIC. NSIC changes the security model from reactive to proactive, supports more effective responses to IS incidents, enhances communications between the network and security teams, management and board members, drives IS investment strategies, and more directly connects IS priorities with business risk management priorities. The research in this area has just begun.

As for the work about laboratory support of IS education, we mention only the pioneers like [18–21], followed by many lab descriptions worldwide in the next years. These works provide useful instructions in designing labs and developing an education process based on them. The authors also have their own experience in starting the "Network Security" laboratory in 2000 [22], and continuing through the present [23]. Subsequent publications show how to use virtualization technologies in the education process (like [24]). These technologies are very useful as they have the necessary tools to build complicated virtual networks on virtual machines and show all the IPTs' functionality.

3   General NSIC Description

Automating all routine operations and IS incident response that do not require expert decision-making is an urgent need for any modern organization. It should set up a more advanced IS management center than a traditional SOC. The so-called SIC with an integrated attack defense architecture provides full visibility, control and context-driven security intelligence (SI) in one place to temporarily deal with higher-level IS events. By implementing SICs, organizations get a holistic, in-depth view of their "IS health" and can not only detect and recognize attacks, but also effectively predict, prevent, and address IS incidents before they cause harm, thus constantly gathering data and producing new IS-related knowledge. The SI concept emphasizes the need to not just collect data but also learn from it in order to continually stay ahead of intruders. Viewing time-stamped historical data or logs is very important for IS incident investigation. But stopping IS incidents is possible only when you have a real-time view in a concrete context of what is happening right now so you can find something unusual, across the entire network. Any delay, and only reactive actions, put an organization's assets at risk. Hence, the goal of SI is to provide proactive, predictive (forward-looking), actionable and comprehensive protection and insight into IS that reduces the IS risks and operational effort through advanced analytics. All information that SI deals with is processed, sorted, aggregated from reliable sources, cross-correlated for accuracy, assessed for relevancy, evaluated and interpreted by analysts at the final stage if needed.

The NOC's aim is to support a centralized place from which network administrators can remotely supervise, maintain and monitor their telecommunications networks using appropriate management software, and visualize their detailed status with all devices that are being monitored. The NOC can be considered the focal point for the following typical activities: network discovery, assessments and management; optimization and quality of service management and reporting; domain name management; constant research of anomalies and problems (troubleshooting) to make adjustments, marshal resources and respond to emergency situations; application software installations, distribution, troubleshooting and updating; performance monitoring, reporting and improvement recommendations; backup and storage management; email management services; voice and video traffic management; basic (elementary) IS controls like authentication and authorization, IP- and MAC-address filtering, etc.

The NSIC's key objective is to move SI to organizations' NOCs, allowing them to stay ahead of IS challenges while being fully integrated around their main business processes. To implement this idea of migration to the NSIC is possible because both the SIC and NOC operation functions are frequently organized in a similar way, which is based on a tiered approach with similar roles, and share some tools. Their union would be very beneficial in the long-term as the NOC's primarily concern is serving the business, while the SIC's main focus is to ensure its security. When an outage is detected, the NOC's staff is likely to attribute the disruption to device malfunction or system issues and attempt to address it through hardware replacement or configuration adjustment. But the SIC's personnel are likely to attribute the problem to malicious activity and will thus prompt an investigation before initiating IS event response actions.

While designing the NSIC, we have focused first on its self-protection. For that purpose, we defined all information resources that are to be protected within the NSIC (using the common approaches of asset inventory and categorization as the initial steps of IS risk assessment [25]). It is typically sensitive data used in a typical network of an educational institution, for example proprietary information of limited propagation, sensitive information related to the NSIC's activities, personally identifying information (PII) of its staff and trainees, learning and testing materials protected by copyright, keys, credentials and passwords, etc.

Then, based on a comprehensive analysis of the security level of our department network (investigating logs, using security scanners, for example), we worked out two generalized IS models for the given network, presented in documents of many pages. The first one – an IS threat model – included a formalized description of IS threat sources [26], vulnerabilities exploited by them, objects suitable for the threats' realization, threats implementation techniques (actual attacks), types of possible loss, extent of the potential damage and some additional information such as likelihood of threats implementation; destructive impact (including interconnecting); damage elimination/limitation; impact frequency and duration, etc. The second model (an IS intruder model) contained a formalized intruders' classification and description of their experience, knowledge, available resources for IS threats implementation, possible motivation of their actions and IS threats implementation techniques.

After that, we developed an IS policy for the NSIC that ensured meeting the key goal of its IS, namely achieving adequate protection of NSIC's information assets and business processes, and allowing its continuous operation under IS threats. Among the most important IS policy requirements are the following:

- Usage of all applicable IPTs and IS controls;
- Establishing monitoring and auditing policies and procedures;
- IS event and incident processing;
- Vulnerability management;
- Configuration and changes management;
- User' s activity registration;
- Filtering of incoming and outgoing traffic;
- Protection against computer viruses and unauthorized software modification and insertion;
- Control over all NSIC's computer port usage;
- Protection against DoS attacks and unauthorized scanning; and
- Setting responsibilities for IS policy violation, etc.

4   NGFW Study

Now, the most common IPTs are hardware and software firewalls (FWs), which provide network traffic control based on packet filtering in accordance with the rules of organization's IS policy. As a result of their evolutionary development, the first specialized solution with Deep Packet Inspection (DPI) and detailed and customizable control at the application level appeared in 2007. NGFW unites on one platform multiple IPTs such as FW, IPS (Intrusion Prevention System) and Web security gateway. Policies for applications, users and sessions are defined in a NGFW within certain contexts, not just for ports and IP addresses. User identification, which allows integration with various organization's directory services, is implemented in a NGFW. A NGFW can work with encrypted SSL-traffic on all ports. This IPT can receive black and white address lists from trusted external sources and apply them to the relevant filtering rules. Indeed, NGFWs work faster and support more complex rule sets than their predecessors. According to a Gartner survey [27], 40% of companies use NGFWs to protect their intranets, and by 2018, 85% of all FWs will be NGFWs.

Based on the analysis of the leading vendors for NGFW, as well as NGFW functionality, we concluded that the Palo Alto Networks NGFW [http://www.paloaltonetworks.com] meets the requirements of our NSIC. It also can be implemented in the VMware environment (as a virtualized NGFW) that is well suited for carrying out laboratory work with NGFWs. Due to our collaboration with Palo Alto Networks, we obtained this solution for our educational purposes.

To develop students' skills in configuring NGFW settings and customizations and taking into account its capabilities, we created a laboratory bench. The laboratory bench is designed to test all basic NGFW functionality (Fig. 1) in the form of a one-way gate. One student uses one computer with VMWare Player and one image of the VM-300 (Palo Alto Networks) virtual machine. All computers in the classroom are connected in a single local network and receive their IP addresses using DHCP from the 192.168.1.0/24 network. The students run a virtual machine image, configure NAT and routing for the virtual 172.168.1.0/24 network. When they are trying to connect to the Internet, the traffic generated passes through the NGFW.

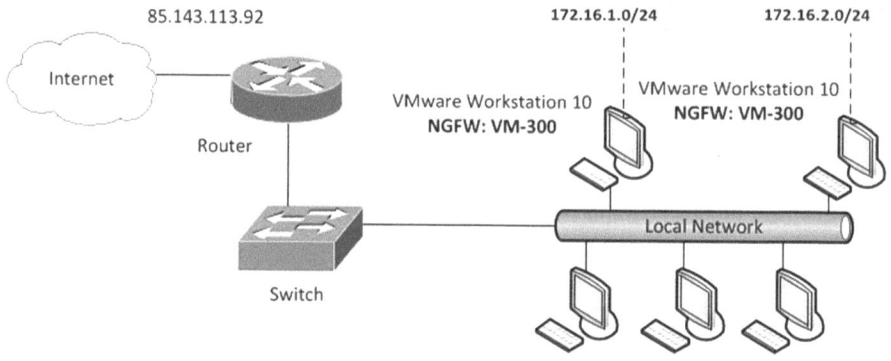

Fig. 1. The scheme of a one-way gate

This laboratory bench meets the following requirements:

- Flexibility, as its structure should be easily reconfigurable: different lab tasks require specific network topologies and host configurations,
- Scalability, for simultaneous task performance by 16 students in the NGFW laboratory and two others (with DLP and SIEM systems); the main resources are located on each computer, and we have a distributed network which does not depend on a centralized server;
- Profitability, as the cost of NGFW installation and maintenance in the laboratory is significantly less than the cost in the real intranet, taking into account that the lab should effectively simulate the processes in real networks;

- Reliability, as the laboratory should be able to easily recover from accidental damage by the students, as well as be able to quickly restore the default settings and network configurations; and
- Isolation, as it should be isolated from the remaining part of the NSIC and not affect its operation; the internal LAN is isolated from the outside NSIC's network. Each student works within the same LAN. The work task implementation will not cause any inconvenience to other NSIC users. Thus, the laboratory bench allows each student to test the NGFW functionality by himself.

On the basis of the rules of the IS policy (Sect. 3), the following context for laboratory work was defined:

1. To prohibit all traffic between some subnetworks, except for that authorized by a network administrator;
2. To use the NGFW only in a router mode;
3. To allow all hosts from 192.168.2.0/24, 192.168.20.0/24, 192.168.21.0/24, 192.168.200.0/24 networks to access the Internet;
4. To identify the applications at OSI layer 7 by signatures;
5. To decrypt all SSL traffic from the 192.168.200.0/24 network, and if that fails, then block this traffic;
6. To allow access to the DMZ servers from the internal network;
7. To permit only those web-mail applications that use MEPhI's email;
8. To block access to phishing and malicious URL-addresses from the 192.168.200.0/24 network;
9. To analyze the frequency of HTTP, TCP, UDP, ICMP packets to web and DNS servers;
10. To analyze .exe, .dll, .bat, .sys, .flash, .jar, .doc, and .pdf files for malware using behavioral anti-virus mechanisms; and
11. To block encrypted documents and files downloaded to the 192.168.200.0/24 network, etc.

To start with, we created 5 laboratory exercises, and will be adding more to these in the future. Each lab is designed for 4 academic hours (with all controls and tests).

1. Lab #1 "First NGFW installation and configuration".

Objective: to get skills in installing a NGFW, configuring routing rules, and defining user accounts and security certificates (create, import, and export).

Student assignment: to configure the static routing rules (e.g., all incoming traffic is redirected to the next router at 192.168.1.1); to configure the network address translation (NAT) rules (for example, translate dynamic IP and port type, interface address type, Ethernet ½ interface, etc.); to create a trusted client's connection to the NGFW; to create a user with administrator privileges; and to set up two-factor authentication for the NGFW administrator.

To confirm the successful task execution, it is necessary to demonstrate to an instructor the following features (controls): the ability to connect to the Internet from the 172.16.1.0/24 network; a trusted connection to the Palo Alto Networks Web interface; multiple users authenticated as administrators; two-factor authentication of an administrator, using a password and a client certificate.

2. *Lab #2 "SSL/SSH traffic decryption"* (Fig. 2).

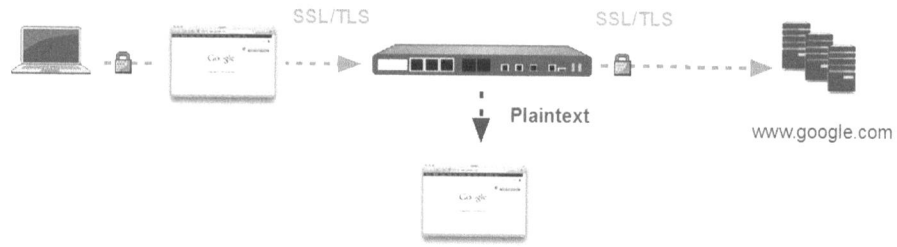

Fig. 2. SSL traffic decrypting scheme

Objective: to gain skills in installing a security certificate, decrypting SSL/SSH traffic, and intercepting and analyzing packets captured with the Wireshark traffic analyzer software.

Student assignment: to create a self-signed certificate; to configure SSL decrypting rules; to capture packets using the Packet Capture technology; to analyze packages using Wireshark.

Controls: interception and decryption of https traffic from the student's computer; filled-in data from an authentication form (such as https://accounts.google.com/) found by the Wireshark.

3. *Lab #3 "User identification (User-ID)".*

The authentication profiles define the configuration of a local database, RADIUS, LDAP and Kerberos, and can be assigned to administrative accounts and provide VPN access. The NGFW checks the authentication profile assigned to the account and authenticates the user based on the specified settings.

Objective: to gain skills in identifying the users who have requested access to the Internet, configuring the authentication profiles, creating a local user database, configuring LDAP server settings, and using security certificates for authentication.

Student assignment: to configure user authentication rules; to set up forwarding to a Web form to enter a login name and password; to set up a security policy based on user ID.

Controls: redirection to a web form and user network authentication; the use of various filtering rules depending on the user authenticated in the network.

4. *Lab #4 "Identification of applications (App-ID) and data control (Content-ID)".*

Creating and managing security policies based on application and user identification, regardless of device or location, is more effective for network security than making a decision based solely on ports and IP addresses. Integration with enterprise user directories allows the users of Microsoft Windows, Mac OS X, Linux, Android, and iOS, who are accessing the applications, to be identified. The combination of application usage monitoring and control means that the protected usage of Oracle, BitTorrent, Gmail or any applications used in the network, regardless of where and how the user accesses it, can be ensured.

Objective: to gain skills in identifying applications (regardless of port, protocol, encryption or masking techniques used), traffic analysis, limiting unauthorized transfer of files and data traffic, filtering by URL addresses, and blocking unknown or targeted malware.

Student assignment: to add new URL filtering rule; to set the time interval following the Continue action of the user; to set the time interval after the user enters the admin override password; to apply different filtering rules to the URL categories; to select different filtering rules for all the proposed file extension types; and to apply the filtering rules created in the policies section.

Controls: the use of different filtering rules depending on the application, for example, to block all Tor connections; the use of different filtering rules depending on the extensions of transmitted files, for example, to block downloading executable files; the use of different filtering rules depending on the web page category or URL, for example, to block all anonymizer sites; the application of any method of traffic masking, such as TCP over DNS tunneling; and a demonstration of the ability to protect different applications used in the network.

5. Lab #5 "Prevention of threats and vulnerabilities".

An NGFW with an Intrusion Prevention System (IPS) inside neutralizes the threats associated with network blocking, application level vulnerabilities exploitation, buffer overflows, DoS attacks, port scanning, etc. Antivirus and antispyware software blocks malware, as well as command and control traffic generated by malware, viruses in PDF files and malware hidden in compressed files or web traffic. Based on security policies, the decryption of SSL traffic for all applications and ports provides protection against malware that attempts to gain access through applications using the secure SSL protocol.

Objective: to gain skills in protecting networks against computer viruses, worms, spyware and other malicious traffic using security profiles; detecting and eliminating vulnerabilities of network applications inside the LAN; identifying hosts infected with bots; and detecting and preventing known attacks.

Student assignment: to set the rules for signature-based anti-virus tools; to set the rules for behavioral anti-virus tools; to set the rules to detect attacks such as HTTP, ICMP, UDP and SYN flooding.

Controls: blocking malicious files by the signature-based anti-virus tools; blocking computer virus (obtained from the instructor) by the behavioral anti-virus tools; any method known to the student to conduct HTTP, ICMP, UDP and SYN flooding and its detection and prevention using the NGFW.

We make one short note on the current context, in which the students carry out their exercises: all of them are given the lab descriptions (30 pages in total) in advance, to provide the opportunity to be better prepared to work and demonstrate their knowledge on the progress test after it. In order to complete the labs successfully, the students must pass tests consisting of 30 questions.

Another note concerns privacy. It is a separate issue that requires special study in the framework of different disciplines (not only technical network security). That is why it is not been considered in this paper.

The labs have been successfully tested within the "Information Security of Open Systems" course for the 5th year Specialists (2 groups, 40 students) and the "Objects' Information Security Maintenance Technologies" course for the 2nd year Masters (5 groups, 60 students).

5   Conclusion

All scientific studies facilitate new learning and vice versa – some interesting issues that require additional investigation can be found during practical work. An NSIC can be regarded as expanding knowledge and skills through creative research and discovery. Consequently, the NSIC's project relevance is determined by the urgent needs to create a scientific, methodical and material base for network security professional training through the use of modern and advanced ICT and educational technologies, as well as the conditions necessary for MEPhI to compete successfully among world educational centers. The vision of the center is to be recognized at national and international levels for excellence in advanced network security management and professional training.

We shared our short-tem experience in starting the development and use of our NSIC in the framework of the MEPhI ICIS. As can be seen, it is a work in progress and there is still much to do. Our future work is intended to finalize the creation of the second and third NSIC's DLP and SIEM laboratories. After that, all three core IPTs (NGFW, DLP and SIEM systems) for the NSIC will be deployed.

We presented the NSIC's usage only in term of educational process improvement, in particular for studying NGFWs. Our ambitious plans in this direction include but are not limited to the following: development and subsequent implementation of educational standards; new programs (curricula) and competency models for different educational levels for specialized professional training in the field of network security; supervising PhD students carrying out their research within the NSIC's topics; conducting summer schools with intensive network security programs, etc. NSIC can be reasonably used to create a trusted educational environment for blended learning with a set of e-learning courses on network security management.

The created center is also expected to carry out research on the NSIC's design, effective network security management practices based on intelligent approaches and applications, the use of Big Data technologies for IS-related data processing, and the study of the compatibility between different IPTs and make recommendations to address arising issues, as well as evaluating network security.

To publicize the NSIC's activities and to post its news and offers in education and joint research, we are creating a secure web site for it.

Acknowledgement. This work was supported by Competitiveness Growth Program of the Federal Autonomous Educational Institution of Higher Education National Research Nuclear University MEPhI (Moscow Engineering Physics Institute).

References

1. e-Skills for the 21st Century: Fostering Competitiveness, Growth and Jobs. http://ec.europa.eu/growth/sectors/digital-economy/e-skills_en. Accessed 03 Nov 2016
2. Progress made in the implementation of and follow-up to the outcomes of the World Summit on the Information Society at the regional and international levels. Report of the Secretary-General. United Nations. General Assembly. Economic and Social Council. http://unctad.org/en/PublicationsLibrary/a71d67_en.pdf. Accessed 03 Mar 2017
3. 2016 Cybersecurity Skills Gap. ISACA. http://www.isaca.org/cyber/PublishingImages/Cybersecurity-Skills-Gap-1500.jpg. Accessed 03 Mar 2017
4. Gartner's Top 10 Strategic Technology Trends for 2015. http://www.gartner.com/smarterwithgartner/gartners-top-10-strategic-technology-trends-for-2015/. Accessed 03 Mar 2017
5. Miloslavskaya, N., Tolstoy, A.: Application of big data, fast data and data lake concepts to information security issues. In: Proceedings of 2016 4th International Conference on Future Internet of Things and Cloud Workshops. The 3rd International Symposium on Big Data Research and Innovation (BigR&I 2016), Vienna, Austria, 22–24 August, pp. 148–153 (2016)
6. Bidou, R.: Security operation center concepts & implementation (2005). http://iv2-technologies.com/~rbidou/SOCConceptAndImplementation.pdf. Accessed 31 Jan 2016
7. Miloslavskaya, N.: Security operations centers for information security incident management. In: Proceedings of the 4th International Conference "Future Internet of Things and Cloud" (FiCloud 2016), Vienna, Austria, pp. 131–138 (2016)
8. Security operations center: building, operating, and maintaining your SOC. Cisco Press (2015)
9. Sanders, C., Smith, J.: Applied Network Security Monitoring: Collection, Detection, and Analysis. Syngress, Boston (2013)
10. Bejtlich, R.: Practice of Network Security Monitoring. No Starch Press, San Francisco (2013)
11. Insights on governance, risk and compliance. Security Operations Centers — helping you get ahead of cybercrime. EY GM Limited (2014)
12. Burnham, J.: What is Security Intelligence and why does it matter today? https://securityintelligence.com/what-is-security-intelligence-and-why-does-it-matter-today/. Accessed 03 Mar 2017
13. Hutchins, E.M., Clopperty, M.J., Amin, R.V.: Intelligence-driven computer network defense informed by analysis of adversary campaigns and Intrusion Kill Chains. Lockheed Martin Corporation (2013)
14. Threat intelligence platforms. ThreatConnect, Inc. (2015). http://www.informationweek.com/whitepaper/. Accessed 03 Mar 2017
15. Security Intelligence. Prevent fraud. Achieve compliance. Preserve security. https://www.sas.com/en_us/software/fraud-security-intelligence.html. Accessed 03 Mar 2017
16. SOC vs. SIC: the difference of an Intelligence Driven Defense® Solution. A White Paper Presented by: Lockheed Martin Corporation (2015)
17. What is a Network Operations Center (NOC)? http://www.continuum.net/msp-resources/mspedia/what-is-a-network-operations-center-noc. Accessed 03 Mar 2011

18. White, G.B., Sward, R.E.: Developing an undergraduate lab for information warfare and computer security. In: Proceeding of the IFIP TC11 WG11.8 First World Conference on Information Security Education, Kista, Sweden, 17–19 June 1999, pp. 163–170 (1999)
19. Armstrong, C.J., Armstrong, H.L.: The virtual campus. In: Proceeding of the IFIP TC11 WG11.8 Second World Conference on Information Security Education, Perth, Australia, 12–14 July 2001, pp. 161–168 (2001)
20. Gritzalis, D., Tryfonas, T.: Action Learning in Practice: Pilot delivery of an INFOSEC University laboratory course. In: Proceeding of the IFIP TC11 WG11.8 Second World Conference on Information Security Education, Perth, Australia, 12–14 July 2001, pp. 169–182
21. Hoffman, L.J., Dodge, R., Rosenberg, T., Ragsdale, D.: Information assurance laboratory innovations. In: Proceedings of the 7th Colloquium for Information Systems Security Education, Washington, DC, USA (2003)
22. Miloslavskaya, N., Tolstoy, A.: Network security scientific and research laboratory. In: Proceedings of the 3rd World Conference on Information Security Education WISE3, USA, Monterey (2003)
23. Ismukhamedova, A., Satimova, Y., Nikiforov, A., Miloslavskaya, N.: Practical studying of Wi-Fi network vulnerabilities. In: Proceedings of the 3rd International Conference DIPDMWC2016. 1st International Workshop on Education for Secure Digital Information Processing, Data Mining and Wireless Communications (ESDIPDMWC2016), 6–8 July 2016, Moscow, Russia, pp. 227–232 (2016)
24. Hay, B., Dodge, R., Nance, K.: Using virtualization to create and deploy computer security lab exercises. In: Jajodia, S., Samarati, P., Cimato, S. (eds.) SEC 2008. IFIP, vol. 278, pp. 621–635. Springer, Boston, MA (2008). doi:10.1007/978-0-387-09699-5_40
25. ISO/IEC 27005:2011 "Information technology – Security techniques – Information security risk management"
26. Malyuk, A., Miloslavskaya, N.: Information security theory for the future internet. In: Proceedings of the 3rd International Conference « Future Internet of Things and Cloud » (FiCloud 2015), Rome, Italy, 24–26 August 2015
27. Magic Quadrant for Organization Network Firewalls 2015 (2015). http://innetworktech.com/wp-content/uploads/2015/04/Magic-Quadrant-for-Organization-Network-Firewalls.pdf. Accessed 03 Mar 2017

Author Index